Grayslake Area Public Library District
Grayslake, Illinois

THE SWEET LIFE IN PARIS

Also by David Lebovitz

Room for Dessert

Ripe for Dessert

The Great Book of Chocolate

The Perfect Scoop

THE SWEET LIFE
in Paris

Delicious Adventures in the World's Most
Glorious—and Perplexing—City

DAVID LEBOVITZ

BROADWAY BOOKS

NEW YORK

Published in the United States by Broadway Books,
an imprint of The Crown Publishing Group,
a division of Random House, Inc., New York.
www.broadwaybooks.com

BROADWAY BOOKS and its logo, a letter B bisected on the diagonal,
are trademarks of Random House, Inc.

Book design by Elizabeth Rendfleisch

Library of Congress Cataloging-in-Publication Data

Lebovitz, David.
The sweet life in Paris: delicious adventures in the world's most
glorious—and perplexing—city / David Lebovitz. — 1st ed.
        p.   cm.
1. Gastronomy. 2. Cookery, French. 3. Paris (France)—Social life and customs.
4. Americans—France—Anecdotes. I. Title.

TX637.L42 2009
641'.013—dc22
2008025955

ISBN 978-0-7679-2888-5

PRINTED IN THE UNITED STATES OF AMERICA

1   3   5   7   9   10   8   6   4   2

First Edition

CONTENTS

ACKNOWLEDGMENTS

The last thing I thought while frantically cramming everything I owned into a couple of suitcases was that I'd ever write a book about my life to come in Paris. But as I acclimated to my new home, I started writing about Paris, turning my Web site into a blog, chronicling my travails (which included learning to live by arcane rules and rituals that haven't changed for centuries), meeting a lot of marvelous people, and most important, discovering an abundance of wonderful things to eat along the way.

Many of my French friends and readers enjoyed and commented on my observations, which were always written with humor and in the spirit of goodwill, even when critical. Despite what many tourists think, Paris is not a museum; it's a big city with flaws just like any other major metropolis, and any frustrations and negative impressions I encountered are balanced by my love for the city and its people.

Well, most of them.

Thanks go to all who helped smooth out the rough edges and who contributed something special to my life in Paris: Gideon Ben-Ami, Paul Bennett, Lani Bevaqua, Anne Block, Randal Breski, Cliff Colvin, Lewis Fomon, Julie Getzlaff, Rik Gitlin, Mara Goldberg, Dorie Greenspan, Jeanette Hermann, Kate Hill, Dianne Jacob, David Lindsay, Susan Herrmann Loomis, Nancy Meyers, *la famille* Pellas, John Reuling, Mort Rosenblum, Lauren Seaver, Heather Stimmler-Hall, David Tanis, and Claude and Jackie Thonat.

Much gratitude goes out to my virtual friends, who became real-life pals along the way. There are way too many to mention here, but I would especially like to *embrasse* Shauna James Ahern, Matt Armendariz, Elise Bauer, Sam Breach, Louisa Chu, Michèle Delevoie, Clotilde Dusoulier, Brett Emerson, Keiko Oikawa, Béatrice Peltre, Deb Perelman, Adam Roberts, Derrick Schneider, Amy Sherman, Nicky Stich and Oliver Seidel, Susan Thomas, Heidi Swanson, Pim Techamaunvivit, Pascale Weeks, and Luisa Weiss.

Beaucoup de kudos to Cindy Meyers for being the tester *extraordinaire aux États-Unis.* And to Carrie Brown of the Jimtown Store in Healdsburg, California, Gérard Cocaign, Meg Cutts, Rosa Jackson, Marion Lévy, and Thérèse Pellas for sharing recipes.

Special thanks to Romain Pellas who, even though he didn't always understand what I was saying, somehow understood me anyway. *Merci toujours.*

Many thanks go to the shopkeepers and artisans in Paris who have gone out of their way to be helpful to me, sharing their craft and knowledge: Jean-Claude Thomas at G. Detou, Régis Dion of Tradition Guérande, chocolatier Jean-Charles Rochoux, and Corinne Roger at Patrick Roger chocolatier. *Remercie* to the *mecs* at Paris Pêche who patiently tried to teach me how to fillet fish. And apologies to the customers who, when they got home, found a badly mangled scrap of fish when they were expecting a nicely trimmed fillet.

To my agent Fred Hill and his associate, Bonnie Nadell, for their amazing support and moxie. To editorial assistant Anne Chagnot for making sure everything was in the right place, and editor Jennifer Josephy who told me, "Be yourself!" but didn't realize what she was getting into. And to Charlie Conrad for steering the book home.

I'd also like to thank the people who read my writings, left comments that made me laugh, and followed along while I began a new life in Paris. To all of you who said that I should write a book about Paris—here it is!

THE SWEET LIFE IN PARIS

INTRODUCTION

I distinctly remember the exact moment when I became Parisian. It wasn't the moment when I found myself seriously considering buying dress socks with goofy cartoon characters on them. Nor was it the time I went to my bank with €135 in hand to make a payment for €134, and thought it completely normal when the teller told me that the bank didn't have any change that day.

And I'm sure it wasn't when I ran into the fifty-something receptionist from my doctor's office sunbathing topless by the Seine, *à la française,* and I didn't avert my eyes (much as I wanted to).

It wasn't when my shoulder bag caught the sweater of a young boy in La Maison du Chocolat and, as it started to unravel, I ignored his woeful cries. "*C'est pas ma faute!*" I reasoned to myself before walking away. After all, who in their right mind would wear a sweater to a chocolate shop, anyway?

It could have been the moment when I listened intently as two Parisian friends explained to me why the French are so determined to clip the pointed tips off *haricots verts* before cooking them. Was it because that's where the radiation collects in the green beans, as one person insisted? Or was it to prevent the little points from getting stuck in your teeth, which the other one assured me would happen? Even though I didn't remember ever getting a string bean end lodged between my teeth, nor did I think radiation had the ability to slide around in vegetables, I found myself nodding in agreement.

No, the exact moment happened just a few months after I'd arrived in Paris. I was spending a lazy Sunday in my apartment lounging around in faded sweatpants and a loose, tattered sweatshirt, my ideal outfit for doing nothing in particular. By late afternoon, I'd finally mustered the energy to take the elevator downstairs to the inner courtyard of my apartment building to empty the garbage.

With the elevator door exactly three steps from my front door and the garbage room just five steps from the elevator landing at the bottom, the trip involves basically four movements—walk out the door, take the elevator down, dump the garbage, and go back up.

The whole process should take maybe forty-five seconds.

So I extracted myself from the sofa, shaved, changed into a pair of real pants, tucked in a clean wrinkle-free shirt, and slipped on a pair of shoes and socks before heading toward the door with my little plastic *sac* for the *poubelle.*

God forbid I should run into someone from my building while wearing my Sunday worst.

And that, *mes amis,* was when I realized I had become Parisian.

The unspoken rule if you plan to live here—but equally good to adopt even if you're just coming for a visit—is knowing that you're going to be judged on how you look and how you present yourself. Yes, even if you're just dumping your garbage. You don't want anyone else, such as a neighbor (or worse, one of those garbagemen in their nifty green outfits), to think you're a slob, do you?

Since only 20 percent of Americans have passports, we don't get out as much as we should, and our dealings with foreigners are usually on our own turf where they have to play by our rules. We're not so good at adapting to others, since we're rarely in a position that requires us to do it. I've heard a variety of complaints from visitors (and uttered a few myself) expecting things to be like they are back home: "Why don't they have doggie bags?" "How come there's no ice?" "Why can't I pick something up off the store shelf?" or "Why is our waiter flirting with those Swedish girls and having a cigarette when we asked for our check over thirty minutes ago?"

I wonder why when we travel outside the United States we expect people to behave like Americans—even in their own country. Think about it for a minute: how many waiters, taxi drivers, hotel clerks, shopkeepers, and others in your hometown could or would respond to a French person who spoke only French? If you don't speak French and have traveled to Paris, you were probably helped by a number of people who speak pretty good English. And almost all Europeans coming to our shores make it a point to adapt to our customs. Well, almost all. Don't ask a waiter who's just been stiffed on his 18 percent tip.

Every culture has certain rules. In America for some unknown reason, you can't get wine at fast-food restaurants, and spending a few minutes digging deeply inside your nose on public transit is frowned upon. In Paris, the rules dictate one shouldn't dress in grungy jeans and a ripped T-shirt, unless it says "Let's Sex! . . . NOW!!" painted in gold lettering across the front. To life in a foreign country you need to learn the rules, especially if you plan to stay. And I had to learn plenty.

⌒

Like so many other people, I dreamed about living in Paris ever since my first visit in the '80s, during that rite of passage every American student fresh out of college used to embark upon, before kids decided it was less of a hassle to explore the world with RAM rather than a Railpass. Why bother getting lost in the labyrinth of historic cities, dining on regional delicacies, sleeping with total strangers in youth hostels, and soaping up in communal showers with a team of Italian soccer players? Yes, I suppose it's far better to stay home and experience Europe though a computer screen. But back then, I had quite a time doing most of those things. (I'll leave it to your imagination to guess which ones.)

But explore I did. I spent almost a year traipsing around the continent after college doing nothing in particular except learning about European cultures, primarily by pulling up a stool or chair and eating what the locals ate. During that time, I made it through almost every country in Europe and tried whatever local delicacies were to be had: oozing raw-milk cheeses in France and hearty, grain-packed breads in Germany; Belgian milk chocolates that when sniffed, could transport you to a dairy farm in the countryside; and crispy-skin fish grilled over gnarled branches in the souks of Istanbul. And of course, lots of buttery pastries and crusty breads smeared with plenty of golden-yellow butter in Paris, the likes of which I'd never tasted before.

After months of criss-crossing Europe, in dire need of a good, deep scrubbing and a proper haircut to rein in my unruly mop of curls (which definitely earned me the term dirty blond), I eventually ran out of steam—and money—and returned to the States. During the carefree time I'd spent traipsing from country to country, I hadn't given any thought to my future and what I'd do after I returned. Why spoil the fun? Back in America, after seeing a world outside of our sometimes isolating borders, I didn't quite know where I would fit in and hadn't a clue as to where to go or what to do with my life.

I'd read about "California cuisine," which was a new and exciting concept just emerging back then. And something to do with food seemed like an interesting option, since I didn't see Europe through my eyes, but my stomach. Everything I'd tasted was a far cry from my college days, when I worked at a vegetarian restaurant ladling out peanut butter–thickened soups and dishing up desserts made by our long-haired baker, who added his own unique touches to anything he baked. In fact, I can still smell his fruit cobblers filled with apples and kidney beans, baked and scented with his signature handful of cumin, which gave them a distinctly unpleasant odor.

On second thought, that might have been him.

Fortunately, the European style of cooking was gaining a foothold in northern California, and there was a new appreciation for fine foods and cooking *du marché:* buying locally produced foods at their peak of freshness, which was a daily ritual in Europe. It seemed like common sense to me, and simply the right way to eat. So I packed up and moved to San Francisco, just across the bay from Berkeley, where an exciting culinary revolution was simmering. And I hoped cumin-scented desserts weren't a part of it.

Shopping the outdoor markets of the Bay Area, I discovered farmers who were raising things like blood oranges with tangy, wildly colored juices and tight bunches of deep-violet radicchio, which people at the time assumed were runty heads of cabbage. Laura Chenel was producing European-style moist rounds of fresh goat cheese in Sonoma, which were so unfamiliar that Americans were mistaking them for tofu (especially in Berkeley). And viticulturists in Napa Valley were producing hearty wines, like Zinfandel and Pinot Noir, which had a great affinity for the newly celebrated regional cuisine, which was liberally seasoned with lots of fragrant garlic, branches of rosemary and thyme, and drizzled with locally pressed olive oil—a big improvement over the bland "salad oil" I grew up with.

I was thrilled—no, *astounded*—to find the culinary counterparts to everything I had eaten in Europe. I savored the hand-dipped ultrafine chocolates of Alice Medrich at Cocolat, which rivaled those I had swooned over in swanky French chocolate boutiques. I'd line up daily for a *boule* of *pain au levain* that Steve Sullivan would pull out of his fired-up brick oven every morning over at Acme Bread, and was ecstatic to find many of the pungent cheeses I remembered so fondly from Europe stacked up at the Cheese Board Collective in Berkeley, just across from Chez Panisse.

Since I believed that if I was really going to pursue a restaurant career I should start at the top, I applied for a job at Chez Panisse, where Alice Waters was leading this culinary revolution I wanted to enlist in. I sent a letter to the restaurant, waited a few weeks, and got no response. Despite the lack of acknowledgment or enthusiasm on their part, I presented myself at the now-famous redwood archway, ready to embark on my lifelong career as a chef. I marched inside, where a busy waiter, who was rushing by holding a tray of wineglasses and wearing a white shirt, tie, and long apron, looking remarkably like a *garçon* in Paris, pointed me toward the bright kitchen in the back of the dining room.

The kitchen staff was working at full throttle. Some were maniacally rolling out ultrathin, nearly transparent sheets of pasta. Others were painstakingly trimming carrots tinier than a baby's pinky, their peelers thwacking against the countertop at warp speed, spewing bright orange curlicues, then tossing each denuded root into a stainless steel bin with a little plunk before seamlessly moving on to the next one.

One cook was busy layering moist rounds of goat cheese in well-worn earthenware crocks, ripping apart bunches of thyme and layering them between whole cloves of garlic and pinelike branches of rosemary. In the back, I noticed some women intently guarding the oven doors, checking inside every few moments. I had no idea at the time that they were scrupulously watching the progress of Lindsey Shere's famous almond tarts—making sure they didn't cook a second too long and were taken out just when they reached their precise degree of caramelization.

I went over to speak with the chef, who was at the epicenter of it all, directing the chaos around her. Overwhelmed by it all, I asked in my most timid voice if there was any possibility . . . any way at all . . . she could perhaps find a place for me at Chez Panisse—the Greatest Restaurant in America.

She closed her eyes and put down her knife midslice, then turned around to look at me. And in front of the entire kitchen staff, she proceeded to tell me off, saying she had no idea who I was and how could I think that I could just walk into the restaurant unannounced and ask for a job? Then she picked up her knife and started chopping again, which I took as a pretty good indication that I should leave.

And that was the end of my first job interview in laid-back California.

So I went to work at another restaurant in San Francisco, where I found myself in way over my head and in a job that was downright horrible. The chef was a complete nutcase and should have traded his chef's jacket for a more restrictive padded one, with buckles in the rear. My Sunday brunch shift would begin with his breaking open and smashing to bits all the scones I had carefully rolled out, cut, and baked that morning, verifying that each one was, indeed, flaky. And by my last shift (ever), I was so flustered by it all that, as I struggled to keep up with the barrage of orders that came streaming in, I neglected a pot of simmering fryer oil, which turned into a raging fire.

Cumin-scented cobblers were beginning to seem not quite so bad after all.

(I do have a few good memories of that place, though. I still get a chuckle when I think how one of my coworkers, who was teaching me a few words in Vietnamese, taught me how to say "sweet potatoes" in his native language, which actually meant "blow job." Nowadays I wonder what the other prep cooks were thinking when I called downstairs and asked one of them to come upstairs because I desperately needed some "sweet potatoes.")

After each day of work, I'd drag myself home and collapse in a defeated heap, near tears. Waking up the next morning, I found myself filled with so much dread that I could barely heave myself out of bed. So when I heard the news that the chef at Chez Panisse was leaving to open her own place, I plotted my escape—a triumphant return to where I rightfully belonged. At least *I* thought so. After scoring an interview with the new chef and undergoing the final scrutiny of Alice Waters herself, I was soon proudly working at Chez Panisse.

(I have to mention that the original chef who disparaged me turned out to be a terrific person, warm and supportive of up-and-coming chefs, and someone I like and respect very much. Although not French, she was my first encounter with a short-fuse French-style temperament and good practice for things to come.)

In all, I spent nearly thirteen years cooking at Chez Panisse, most of it working in the pastry department, joining the select few who've mastered Lindsey's famed, and notoriously tricky, almond tart. I'm not one for hero worship, but I will certainly say that Alice Waters was a formidable force, and she kept the hundred-plus cooks who worked there on their toes at all times. Someone once said, "You don't know terror until you've heard the sound of Alice's footsteps coming toward you."

And how true that was. I quickly learned that the faster those little feet were racing toward me, the more trouble I was going to be in. For all my smart-alecky retorts, though, Alice was almost always right, and each upbraiding was actually a valuable lesson for a young cook like me. Alice was committed to instilling in us her ideas for using seasonal and local ingredients long before the idea became such an overused cliché that airline menus are now touting "locally grown" ingredients. And she inspired us to put those ideas into action in the food we were cooking.

Lindsey Shere, the co-owner of the restaurant and executive pastry chef, was also a constant, and lasting, source of inspiration. From Lindsey, I learned that making our deceptively simple desserts was often far more difficult than creating complex, multitiered, over-the-top sugary extravaganzas. Simplicity meant our ingredients—fruits, nuts, and chocolates—needed to be absolutely top-notch, and sourcing the best of them was an integral part of our job.

Lindsey constantly surprised me with a taste of something new and unexpected—like fresh, tender apricots gently poached in sweet Sauternes to complement their tang, or a scoop of freshly churned rose-flavored ice cream, its perfumed aroma infused with the fragrant petals she'd plucked from her dewy garden that morning. There were golden-brown biscotti with the crunch of toasted almonds, each bite releasing the curious scent of anise, and what became my absolute favorite: wedges of very dark chocolate cake, made with European-style bittersweet chocolate, which were barely sweet. I gobbled up hunks of it every chance I could.

Each day was a revelation to me, and I learned restraint in a profession where the prevalent wisdom had always been not to let guests leave unless they were gut-bustingly full. I knew I was in the right place when I was told "This is the one restaurant where the customer isn't always right."

When I started, I worked in the café upstairs, and learned how to let the leaves of just-picked lettuce fall from my hands into an airy heap on the plate just so. Later, when I moved to the pastry department, I reveled in the *fraises des bois*, tiny wild strawberries raised especially for us, each one a tiny burst of the most intense strawberry flavor imaginable, which we'd serve with just a scoop of nutty crème fraîche and a sprinkle of sugar, letting the flavor of the wild berries shine. We were making food that was meant to inspire, not be mindlessly ingested. With each flat of picture-perfect fruit or berries I tore into, I realized I was part of something very special.

While I happily learned dessert making surrounded by the most dedicated cooks imaginable, as the years wore on something else was happening: My back and brain were suffering under the stress and brutal demands of restaurant work. Cooks are known to move rapidly from job to job, but they stay put at Chez Panisse. When only the highest-quality ingredients are available to you and you're surrounded by a terrific crew of people with the same passionate interest in sending out the best food possible, where do you go next? What do you do?

So after over a decade, I left Chez Panisse. But then had to ask myself, "What should *I* do?" I didn't really know, but Alice suggested I write a book of desserts. So I started by plucking my favorite cookbooks off the shelf and seeing what features appealed to me most. I had created quite a few recipes and adapted some that were inspired by others, and I wanted to share them in a friendly, approachable style. Most of them were simple to make and didn't require an arsenal of fancy equipment.

I also wanted to shift people's perception of dessert from being the rich overload, the proverbial "nail in the coffin" that seals one's fate after dinner, to simpler sweets that concentrated on the pure flavors of fresh fruits and dark chocolate. I was delighted when people reported back that my recipes had become part of their permanent repertoires and happy to be carrying on with the foundations that Lindsey and Alice had instilled in me.

After a few years in the pajama-clad workforce of folks who work at home (or in my case, specifically, in the kitchen), I had a life-changing experience: I unexpectedly lost my partner, who had been the vision of health and vitality. It was one of those unimaginable experiences in life where everything around you stops and you go into shock, able to do only what's necessary to stay afloat. I was devastated, and as Joan Didion wrote in *A Year of Magical Thinking,* I found myself in that "place none of us know until we reach it."

Eventually, after months and months of numbness, I realized I needed to rejoin life. After learning that life can take an unexpected turn when you don't think it will, I sought to regain my footing and felt ready to move forward.

It was an opportunity to flip over the Etch A Sketch of my life, give it a good shake, and start again. I had so much: a job in one of the best restaurants in America, a few well-received cookbooks, a beautiful house in San Francisco with a professionally equipped kitchen, and lots of really close friends who meant the world to me. But all that wasn't fueling me anymore. After all I'd gone through, I was emotionally exhausted and in need of something to recharge me.

So I decided to move to Paris.

My friends reacted by saying, "You can't run away, David." But I didn't feel like I was running from anything; I was heading in a new direction.

Why would anyone run from a beautiful city like San Francisco, where I had lived most of my life, and where all my friends were? Well, because there was Paris.

I had fallen in love with Paris when I had attended some advanced pastry classes at the prestigious Ecole Lenôtre a few years earlier. One night after a lively dinner with friends, I was walking alone across one of the graceful bridges that cross the Seine. If you've ever walked through Paris at night, you can't help noticing that its beauty is magnified in the darkness; lights glow softly everywhere and frame the centuries-old buildings and monuments in spectacular ways. I remember that evening breathing in the damp air rising off the Seine, watching the Bateaux Parisiens gliding on the river, loaded with awestruck tourists, and illuminating the monuments in their wake, the dramatic light hitting a building for just a few moments before moving on to the next.

It's the life of the city, though, that held the most appeal for me and inspired my move. Paris is a major metropolis, yet has all the peculiarities and charms of a small town. Each neighborhood has a special personality, its butchers and bakers, the *maraîchers* at the open-air stalls selling fruits and vegetables piled high, and the cafés, which Parisians use as makeshift living rooms to mingle with friends over a glass of wine, or just to sit by themselves with a chilled kir, content to do nothing more than gaze off in the distance.

It all seemed good to me. So off I went.

KIR

MAKES 1 SERVING

Kir is a popular apértif named after the former mayor of Dijon who dedicated himself to reviving the café culture in Burgundy after it had been devastated by World War II. He was a big proponent of this apértif, which featured a splash of crème de cassis, a fruity liqueur made with locally produced black currants. This further endeared him to the locals, as well as to me.

Substitute Champagne for the white wine and you've got a kir royale. Just be sure to serve it in a Champagne flute, which even the humblest and funkiest café in Paris will do. I prefer my kir on the lighter side, although it's very *au courant* to use a bit more cassis than suggested here.

$1^1/2$ to 2 teaspoons crème de cassis

1 glass well-chilled dry white wine, preferably Aligoté, or another tangy-dry white wine, such as Chablis or Sauvignon Blanc, will also do

Pour the crème de cassis into a wineglass. Add the wine and serve. The accompaniment of choice, in Paris, is salted peanuts.

NOTES ON THE RECIPES

All the recipes in the book were tested in my Parisian kitchen using a combination of French and American ingredients, and in an American kitchen using all-American ingredients.

Where certain items may be unavailable, I've offered substitutes that will yield excellent results no matter where your kitchen is. I've listed mail order and online sources (see Resources, page 271), although almost everything should be available in well-stocked su-permarkets, and I encourage you to use local ingredients whenever possible.

Because there are so many kinds of salt to choose from, I often call for "coarse salt." Kosher salt and sea salt are both appropriate. If not specified, you can use whatever you prefer. I don't use fine table salt, which I find too harsh and acrid. If that's what you pre-fer, cut the amount of salt in half to compensate.

If sugar is called for in recipes, it's white granulated sugar, sim-ilar to what's called "castor sugar" in some countries. Powdered sugar, also called confectioners' sugar, is known in other English-speaking countries as "icing sugar." Flour is always all-purpose, un-less noted otherwise.

While prevalent wisdom has decreed that we should use only unsalted butter for baking, you can use salted butter and omit the salt in the recipes. (I'm considering leading a return-of-salted-butter movement.)

Last, a few of the recipes in this book may appear in another form on my Web site. Recipes evolve over time, and it's interesting to go back and see how my tastes and techniques have progressed. In spite of the fact that technology makes it possible to "turn back time" and make changes, I chose to keep them intact online since those entries are a record of what I made at that particular time. Any recipes in this book that originally appeared on the site are the result of revisions and refinements.

JE SUIS PARISIEN

My first day in Paris, I was already in a fight—with three ridiculously overstuffed suitcases containing everything I couldn't bear to live without. For most people, it would be clothing, a stockpile of their favorite shampoo, and maybe a photo album or two. Me? My suitcases were jam-packed with Sharpies, crunchy peanut butter, and measuring cups.

The four of us wrestled through the massive wooden doorway of my unfamiliar apartment building and landed in a deserted courtyard. After twenty years of living in San Francisco, I had sold virtually everything I owned, and the rest I brought with me.

In addition to the cherished items in my suitcases, a few weeks earlier I had packed up two cases of my absolute favorite, most cherished cookbooks from a collection that I'd amassed over the years at Chez Panisse, all signed by the authors whom I'd met and cooked with, timing the boxes' arrival to coincide with mine.

This year marks the sixth anniversary of my expectation that any day now, *La Poste* will knock on my door and reunite me with my long-lost collection of cookbooks. I refuse to give up hope. As a Frenchman at a dinner party said to me shortly after I arrived, and recounted my first troubled weeks in Paris, "I love Americans. You're all so optimistic!"

Realistically, I have to assume by now that somebody, somewhere, has a fabulous library of personally autographed cookbooks by Julia Child, Richard Olney, and Jane Grigson. I just hope his name is David, he's into cooking, and he treasures them as much as I did.

After stuffing myself and my luggage into the impossibly cramped elevator, the suitcases wobbling one on top of the other in a space half the size of an airplane bathroom, the door struggled to close, and I prayed I'd make it to the top floor without being crushed to death.

The door opened at the top and we all stumbled out. I dug out of my pocket the grandiose key that had been mailed to me for my dream *appartement,* which I'd optimistically fallen in love with from the pictures on the Internet. The place had looked perfect—ceilings mirroring the mansard roof, a compact but wide-open kitchen, an expansive rooftop view of Paris, and a peaceful, Zen-like bedroom.

Turning the key in the little slot, I swung open the door.

I stepped inside and pushed my way through the vastly overgrown and spindly tendrils of a dried-up and long ago given-up-for-dead plant whose withering branches were nailed firmly in place across the entryway. Once I managed to hack through the urban jungle, I looked around and took in my new home.

Where one might traditionally find, say, ceilings, big pieces of crumbly stucco dangled instead, collapsing in shards of papery stalactites, littering everything with dusty flakes of plaster. I kicked aside some of the debris and looked down at the carpet, which was so dank and filthy I didn't want to soil the bottoms of my shoes by walking on it.

The Japanese-inspired bedroom was indeed an oasis of tranquility, except for the futon bed, which was splattered with some stains that made me more than a little uneasy. And the previous tenant had left a collection of beer bottles by the bedside. Ever the optimist, I wanted to assume they were intended as a welcome-to-Paris gesture, but since they'd been polished off before my arrival, I could feel my optimism slipping away. At least my predecessors were kind enough to dispose of their stinky cigarette butts, which filled the inside of the bottles, rather than messing up the floor.

So what does one do when faced with this kind of situation?

In Paris, there's only one thing you can do: eat. And have a glass of wine. Or maybe two. So I left, closing the door and locking it behind me. (As if anyone was going to steal my old socks and measuring cups.) Hungry for my first Parisian lunch, I took a walk and stopped at a small café. Flustered and overwhelmed by my less-than-successful arrival, I ordered a *salade* and the first of many glasses of wine, which I quickly surmised would become a good coping strategy for any problems that were to come.

After lunch, I went back to the apartment and made an anguished call to the landlord, who lived abroad. He managed to find a painter to rehabilitate my two-room apartment, which meant I had to move out before I could move in, the first of many mind-skewing French paradoxes. I expected a small job like painting two rooms might take a normal painter about a week.

Except the landlord hired a French painter.

～

One of the most important things I would tell anyone moving to France is not to expect anyone to be particularly concerned about finding the most expedient path to the end result.

If you don't believe me, join the queue of Parisians waiting for their baguettes at the *boulangerie* and you'll see what I mean. You've never heard so many elaborate discussions over which baguette is better: *pas trop cuite* or *bien cuite* (pale and soft versus well-baked and crunchy), *traditionnelle* or *ordinaire, demie* or *entière . . .*

Listen as you wait in line at the *volailler:* Is that *poularde* in the case going to make a more flavorful bouillon than the *poulet fermier* in the window? Could that chicken on the left be exactly the same size as the one next to it? Is it *really* the same price? Can you weigh them both and check just to be sure? Do you have others in the back?

The negotiations, gesticulations, and debate are far more important than the final result, which is getting the goods and getting out of there. And when it's time to pay, that simple act can last an eternity too, as each precious centime is extracted and painstakingly given up to the cashier. For some reason, to the French, it always seems like a total surprise when the time comes to pay up. As if the customers are saying, "After all that, you expect me *to pay*, too?"

"What do you do all day in Paris?" is something I'm often asked by people who think I spend my days hopping from chocolate shop to patisserie. I know it's not very interesting or romantic for them to hear, "Well, yesterday I bought paper clips." Or "On Monday, I tried to return something that was broken. Tuesday, I went searching for shoelaces."

I've learned to give myself p-l-e-n-t-y of time to run errands, and I realized the rule, rather then the exception, is that either the place will be closed when I get there (albeit with a polite *excusez-nous* taped to the door) or it will have every item, such as each and every kind of herb tea imaginable, *except* for the most common one of all—like chamomile. Which, *of course*, is the one my queasy tummy desperately needs.

The first time I had to return something in Paris, I naïvely thought I could take care of it in just a few minutes. The phone battery I had bought to replace the dead one in my new apartment at the electronics chain, Darty, didn't work. Since the store advertises in big letters painted on the wall: *Notre Objectif: 100% de clients satisfaits,* I thought it would be a breeze. I'd pop in, get a replacement, and join the happy ranks of the 100 percent satisfied customers.

I entered the store and waited in the short line at the *acceueil* counter, which, even though the word means "welcome," is, paradoxically, the most unwelcoming place in France. There I waited and waited . . . and waited and waited . . . and waited and waited. Even though there were just a couple of people in front of me, a half-hour passed before it was my turn. Each transaction seemed to take forever, with lots of back-and-forth negotiations on both sides, ending with either reluctant acceptance by the cashier, or an admission of defeat by the customer, who would shrug his shoulders and walk away.

Americans don't like to accept defeat, which is why the phrase, "Can I speak to the manager?" is so often used. In the United States, the manager sides with the customer and usually clears up the problem in your favor. In France, the manager isn't there to help customers. His job is to watch out for fellow employees. So you're better off not asking, unless you're confident enough to take on two adversaries instead of one.

When it was my turn, I figured I'd hand off the bad battery and they'd simply hand me a new one, or give me a refund. Instead, I was directed downstairs, to the *service clients* desk.

After shuffling through a mound of paperwork jammed into several bulging three-ring binders, the clerk began to compile a dossier. A stack of forms was filled out, date-stamped multiple times, then photocopied. Afterward, a manager was called to sign his approval, which he grudgingly did after studying the contents of the thick folder for a few minutes, suspiciously looking for some clue that I was fudging my bum battery claim. Then I was directed back upstairs, presumably to pick up my refund.

Relieved to be done, I proudly presented the supremely uninterested woman behind the register with my folder of paperwork, expecting to be united with a new battery. Instead, I needed to go to *another* desk, where my dossier would be reinspected and a new battery *might* be located for me.

The woman at that desk spent what seemed an inordinate amount of time searching for my replacement on her computer. When she couldn't find one in stock, I asked, optimistically, "Could I please just get a refund then?"

Let's just say that if there's supposed to be truth in advertising, they need to lower their 100 percent *satisfait* number by one.

Back at home, equally low on my customer-satisfaction scale was my resident *artiste*. After two weeks, he'd nearly finished the painting but was finding it impossible to make that last definitive brushstroke and leave. I could again feel my cheery optimism slipping away day by day. After leaving him alone to work and camping out at a friend's apartment, I'd foolishly assumed that if I moved back in and started setting up house around him, he'd take the hint, finish up, and split.

Instead, he left all his gear lying about, and would come back daily to do something—anything—no matter how trivial: repaint the bottom of a door, give the ceiling of the closet another coat, or touch up the baseboard behind the refrigerator. Then he'd leave, saying he'd be back tomorrow to finish up a few more critical areas. After a couple more weeks of this I realized that the concept of "finishing" wasn't part of his agenda, which was odd, since he'd already been paid and I'm sure he had better things to do than spend his afternoons dragging his ladder and drop cloth around my apartment looking for obscure corners to repaint.

Because it's kind of pathetic to see a man in his forties cry, my friends David and Randal offered to perform a "French-painter intervention" and get rid of him once and for all. They called him up and gave him his marching orders, informing him they were piling all his gear outside the apartment door and that he'd better come over to get it as soon as possible. Then we left for a very long walk, stopping in a café for a glass of wine. And when we came back, he and his equipment were out of my life, for good.

Or so I thought.

Fortunately, this was also the same time that I got a new number and learned about *la liste rouge*, a telephone feature that allows you to block your number from anyone you choose, including hostile French painters. And with the touch of a few buttons on my brand-new telephone, I began to feel like I just might be home.

===

WARM GOAT CHEESE SALAD

MAKES 1 SERVING

The very first thing I ate on my first day in Paris was a *salade de chèvre chaud*, while I dined alone at the Café Le Moderne in the Bastille and pondered my predicament.

After I sat down, I gathered up my courage, linked together the few words of French I knew, and ordered a simple salad topped with rounds of warm goat cheese along with a glass of crisp white wine, the first of many to come.

Goat cheese toasts

2 slices of hearty bread, such as pain au levain,
    or good white bread

Extra virgin olive oil

3-ounce (90 g) round, or crottin, of goat cheese,
    sliced in half horizontally

Salad

1/2 teaspoon red wine or sherry vinegar

2 teaspoons extra virgin olive oil

1/8 teaspoon Dijon mustard

Coarse salt

2 cups (100 g) torn green lettuce leaves, rinsed and dried

Freshly ground black pepper

1/4 cup (25 g) walnut halves, toasted, optional

1. Preheat the broiler and set the oven rack 4 inches (10 cm) below the heating element.

2. Brush the bread with just enough olive oil to moisten it. Place half of the cheese on each slice. Broil on a baking sheet in the oven until the cheese is soft, warmed through, and a little browned on top. This should take 3 to 5 minutes, depending on your broiler.

3. While the toasts are baking, make a vinaigrette in a large bowl. With a fork, stir the vinegar, olive oil, mustard, and a nice pinch of salt.

4. Toss the lettuce in the vinaigrette and pile on a plate. Grind fresh pepper over the top, rest the warm toasts over the lettuce, and scatter with walnuts, if using.

SERVING: Serve with a chilled glass or *fillette* of white wine, such as Muscadet, Sancerre, or Sauvignon Blanc. Enjoy by yourself.

MA PETITE CUISINE

In order to finalize some of my affairs stateside, later that same year I had to head back to the States for six months. So I decided to sublet my recently painted, state-of-the-art telecommunications-equipped apartment. I posted a listing on a popular Web site and got a few encouraging responses. The most enthusiastic of the lot was from a potential *sous-locataire* who "couldn't wait to be cooking and baking away in the well-stocked and professionally equipped kitchen of—*David Lebovitz!*"

I must not be that good with a camera, because the pictures I sent in response didn't quite seal the deal, and I never heard from him again. Even with my wide-angle lens, it's hard to hide the fact that my kitchen is barely big enough for one person, let alone any professional equipment. And apparently my renown with this fellow wasn't enough to overcome my kitchen's shortcomings.

Coming from America, where the average kitchen is the size of my entire apartment (and often larger), it was quite an experience learning to bake on a counter so small I had to lift one bowl up before I could set down another. I wasn't baking so much as practicing crowd control. People see my kitchen and think it's so cute: *"C'est très parisien!"* they say as they lunge forward in excitement. It's not until they lift their heads back up and thwack it hard on the sloped ceiling that they begin to understand some of the challenges I face. I learned to watch out for the ceiling eventually. But in the beginning, my head got banged more times than the gals up in Pigalle.

When I moved in, the kitchen was no different from the rest of the apartment: a complete disaster. The refrigerator looked as though it hadn't been cleaned since the all-out strikes of May 1968. The dishwasher pipes were so caked with Paris's insidious *calcaire* that when you switched the washer on, instead of humming to life, it would start off with a hopeful buzz that soon led to convulsive wheezing, with plates clattering inside. Shortly afterward, it would progress to violent shaking and begin body-slamming everything around it, wrenching itself loose from the confines of the cabinets, forcing me to race across the room to pull the plug before the plate-shattering *grande finale*.

Just behind the dishwasher, tucked in the corner, is a small washing machine. For the life of me, and every other American living in Europe, I can't figure out why it takes two hours to wash a load in a European machine in Europe, whereas washing a load in a European machine in America takes only forty minutes.

That, coupled with the subsequent drying for those of us who don't have a dryer (which is almost everyone in Paris), means having to be creative about hanging your clothes in every spare space available in your apartment, *à la Napolitana*, as they say: in the style of a Neapolitan washer woman. Which means if you have guests, you can't be too shy about their knowing whether you're a boxers or briefs kinda guy. Unlike the Neapolitans, I keep mine indoors, since I don't want my neighbors, especially *le voyeur* with the binoculars across the street, to know that much about me. Although he seems to be pretty fixated on whatever's going on in the apartment below mine. (And because of him, now I am, too.)

Part of becoming Parisian means an initiation into the surely decades-old tradition of buying your first drying rack, which requires as much thought, reflection, and comparison of features as your very first car purchase. My initial foray into the world of drying racks required a hands-on demonstration that lasted well over thirty minutes. The eager salesman, whose talents eclipsed those of hyper-hawker Ron Popeil, unfolded and flexed and contorted every single drying rack in his department. I wondered whether he was on commission or just bored, standing among all those drying racks each and every day. Regardless, I was won over not just by the sturdy, well-designed rack I went home with, but by the fact that I actually got a salesperson's undivided attention for more than thirty seconds in a French department store.

Aside from my new part-time job as an Italian washerwoman, I had to think about my real-life job, which involved a lot of cooking and baking. How could I work in such a petite *cuisine américaine*? And when I say "American kitchen," you're probably conjuring up images of expansive granite countertops, shelves stacked with shiny cookware, all the latest gadgets, and restaurant-style appliances.

Here in Paris, *"cuisine américaine"* translates to "completely impractical." My counter is so high that if a spoon handle is sticking over the edge of a bowl, I'm in danger of putting an eye out. It also means that even though I'm close to six feet tall, when folding batters and such, I can barely see into the bowl and I have to assume things are getting mixed in properly way up there. I suppose I could put a mirror on the ceiling, but when I moved in, the painter removed all the seventies-style mirrors, which covered every conceivable surface of the apartment, and I wasn't about to call him up to find out where he'd put them.

What the countertop lacks in practicality, it makes up for by not imposing itself and taking up too much space in my apartment. Consequently, my entire cooking area is roughly the size of a rectangular gâteau Opéra, the size that serves eight. And we're talking eight French-sized servings, not American-sized slabs.

The first thing you realize when horizontal space is at a premium is that there's only one way to go, and that's up. So things get stacked one on top of the other, which is more than mildly annoying. If I need the sugar bin, it's invariably the one at the bottom of the stack, and to get it I have to move everything else on top of it, which may include any or—if I hit it at the wrong time (which I always seem to do)—all of the following: flour, cocoa powder, cornstarch, confectioners' sugar, cornmeal, brown sugar, and oats.

My precious stash of American goodies—molasses, organic peanut butter, dried sour cherries, non-stick spray, wild rice, and Lipton Onion Soup Mix—get crammed in the back of one of my two cabinets, reserved for special occasions. The onion soup mix is especially rare around here, and a guest has to be someone pretty dip-worthy for me to tear into one of my prized foil-wrapped pouches.

Baking as much as I do, I stockpile ingredients. Everything closes at 9 p.m., and there's nothing worse than running out of sugar at 8:40, the time when the employees actually decide they're ready to call it quits and lock the door. So I bought a sturdy bakery-style chrome rack to store sacks of flour, big bags of nuts, massive blocks of chocolate, and kilos of sugar, which keep the ice cream, cakes, and cookies flowing at all hours.

This absolutely stuns French guests who are only used to seeing twenty or thirty bags of sugar and flour being delivered to their local pâtisserie, not in someone's apartment. And I've got one whole shelf devoted entirely to French chocolate, which I buy in enormous tablets, as well as sacks of *pistoles:* those small, round disks that are great when you need 247 grams of chocolate and don't want to spend the time—or in my kitchen, lack the space—to lop off hunks from a jumbo slab of *chocolat noir.* The only problem is those little suckers are a little *too* convenient, and as much as I keep hiding that box away in the back corner, a few hours later it seems to find its way up to the front with my arm digging around up to my elbow, like a kid rifling through a box of cereal, half-crazed, searching for the prize.

Frustratingly, I can't stockpile everything and have to keep other necessities, like popcorn and polenta, to a bare minimum because of space constraints. Since I have good friends who work for major cookware and appliance companies, I'm sometimes offered gifts that I simply can't refuse. But refuse I do.

Well, most of the time. How does one turn down a professional blender or a copper roasting pan? So add a blender, espresso maker, and ice cream freezer to my kitchen, then do the math: with 25 percent of the space devoted to an electric mixer, 10 percent to a blender, and 54 percent to my Italian espresso maker, I'm left with only 11 percent of usable counter space.

Although I considered not replacing the dishwasher and resigning myself to the drudgery of hand washing, my painter-pushing friend Randal slapped some sense into me. One day shortly thereafter, two hunky Frenchmen showed up at my apartment, muscles bulging and a fine mist of sweat glistening on their chiseled features. Which was great, but what was even more appreciated than their presence was the new dishwasher they'd hauled up the six flights of stairs.

 ⌒

The longer I've lived *chez* David, the more creative I've become with space, and my apartment is now really just one giant kitchen, closer in size to the *cuisine américaine* I had back in San Francisco, and which I miss more than shopping at Target. I've even co-opted the adjoining rooftop, which holds the distinction of being the most beautiful cooling rack in the world; my cookies cool with a view of the Eiffel Tower, overlooking the elegant place des Vosges. With the gentle breezes of Paris blowing, it's actually quite a model of efficiency—provided you make sure no wildlife is lurking about. I've learned the hard way, deduced from a few telltale feathers embedded in a block of barely cooled toffee, that Parisian pigeons have just as much of a sweet tooth as I do.

And why limit the bathroom to personal grooming? My dated, but thoroughly utilitarian, marble bathroom shelves are a perfect pigeon-proof environment for cooling candy. When there are lots of pots and pans to be tackled, there's much more room in my generously sized bathtub than in my dinky kitchen sink, which would frustrate even Barbie if it were installed in her Dream House.

Imagine if you had to scrub clean a stockpot in one of those washbasins on an airplane and you'll understand why my bathtub's the best place for lathering up the Le Creusets. I fill the tub with soapy water, then get down on my hands and knees, like the *lavandières* of yesteryear doing their scrubbing in the Seine.

My toilet, which was on its last gasps when I moved in, is a repository for mistakes, which I'm sure isn't helping it maintain what's left of its vigor. Like the French, it's sometimes a bit rebellious and *fragile,* and I now know it's a wise idea to check to make sure everything's gone after you flush: a failed batch of grass-green mint chip ice cream hadn't quite made it down when a friend who came by. Upon exiting the bathroom, he suggested that I might want to see a doctor.

And is the bedroom off limits? *Pas du tout!* Because these days, there's not as much activity going on in there as I'd hoped, so I've turned it into a full-on *glacière.* My bedroom started multitasking when I was writing a book on ice cream and found myself churning out batches of ice cream and sorbet all day long—and sometimes into the night, which I'm sure made the neighbors downstairs wonder what I was up to.

I had three machines that I was rotating batches through, and each made a terrible racket. So into the bedroom they all went, which was such a great solution that that's where they now all stay. The only difficulty is explaining to my cleaners why there's toffee stuck to my sheets. When I tell them I'm rippling ice cream, I get quite a few funny looks. Although the French have a reputation for bedroom antics, I think I have them beat.

===

FLOATING ISLAND

MAKES 6 SERVINGS

I don't recommend flushing meringue down the toilet, especially if you live on the top floor where the water pressure may be less than optimal. I speak from experience since I tried it with a batch when I was testing this recipe, and the fluffy egg mass refused to budge for a couple of days. In frustration, I finally took a knife to it, and the meringue disappeared once and for all.

But I got it right with this version and it's so good, you won't want to throw any of it away.

Crème anglaise

4 large egg yolks

1 1/2 cups (375 ml) whole milk

1/4 cup (50 g) sugar

1 vanilla bean, split lengthwise

Meringue

4 large egg whites, at room temperature

Pinch of salt

1/8 teaspoon cream of tartar, optional

6 tablespoons (75 g) sugar

Caramel sauce

1 cup (200 g) sugar

3/4 cup (180 ml) water

Toasted sliced almonds or chopped pistachios

1. For the crème anglaise, make an ice bath by filling a large bowl with ice and a bit of water. Nest a smaller metal bowl inside it to hold the crème anglaise. Set a mesh strainer over the top.

2. In a medium bowl, whisk the egg yolks. Heat the milk, 1/4 cup (50 g) sugar, and vanilla bean in a saucepan. Once warm, very gradually pour the milk into the yolks, whisking constantly. Scrape the mixture back into the saucepan and cook, stirring constantly with a heatproof spatula, until the custard begins to thicken and leaves a clean trail when you run your finger across the spatula.

3. Immediately pour the custard through the strainer into the chilled bowl. Pluck out the vanilla bean and add it to the custard, then stir gently until cool. Refrigerate until ready to use.

4. For the meringue, preheat the oven to 325°F (160°C). Very lightly oil a 2-quart (2-L) loaf pan. Set the loaf pan inside a shallow roasting pan.

5. Start whipping the egg whites with an electric mixer on medium speed or by hand. Add the salt and cream of tartar (if using) and beat until the mixture is frothy. Increase the whipping speed to high and when the whites start to hold their shape, add the 6 tablespoons of sugar one spoonful at a time. Once you've added all the sugar, beat for a few minutes, until the meringue is stiff and shiny.

6. Spread the meringue into the prepared loaf pan, being careful not to create any air pockets, and smooth the top with a damp spatula. Add enough warm water to come three-fourths of the way up the sides of the roasting pan.

7. Bake for 25 minutes, or until a toothpick inserted into the center comes out clean. Remove the meringue from the water bath and cool on a wire rack.

8. To make the caramel, spread 1 cup sugar in an even layer in a heavy-bottomed skillet. Cook over medium heat until the sugar begins to liquefy at the edges. Use a heatproof utensil to stir the sugar slightly to prevent the edges from burning.

9. As the sugar melts and begins to caramelize, stir gently (which may cause the sugar to become crystallized, which is fine) until the sugar is a deep bronze color and begins to smoke slightly. Remove from heat and add the water, being careful of the hot steam that rises.

10. Return the pan to the heat and stir until any pieces of molten sugar are melted. You can strain the caramel to remove any stubborn bits.

SERVING: Chill individual serving bowls. Put about 1/3 cup (80 ml) of crème anglaise in each bowl. Run a knife around the edges of the meringue to turn it out onto a platter. Using a thin, sharp knife, slice the meringue into six portions and place them on top of the crème anglaise. Drizzle with a heaping spoonful of caramel sauce and sprinkle with toasted nuts. (You can also use the Candied Almonds, page 51.)

STORAGE: The crème anglaise can be kept covered in the refrigerator for up to three days. The caramel, which will be more than you need for the recipe, will keep for several months in the refrigerator and can be used to garnish another dessert. The meringue can be made one day in advance and refrigerated, loosely covered. The crème anglaise should be very cold and the caramel should be brought to room temperature for serving.

═══════════

CLAFOUTIS AUX PRUNEAUX-FRAMBOISES

PLUM AND RASPBERRY CLAFOUTIS

MAKES 8 SERVINGS

No matter how *faible* (feeble) your kitchen is, clafoutis is easy to make and requires no special equipment: just an oven, a bowl, a whisk, and a baking dish. It's not a fancy dessert—it's meant to be homey and simple, and it's a no-brainer when marvelous summer fruits and juicy berries are in season.

Especially good to use are *quetsches*, which are known as Italian prune plums in the United States. They're generally available late in the season, or you can substitute fresh apricots, which become pleasantly tangy when baked.

4 tablespoons (60 g) salted or unsalted butter, melted, plus more
    for preparing the dish
1 pound (450 g) firm, ripe plums
1 cup (115 g) raspberries
3 large eggs
1/2 cup (70 g) flour
1 teaspoon vanilla extract
1/2 cup (100 g) plus 2 tablespoons (30 g) sugar
1 1/3 cups (330 ml) whole milk

1. Position the rack in the top third of the oven. Preheat the oven to 375°F (180 C).

2. Liberally butter the bottom and sides of a 2-quart (2-L) shallow baking dish. Halve the plums, remove the pits, and place them cut side down over the bottom of the baking dish. If the plums are quite large, cut them into quarters. Scatter the raspberries over the plums.

3. In a medium bowl, whisk the eggs until smooth. Whisk the butter and flour into the eggs until completely smooth, then add the vanilla. Whisk in 1/2 cup (100 g) of the sugar, then the milk.

4. Pour the custard mixture over the fruit and bake for 30 minutes.

5. After 30 minutes, slide out the rack that the clafoutis is resting on (rather than lifting the clafoutis and breaking the tenuous crust that's starting to form on top) and sprinkle 2 tablespoons (30 g) of sugar over the top.

6. Continue baking the clafoutis for about 30 more minutes, until the custard feels slightly firm in the center and the top is a nice golden brown.

SERVING: Serve warm or at room temperature. Clafoutis is best served shortly after it's baked. I prefer it without any accompaniment, as it's traditionally served, although I'll allow you to serve vanilla ice cream or softly whipped cream alongside.

THE MOST IMPORTANT WORDS TO KNOW IN PARIS

So you're in Paris and you need something.

Let's say you're shopping for, I don't know—a pair of gloves. Or a hammer. Or shoelaces. A new battery for your telephone. Or just a *baguette ordinaire*. Whatever. It doesn't really matter how large or small it is. You step inside a shop, but can't find what you're looking for, so you ask the salesperson who ostensibly is there to help you, the all-important customer.

In lieu of a response, you're met with a *réception glaciale*, and on your way out, you wonder, "Why are Parisians so nasty?"

It's probably because you've insulted them—deeply—which you might think is strange, since all you did was ask them a question. And that's the problem.

It is imperative to know the two most important words in the French language—*"Bonjour, monsieur"* or *"Bonjour, madame"*—which you absolutely must say first thing to the first person you make eye contact with. Whether you step into a shop, a restaurant, a café, or even an elevator, you need to say those words to anyone else in there with you. Enter the doctor's waiting room and everyone says their *bonjours.* Make sure to say them at the pharmacy, to the people who make you take off your belt at airport security, to the cashier who's about to deny you a refund for your used-once broken ice cream scoop, as well as to the gap-toothed vendor at the market who's moments away from short-changing you.

If addressing a single woman, use *"Bonjour, mademoiselle."* When I asked a Frenchman how one might discern the difference, he told me to use *mademoiselle* to address women who haven't had sex yet. I don't know how one can tell, but he assured me that Frenchmen can.

The exceptions to the rule are *les grands magasins,* the multilevel Parisian department stores where the service is generally worse than wretched. The customers aren't seen by the salesclerks as guests or visitors, but as a nuisance that gets in the way of the text message they're composing. Or the chat they're having with their coworkers about their breakup with a boyfriend. Or their interminable wait between trips outside for their next cigarette break.

Yet Americans are forever fixated on the notion of how impolite the French are. Whenever I travel in the States, the number one question I'm asked is, "Do the French really hate Americans?"

No, they don't. But they don't like the rude ones. (I don't blame them; neither do I.) If you don't want to be considered rude and want to be treated courteously, you must practice the rules of politesse, which sometimes seem awkward to Americans who are used to breezing into stores, and splitting without greeting anyone. Nowadays when I'm in the States and exiting any store at all, I make sure to say goodbye to each and every person, including the cashiers, stockboys, and clerks in the film department, as well as the security guards lurking about, which I need to stop doing. In Houston, a thinly veiled all-out alert was issued over the loudspeakers at Walgreens a few moments after I entered and said my usual "hellos" to everyone manning a register.

In Paris, the most unbelievably rude thing you can do—and believe me, I seem to have done them all—is to not acknowledge a salesperson.

One day, I was shopping in a fancy chocolate shop on the uptight Left Bank when an American couple walked in wearing shorts, untied sneakers, and baseball caps (mercifully, not turned backwards), toting hefty *venti lattes* from the nearby Starbucks. In Paris, this is like someone hauling a gallon jug of milk into the middle of Tiffany on Fifth Avenue and taking swigs from it. Their attire, coupled with the way they shoved the door wide open and jammed it into place, would have been bad enough. But they said absolutely not a peep to the shocked saleswoman, who greeted them as they entered the shop and breezed right past her. On my way out, I apologized profusely on their behalf since I have a vested stake in improving the image of Americans around here.

This behavior can feel awkward at first, so it helps to think of shops in Paris as someone's home. Imagine if someone came into your house as a guest and just barged past you at the doorway. I wouldn't want to share my chocolates with them either. Those latte-toting folks weren't being rude intentionally; they were just acting casual, like we normally do in America, where anything goes. Heck, I've even see people wearing sweatpants while doing things like taking out the trash back there—if you can believe it.

GATEAU THERESE

CHOCOLATE CAKE

MAKES 8 TO 10 SERVINGS

Every Frenchwoman I know loves chocolate so much she has a chocolate cake in her repertoire that she's committed to memory, one she can make on a moment's notice. This one comes from Thérèse Pellas, who lives across the boulevard from me; when I first tasted the cake, I swooned from the rich, dark chocolate flavor and insisted on the recipe.

Madame Pellas is fanatical about making the cake two days in advance and storing it in her kitchen cabinet before serving, which she says improves the chocolate flavor. And the Brie she keeps in there as well doesn't seem to mind the company. (For some odd reason, the cake never tastes like anything but a massive dose of dark chocolate.) She uses Lindt chocolate, which is widely available and very popular in France—and whenever I see her out and about, I notice there's always a telltale bit of foil wrapper sticking out of her purse, indicating she's also squirreling a bar away for snacking.

9 ounces (250 g) bittersweet or semisweet chocolate, chopped

8 tablespoons (120 g) unsalted butter

$^1/_3$ cup (65 g) sugar

4 large eggs, at room temperature, separated

2 tablespoons flour

Pinch of salt

1. Preheat the oven to 350°F (180°C). Butter a 9-inch (23-cm) loaf pan and line the bottom with a strip of parchment paper.

2. In a large bowl set over a pan of simmering water, heat the chocolate and butter together just until melted and smooth.

3. Remove from heat and stir in half the sugar, then the egg yolks, and flour. (You don't need to measure the half-quantity of sugar exactly. Just pretend you're a Frenchwoman cooking in her home kitchen and don't worry about it.)

4. Using an electric mixer or a whisk, begin whipping the egg whites with the salt. Keep whipping until they start to form soft, droopy peaks. Gradually whip in the remaining sugar until the whites are smooth and hold their shape when the whisk is lifted.

5. Use a rubber spatula to fold one-third of the egg whites into the chocolate mixture to lighten it, then fold in the remaining egg whites just until the mixture is smooth and no visible white streaks remain.

6. Scrape the batter into the prepared loaf pan, smooth the top, and bake for 35 minutes, just until the cake feels slightly firm in the center. Do not overbake.

7. Let the cake cool in the pan before serving.

STORAGE: The cake can be stored for up to three days. Madame Pellas keeps it in her cabinet, but you may wish to put it under a cake dome. It can also be frozen, well wrapped in plastic, for up to one month.

DINING LIKE A PARISIAN

Before I moved to France, my preferred mode of eating was to belly up to the table, position myself strategically over a plate heaped with food, grab the remote, and obsessively tap the "up" button until I reached whatever Hollywood gossip show I could find.

Then, while watching reports about which supermodel might have swallowed a carrot stick by accident, or waiting for a round-table analysis of why a paparazzi-surrounded celebutant would uncross her legs at the wrong moment, I'd have a go at shoveling whatever was piled on my plate into my mouth. My fork was used to spear chunks of food, and also did double-duty as a makeshift knife—albeit a very dull one. I didn't care how I looked, and I'd attack my plate of food with the fervor of a starving wild beast.

Not wanting to out myself as the ill-mannered *étranger* that I am to my cultivated counterparts, I always, *always* use both knife and fork when dining with the French. Which also forces me to slow down when I eat. Early on, I learned to mimic them, steadying my food precisely in place with a fork while using the knife (a real one!) to cut refined, reasonably sized morsels that traveled from plate to mouth, piece by bite-size piece. Once you've picked up the knife at a French dinner table, don't even think of putting it down until you're done eating.

During my days as a backpacker traveling through Europe, I remember people staring at me as I yanked back the skin of a banana and jammed it in my craw, gnawing away at it like a savage until I reached the last nubbin, then tossing the peel aside. *Quelle horreur!*

Watch a Parisian eat a banana: the skin is carefully peeled back, the fruit is set down on a plate, then eaten slice by painstaking slice, using the tines of a fork with the aid of a knife. I'll admit that I still eat bananas like my primordial predecessors, but only in the privacy of my home. Outside of the house, though, I avoid fruit. It's just too stressful.

Even more *vexant* than fruit are fillets of white-fleshed fish with those little pinlike bones that are barely discernible—until you get one lodged in your throat. The French always leave them in, because they say they keep the fish moister during cooking. (They also don't seem to have any personal-injury lawyers lying in wait either, so there's even less incentive to pick out those little throat-blockers.) I always hate to pluck bones and half-chewed fish out of my mouth, which is the least graceful thing one can do at the table. The French never seem to have any problems and manage to pull it off without jamming their fingers around their gums, like I have to.

Another challenge is salad. I've been warned never, ever to cut lettuce with a knife and fork in France. It just isn't done. Instead, the leaves are speared onto the tines of *la fourchette*, then folded over with the aid of the knife that you've already got a death grip on. It's not too much to ask when dealing with large leafy greens like romaine and *l'iceberg*—but a tangle of weedy *roquette*? I've yet to find a way to enjoy a big mound of those flimsy greens without wayward stems flinging dressing Jackson Pollock–style all over the front of my shirt. So I only eat them at home when no one's looking, from a big, deep troughlike bowl that I can either bring up to my chin or lean my face into.

If you're having trouble mastering the knife and fork, fear not, *mes compatriotes;* a culinary revolution has taken Paris by storm in the last couple of years. It's not those dreaded square plates with a useless scribble of sauce or porcini powder around the rim. Or those silly *verrines*—salads and desserts packed into little glasses—where the more unlikely the pairing of flavors, the more press they get. Nor is it a three-star chef's foamy folly or anything that's been compressed, jellified, aerated, or infused.

It's *le sandwich,* which is eaten—amazingly—while walking!

Some blame the phenomenal success of *le sandwich* on the lack of lunch time allotted during the thirty-five-hour workweek (too much work is the government's fault), or the high restaurant prices in Paris (which the government gets blamed for, too), or simply the desire for something convenient. I think if I spent less time filling out bureaucratic paperwork, photocopying it in quadruplicate, then waiting interminably in line to submit it, I'd definitely have more time to do things around here, like sit down and eat. So I'll blame the government as well.

These days, it's not at all unusual to see time-pressed Parisians barreling down the sidewalks, chomping off a bite from a demi-baguette that's been split open and jammed with a few wedges of Camembert or *jambon,* then glued back together with a big, creamy smear of butter. I find lunching while en route nearly impossible, since I'm such a messy eater and whatever I'm wearing gets littered with too many of those invasive little crumbs. So I stick to eating sandwiches in public using a knife and fork, like Parisians still insist on doing with their burgers. "It's not *possible* to pick this up!" they'll exclaim. And yet I do it, much to their amazement.

But I wouldn't dream of stopping into a branch of the nefarious McDo, which Parisians flock to with surprising fervor. I've gone only once since I've been in France, breaking my fifteen-year boycott in a weak moment when I was on the brink of starvation on a French autoroute. I noticed that the traditional rules of etiquette were tossed aside by McDo diners, as evidenced by the multitude of paper and plastic wrappers that littered the tables and floors from the overstuffed trash cans. The other diners around me were picking up their food with their fingers—even their hamburgers!—and drinking soda with their meal (which is odd, considering wine was happily available) amid a few nods to the region, like the faux farm scenes painted on the walls, the chèvre option on the cheeseburgers, and the merciful absence of plaster clowns lurking about.

It wasn't especially fast nor was it especially cheap. Nor was it any good. Other than the fact that it was open in the late afternoon for lunch, a rarity in the countryside, I didn't see the point of ever returning to one; unlike the French, who like it so much that every six days, somewhere in France, a new McDonald's opens.

I think it may be because McDo is one of the few places where the French can let down their guards—and their knives—and relax and enjoy their meals without worrying about minding their manners. In fact, maybe I should give it another try. After all, I'm pretty adept at eating hamburgers. And there isn't any of that annoying fresh fruit on the menu, either.

═══

TAGINE DE POULET AUX ABRICOTS ET AUX AMANDES

CHICKEN TAGINE WITH APRICOTS AND ALMONDS

MAKES 4 TO 6 SERVINGS

The first time I cooked dinner for French people in my little kitchen, I assumed that half a chicken would be the right amount for each person, American-style.

But I've cut back on my shopping, since the French are content, and patient enough, to fuss endlessly with a lone chicken leg for much longer than I thought humanly possible. I derive endless fascination from watching them extract each and every morsel of meat from a bony wing with finely honed, surgical precision.

Although I'm getting over my fear of eating fresh fruits in public, dried fruits don't pose a similar problem. I like to use them when making a *tagine*, a typical North African casserole that Parisians have taken a liking to. I find sun-dried apricots, French prunes, Armenian peaches, and Iranian dates at Sabah, an Arabic market that sits on the corner of the busy marché d'Aligre (see Resources, page 271). The tight aisles are crammed with everything from olives and preserved lemons, bobbing away in their brine, to sacks of nuts and dried fruits from all over the world. Although they have a pretty fascinating selection of spices, I make a trip across town for saffron to Goumanyat (see Resources, page 271), which specializes in saffron and is truly a mecca for spice-lovers as well.

4 ounces (125 g) dried apricots

1 chicken, cut into 8 pieces (2 legs, 2 thighs, and each breast cut in half crosswise, leaving wings attached)

1 teaspoon ground ginger

1 teaspoon ground turmeric

2 teaspoons paprika

1/4 teaspoon saffron threads

1 teaspoon ground cinnamon

2 teaspoons coarse salt

Freshly ground black pepper

2 tablespoons (30 g) butter, salted or unsalted

1 large onion, finely chopped

2 cups chicken stock (if using canned, use a low-salt brand) or water

1/3 cup (10 g) chopped fresh cilantro, plus a bit extra for garnish

1 tablespoon honey

Juice of 1/2 lemon

3/4 cup (75 g) blanched almonds, toasted

1. Preheat the oven to 375°F (190°C).

2. Put the apricots in a small bowl and pour boiling water over them to cover. Set aside.

3. In a large bowl, toss the chicken pieces with the ginger, turmeric, paprika, saffron, cinnamon, salt, and pepper.

4. Melt the butter in a large Dutch oven or similar ovenproof casserole. Add the onion and cook for 5 minutes over moderate heat, stirring occasionally, until translucent.

5. Add the chicken and cook for 3 minutes, turning the pieces with tongs to release the fragrance of the spices. Pour in the stock, add the cilantro, and cover.

6. Bake for 50 minutes, turning the chicken pieces once or twice while they're braising.

7. Remove the casserole from the oven. Use tongs to transfer the chicken to a deep serving platter, then cover with foil. Return the casserole to the stovetop, add the honey and lemon juice, and reduce the sauce over medium-high heat by about one-third. Taste, and add more salt if necessary.

8. Return the chicken to the pot, add the almonds, and reheat in the sauce. Transfer the tagine back to the serving platter. Drain the apricots and spoon them over the top, then garnish with additional cilantro.

SERVING: Although tagine isn't traditionally served with couscous, I do at home, as they serve it at one of my favorite North African restaurants in Paris—L'Atlas, which faces the Institut du Monde Arabe. Another favorite is Chez Omar, a former bistro that's become a rather popular and slightly trendy North African restaurant. They also serve one of the most authentic versions of *steak frites* in town.

DRESSING LIKE A PARISIAN

If anyone had told me ten years ago that I'd be standing over an ironing board, pressing the wrinkles out of pajamas and kitchen towels, I would have told them they were insane. What kind of idiot irons his pajamas, let alone kitchen towels?

Fast forward to today, and you'll find me dutifully each week working a hot iron back and forth over my dress shirts, polo shirts, T-shirts, jeans, pajamas, pillowcases, dinner napkins, and yes, my kitchen towels, making sure I've eradicated every last wrinkle, crease, and dimple.

Shortly after I arrived in Paris, I happily discovered the

vide-greniers, the French version of tag sales, where you snag great deals on household items for much less than in the fabulous, and fabulously pricey, department stores. About the same time I also discovered linen. Specifically, vintage French linen sheets, pillowcases, and kitchen towels. When I took hold of the thick, heavy fabric with its starchy, clinical crispness, I was hooked and began manically stockpiling as much as I could carry home on the Métro.

Each time I came upon a stack, I thought I'd uncovered a rare find and would buy the whole load, certain I'd never see such deals again. Months later, when I could barely close my closet, I learned that fine linen is common in France and all my hoarding wasn't necessary.

Unfortunately, once my cabinets were packed with all those beautiful linens, I also realized they'd come out of my mini washing machine in a wrinkly ball, looking like one of those Danish modern white paper lamps: a tight, wadded-up sphere of sharp pleats and folds. So unless you're a masochist and enjoy waking up after a rough night with bruises and abrasions on your arms and legs—which I don't—those sheets need to be starched, ironed, and pressed into submission.

～

Not that all that many people get to check out my sheets and pillowcases, which I now send to the laundry since if I hang them up to dry for two to three days in my apartment, it's impossible to walk around the Christo-like maze. But in Paris, people *do* check out how others dress. I recall an enlightening story by a travel writer who, because of her profession, had spent time in a lot of unusual and exotic places. If you've traveled to any of them yourself, you know that one of the pitfalls of being a foreigner is that you can become a magnet for hucksters harassing you to purchase something that you probably don't want—jewelry, a carpet, a leather jacket, their sister. ("She is virgin—many times!" was one particularly ineffective sales pitch, I remember.) Most women are certainly no stranger to tenacious, pesky men hitting on them in foreign countries, suggesting a *liaison d'amour*. So the writer decided to start dressing in the native garb when she traveled, and immediately the touts started dropping like dead *mouches*, and people began treating her like a local.

Even though Parisians outfit themselves in nearly the same Western-style garb as we do—some combination of pants, shirts, dresses, and jack-ets—closer inspection reveals subtle, telling differences. And it's helpful to know about them if you want to blend in.

Parisian men wear shoes that are long and skinny with narrow, hard leather soles and, except in August, a scarf tied with great élan. No Parisian would dream of walking around with a scarf just dangling around his neck. It's always arranged with a complex series of knots so elaborate, I think some of them use a sailing primer for guidance. Jeans are *normale*, although you won't see any baggy ones or brands boasting a "relaxed" or "comfort fit." No matter what the material, pants are always form-fitting, to make everyone's butt look good, which I hope is a look that never becomes passé.

Sport coats are much more common than the polar fleece jackets with all those toggles and zippers and pockets that pragmatic Americans tend to favor. I take that back. You do see Parisians wearing them, but it's oblig-atory to have English-language patches with words like "rugged" and "sporty" sewn up and down the sleeves, plus a few arbitrary sailing flags and reflectors, even though we're hours away from any ocean—and I can't imagine a scarier sensation than feeling the spray from the dubious waters of the Seine on my skin.

Speaking of the sea, there's one particularly unfortunate fashion gaffe that's taken Paris by storm: the *gilet de pêcheur*. Yes, the last remnants of your high school French are correct; it's the fisherman's vest. Parisian men have adapted them for everyday wear, and it's not uncommon to see French dudes proudly patrolling the streets in heavy-duty khaki vests laden with pockets and buckles piled on top of each other and straps dangling every which way.

Gilets de pêcheur notwithstanding, you always want to make a *bonne présentation,* so it should be a priority to look your best if you want to fit in. No torn jeans unless they're torn intentionally. Words on clothes are fine, but only if they're printed up the back of your shirt or diagonally across the front. Preferably in gold. And slogans needn't shy away from sex: I was having dinner at Chez Michel, a casual but fairly nice restaurant, when a man entered wearing a T-shirt that said, "If you don't like oral sex, keep your mouth shut." I doubt he knew what that meant. If he did, he was looking in the wrong place. Perhaps the city of Paris needs to add fashion police to the other duties of the gendarmes.

Zippers need not be limited to the groin: shoulders, sleeves, knees, up the legs, behind the legs, and across one's backside are all locations that are acceptable, even encouraged. I'm not sure why anyone needs a zipper across his chest or shoulders, but I sure hope all those folks strutting their stuff on Sunday afternoons in the Marais take extra care when zipping up: the brazen tightness of their clothes makes me certain there's no room for undergarments above (or below) the waist. It's embarrassing enough explaining how certain things get stuck in your zipper; I don't know how you'd explain how you got your shoulder blade jammed in one.

In the old days, before the dangling fanny pack, the most obvious giveaway for Americans was our sneakers. One glance at our padded feet was all it took to peg us as hailing from the home of Air Jordans. Now, thanks to *mondialisation,* you'll find Parisians pounding the pavement wearing sneakers too, especially the younger generation, who've dubbed them *les baskets.* The difference is that Parisians wear *les baskets* because they're stylish, not because they're comfy. So go ahead. It's fine to wear sneakers. But make sure they're hip, racy—and expensive. Or purple. A good rule of thumb is that you can wear them in Paris if they cost you at least half of what your airfare did to get here.

I don't wear sneakers much, but as hard as I try, I'm unable to squeeze my feet into the stiff leather shoes that Parisian men favor. It's beyond me how Parisian gents are able to wear these shoes on the city's hard and treacherously slippery pavement. Consequently, my black, lug-soled Trippen shoes from Germany make me an outcast and invariably draw stares.

Maybe it's because the smooth soles are easier to wipe clean than my deep-grooved soles if you step in the minefield of sidewalk dog droppings. The downside is when racing through the market in the springtime, I have to stop and take a stick to flick out the cherry pits that get stuck in the bottoms or else people look up, expecting to see a seasoned hoofer tap-dancing his way toward them as I click around the city.

Not only is it okay to wear sneakers nowadays, but another recent change you'll notice is that it's now cool (and cooler) to wear shorts in the summer. But wait, don't drop those trousers so fast. If you plan to venture outside in *les Bermudas*, they need to hang below the knee, please. Even in Paris, one must follow the rules set forth in the global transatlantic Treaty of Taste: shorts must never be wider than they are long.

(Exempt from this rule are the big, busty "working women" on the rue Blondel, whose girth generally exceeds their height. They get a pass.)

So sneakers are okay, shorts are sometimes okay, but never wear both in combination with a fanny pack. And, *mon Dieu*, don't even think of adding an oversized water bottle. Because I'd rather have you dying of thirst than dying of embarrassment.

VACHERIN A LA CANNELLE, GLACE EXPRESS-CARAMEL,

SAUCE CHOCOLAT, ET AMANDES PRALINEES

CINNAMON MERINGUE WITH ESPRESSO-CARAMEL ICE CREAM, CHOCOLATE SAUCE, AND CANDIED ALMONDS

MAKES 6 SERVINGS

One combination that always works in Paris is *le vacherin*. You can't miss with a crisp disk of meringue topped with a scoop of coffee ice cream, warm chocolate sauce, and candied nuts.

There's a misconception that the French don't like cinnamon. Once when I was giving a cooking demonstration, a Frenchwoman in the front row spoke up just as I was about to add a heaping spoonful of cinnamon to something: "Why do you Americans put so *much* cinnamon in everything?" It's true, we do tend to be rather generous with it, and it ends up being the predominant flavor. So I've started using less and appreciating it as a subtle, spicy accent rather than giving it star billing.

Although I've given you a recipe for coffee ice cream, feel free to substitute another favorite flavor, or use a store-bought premium brand.

For the meringues

2 large egg whites, at room temperature

Big pinch of coarse salt

6 tablespoons (75 g) granulated sugar

$1/4$ teaspoon vanilla extract

$1/2$ teaspoon ground cinnamon

Espresso-Caramel Ice Cream (recipe follows)

Chocolate Sauce (recipe follows)

Candied Almonds (recipe follows)

1. Preheat the oven to 200°F (100°C).

2. With an electric mixer or by hand, begin whipping the egg whites with the salt at medium to high speed until they thicken and begin to hold their shape. While whipping, add the sugar a tablespoon at a time. Then beat in the vanilla and cinnamon. When done, the meringue should hold a soft but glossy peak when you lift the beaters.

3. Line a baking sheet with parchment paper and divide the meringue into six equal mounds. Dampen a soup spoon and make an indentation in the center, slightly flattening each one as you create the indentation.

4. Let dry in the oven for at least 1 hour, then turn off the oven and let the meringues dry out for another hour. (If you lift one off and it feels dry, you can take them out earlier.) Remove from the oven and cool completely.

SERVING: Place a meringue in the center of a shallow soup bowl. Add two scoops of ice cream, spoon warm chocolate sauce over the top, then sprinkle with almonds and serve.

STORAGE: Baked meringues can be stored in an absolutely airtight container for up to one week.

Espresso-Caramel Ice Cream

MAKES ABOUT 3 CUPS (3/4 L)

1 cup (200 g) sugar

1 cup (250 ml) heavy cream

1^1/2 cups (375 ml) whole milk

Pinch of coarse salt

6 large egg yolks

^{1}/4 cup (60 ml) strong brewed espresso, or more to taste

1. Prepare an ice bath by filling a large bowl with ice and water. Nest another bowl inside it that will hold at least 2 quarts. Set a mesh strainer over the top.

2. Spread the sugar in an even layer in a medium heavy-duty metal saucepan; I recommend one that's 4 to 6 quarts (4 to 6 L). Have the cream ready nearby. Heat the sugar slowly until the edges begin to melt and liquefy. Continue to cook, stirring with a heatproof spatula, until the sugar turns deep brown and begins to smoke.

3. Continue to cook until the sugar just starts to smell slightly burnt, then immediately pour in the cream while stirring. The sugar will seize and harden, so stir the mixture over low heat until the sugar dissolves. (Don't worry about any lumps; they'll dissolve later. But you may wish to wear oven mitts since the steam can be rather hot.)

4. Add the milk and salt and heat until warm.

5. In a separate bowl, whisk the egg yolks. Slowly pour the warm caramel mixture into the yolks, whisking constantly; then scrape the warmed egg yolks back into the saucepan.

6. Stir the custard constantly over medium heat, scraping the bottom as you stir, until it thickens and coats the back of the spoon.

7. Immediately pour the custard through the strainer into the bowl nesting in the ice bath. Cool the custard by stirring it frequently.

8. Once cool, stir in the espresso, then chill the mixture at least 4 hours or overnight.

9. Before churning, taste the custard and add more espresso, if desired. Freeze in your ice cream maker according to the manufacturer's instructions.

Chocolate Sauce

MAKES 1 CUP (250 ML)

You can spike this very easy chocolate sauce with a big pinch of ground cinnamon or a shot of rum to suit your taste. Depending on which brand of chocolate you use, the sauce may be too thick; if so, stir in a few more tablespoons of milk until it reaches the desired consistency.

4 ounces (115 g) bittersweet or semisweet chocolate, finely chopped
$1/2$ cup (125 ml) whole or low-fat milk, plus a few additional tablespoons, if necessary
1 tablespoon sugar

Heat the chocolate, milk, and sugar in a saucepan over the lowest possible heat, stirring constantly with a whisk until the chocolate is melted and the sauce is smooth.

STORAGE: Sauce can be stored in a covered container in the refrigerator for up to two weeks. Reheat gently before using.

Candied Almonds

MAKES 1/2 CUP (60 G) CANDIED NUTS

2 tablespoons sugar

$1/2$ cup (40 g) sliced almonds

$1/8$ teaspoon ground cinnamon

1. Spread the sugar in a heavy-bottomed skillet and strew the almonds over the top.

2. Cook over medium heat until the sugar begins to melt. Start to stir the almonds and sugar with a heatproof spatula or spoon until the nuts start toasting and the sugar begins to darken and caramelize.

3. Sprinkle with the cinnamon and stir a couple of times, then scrape the mixture onto a plate or baking sheet to cool.

4. Once cool, break into small pieces.

STORAGE: Keep in an airtight container until ready to use. The almonds can be made up to one week ahead.

WATER, WATER EVERYWHERE—
BUT YOU CAN'T HAVE ANY

If you ever peered closely into the brackish water of the Seine, you'd probably lose your thirst in Paris. Because that's where most of the drinking water comes from. Yuck!

Over the past few years, the city of Paris has been making a big push to get Parisians to use less of those environmentally unfriendly plastic bottles and head back to the tap. Not only is the tap water safe to drink, or so they say, but its high calcium content is supposedly good for preventing osteoporosis. One thing they did gloss over was the fact that the heavy doses of chalky *calcaire* ruin our wine glasses and block our shower heads. And good wineglasses are as important as good posture in Paris. The calcium requires us to add a dash of environmentally unfriendly *anti-calcaire* to the laundry so that for those of us who bathe regularly, our towels don't scrape off a couple of layers of skin. (Unlike my neighbor down the hall, who evidently doesn't consider showering all that important.)

In response, scare tactics were employed by bottler Cristaline in ads showing a toilet bowl with a big red *X* across it accompanied by the words *Je ne bois pas l'eau que j'utilise* ("I don't drink water that I use"), a campaign intended as a response to our green-spirited Mayor Bertrand Delanoë's attempts to wean us off plastic.

To encourage consumption of *l'eau du robinet,* thirty thousand fashionable glass carafes were given away at a highly orchestrated publicity event at the Hôtel de Ville, the city hall. Styled by some hot-shot French designer and emblazoned with the logo in blocky blue letters, *EAU DE PARIS,* the carafes garnered a lot of publicity because of their sleek design and the massive giveaway. I've yet to see one anywhere—except on eBay.fr.

Paris has always had a pretty close relationship with water, which runs through it and around it. Paris, or Lutetia, as it was originally called, actually began as an island surrounded by the Seine, which explains why the symbol of Paris is a boat. As the city grew larger, Paris spiraled outward and the water continued to shape the city: the name of the trendy Marais refers to its history as a mucky swamp, and there's still a puddle of water in the basement of the Opéra Garnier, although nothing nowadays resembling the deep lake depicted in the popular musical.

With water all around and beneath us, you'd think it would be easy to get a glass of the stuff. But it can take a daunting amount of effort to get a sip. Unlike their American counterparts, who live under some decree that one *must* drink eight 8-ounce glasses per day, you'll never see a Parisian gulping down a tumbler full or chugging a bottle of water. Water for drinking is parsimoniously rationed in tiny shotlike glasses in restaurants and cafés, meant to be consumed in carefully controlled, measured doses. If you're invited to a private home for dinner, water usually won't be offered until the very end of the meal, if at all.

I attended a dinner party where the hostess kept the bottle of water sequestered under the table, guarded by her feet during the entire meal. Midway through dinner, completely dessicated, I could hold out no longer and summoned up the last bit of moisture in my mouth to form the words to ask for a sip. With some reluctance, she reached down to extract the bottle and poured a tiny trickle into my glass. Right after my ration was doled out, she screwed the top back on and stowed away the bottle.

There's a French aesthetic about drinking glasses, whether for wine or water: they're small and they're never filled more than halfway. It's not that everyone is being so parsimonious with wine, it's just that smaller glasses look nicer on the table. Big glasses are considered *pas jolis* (not beautiful), a term the French use to justify any cultural quirk that can't easily be explained. And I agree. After all, what's the point of being in Paris if you're going to be *pas joli*? And you don't want to ruin things for the rest of us by drinking water, do you?

It can be tricky to order water in France, since there's a panopoly of options. Simply saying, "I'd like water," in a café or restaurant is like going into Starbucks and saying, "I'd like coffee," or going to a multiplex cinema and telling the cashier, "I'd like a ticket to see a movie." An online search revealed there are 214 brands of bottled water available in France, versus 179 in America, which has five times the population of France.

Before ordering, you need to decide whether you want a bottle, or *eau du robinet* from the tap. If bottled is your choice, do you want still or sparkling? San Pellegrino or Perrier? Châteldon or Salvetat? Badoit or Evian? If Badoit, do you want *verte* or hyper-bubbly *rouge*? There's also Volvic, Vichy, and Vittel. But wait, you're not done yet! *Demie* or *grande*?

Unless you specify, you're likely to get the biggest and priciest of the lot, since no waiter anywhere enjoys playing twenty questions in his non-native language and that's your punishment. If you're terribly thirsty, spring for a bottle. Ordering *eau du robinet* means you may need to ask the waiter two—perhaps three—times before you get it, if you get it at all. They seem to have no trouble remembering those money-making bottles, but free carafes are somehow easily forgotten.

Yet there's relief for the parched palates walking the streets: a law on the books dictates that all cafés in France have to give anyone who comes in a glass of tap water upon request. Unless they have a sign posted somewhere saying they don't do that. I haven't built up the courage to ask anywhere to see if it's true, but I wish they'd pass a similar law when it comes to another urgent need around here.

$\backsim$

The flip side of finding a drink of water is finding a place to get rid of it. This is nearly impossible if you're out and about, so it's easy to understand why the French avoid drinking it in the first place.

While *la loi* does give you *le droit* to ask for water in a café, there's no law that gives you the right to demand to get rid of it thereafter. Cafés are notoriously less than accommodating about allowing you to use their often shabby accommodations *sans* purchase, unless you're pregnant or can distend your stomach and rub it lovingly to make a convincing demonstration that you might be. Considering how many *macarons* and *pains au chocolat* I tuck in, I may soon be able to pull it off. For the rest of you, if you want to use the bathroom, paradoxically, you must drink something first, thus perpetuating a vicious cycle that works for the café owners, but not so well their patrons.

I used to buy my weekly *carnet* of Métro tickets at a grubby local *tabac* on the rue Faubourg Saint-Antoine. One day I headed to the back of the place to relieve myself of the excitement from making such a transaction. I didn't think it'd be a problem since I was a steady, paying customer.

As I reached for the doorknob, the proprietor hollered across the room, his voice booming to all the patrons (who stopped what they were doing to turn and watch), yelling that that room was off-limits unless I had a drink. He clarified the verbal assault by making a drinking motion, rocking his extended thumb and little finger toward and away from his mouth, in case I didn't get the point.

I got it. But he almost got my middle finger back, and I never got my Métro tickets there again.

He wasn't acting alone, though. Parisians have little sympathy for those who have to go to the bathroom because they don't ever have to go themselves. They have no idea what it's like. I've spent eight to nine uninterrupted hours with my partner, Romain, and not once did he excuse himself to go. I guess they know better, and lay off the water.

When men do get the urge, they simply pull up to a little corner of *la belle France* and take a break. If you've searched your guidebook to find the historical significance of those corners of semicircular iron bars guarding historic buildings, now you know: they're to discourage men from relieving themselves on history.

The problem's gotten so bad that the authorities in Paris came up with *le mur anti-pipi*, a sloping wall designed to "water the waterer" by redirecting the stream, soaking the offender's trousers. The prototype is now being tested on the most *pipi*-soaked street: the cour des Petites-Ecuries. (Don't ask me how they figured that one out. I don't want to know.)

Perhaps you remember the old solution, the city-sanctioned open-air *pissotières*, where men were allowed to do their business *en plein air*. In the early '90s, though, Paris started replacing those stinky yet terribly convenient (for us men) outdoor *pissotières* with Sanisettes, the automated self-cleaning toilets that are installed at various spots around the city. If you're feeling nostalgic, there's one *pissotière* left, the last malodorous holdout, way out on the boulevard Arago.

Some give kudos to the Sanisettes for giving women equal opportunity to use the streets. Except every woman I know refuses to go in one. They're also overclustered in the touristed neighborhoods instead of where the rest of us need them most. No matter where you are, it seems the more urgent the need, the more likely you'll find that the little illuminated button says the cabin is unfortunately *Hors Service.*

So why is it the French never feel the need to go? I searched for the answer from Romain's mother, who raised four children in an apartment that has four bedrooms, but only one *toilette.* That means six people—plus the au pair—shared one bathroom for twenty years.

"*C'est pas possible!*" I exclaimed. She shrugged off my incredulity and said there were never any problems. I guess they coach 'em right from the start, because if I had to share one bathroom with my two parents, three siblings, and a live-in sitter, I'd probably be better trained than I currently am, too.

Although we find it funny, and at times excruciating, that French bathrooms are few and far between, they think it's *très bizarre* that we drag guests on grand tours of our homes, which include the bedrooms and bathroom as part of the itinerary. And when you think about it, isn't it a little odd that we invite strangers for a look at where we conduct our most intimate business?

The French keep those rooms discreetly off-limits and there's no "Come! See the rest of the house!" when you visit someone. Which is great, since you're never subjected to people bragging about their wok burners or $6,800 state-of-the-art wine refrigerators stocked with California Chardonnay. Or maybe I'm just jealous, since I have nothing to brag about in my kitchen but a half-empty jar of molasses and a few bags of dried onion soup mix.

It sure is nice not having to make your bed or scrub the toilet when company's coming, though. Unfortunately, I have a few American friends who have the nerve to use the bathroom when they come over. And admittedly when I visit friends, even though I know the WC is off-limits, if I haven't stopped first at a nearby building (inside or out), I sometimes do need to ask permission to go. Which is, I think, the least embarrassing of my options.

========

CHOCOLATE MOLE

MAKES 1 QUART (1 L)

Aside from a seemingly endless quest for water, one of our other cultural differences is Americans' love of Mexican food. Authentic Mexican products aren't available here. So like many Americans, I lug dried chiles, hot sauce, and corn tortillas back from trips to the States. Then I prepare elaborate Mexican meals that I hope will impress my Parisian friends.

And how can you not love mole? Here's my version, which everyone seems to like whenever I make it. Parisians seem to love anything that has chocolate in it just as much as Americans do.

For any of those "If-it-doesn't-take-ten-hours-to-make-it's-not-mole" folks out there, give me a break since some of the items aren't available in Paris. I'm doing the best I can with what I've got. Because of that, this recipe has about sixty-seven fewer ingredients than the normal recipe and takes a fraction of the time to put together. But it tastes just like the real thing. So if you're the mole police, please put away your handcuffs.

10 dried ancho or poblano chiles

^{3}/4 cup (120 g) raisins

3 ounces (85 g) unsweetened chocolate, chopped

1^1/4 cups (310 ml) water or chicken stock

1 tablespoon canola or neutral-flavored oil

1 large onion, peeled and chopped

3 garlic cloves, peeled and thinly sliced

3 tablespoons (35 g) sesame seeds (reserve a few to sprinkle
    over the finished dish)

^{3}/4 cup (60 g) sliced almonds, toasted

3 tomatoes, peeled, seeded, and chopped (see Note),
   or 1^1/2 cups (375 ml) canned tomatoes and their juice

^{1}/2 teaspoon ground cinnamon

^{1}/2 teaspoon ground cloves

^{1}/2 teaspoon dried oregano

^{1}/2 teaspoon ground cumin

^{1}/2 teaspoon ground coriander seeds

^{1}/2 teaspoon ground anise seeds

1^1/2 teaspoons coarse salt

Freshly ground black pepper

^{1}/2 to 1 teaspoon chile powder, optional

1. Remove the stems from the chiles. Slice them in half lengthwise and scrape out most of the seeds. Put the chiles in a nonreactive pot, cover with water, set a small plate on top to keep the chiles submerged, and simmer for 10 minutes or until tender. Remove from heat and let stand until cool.

2. Put the raisins and chocolate in a blender. Heat the water, then pour it in the blender mixture and let stand for a few minutes to soften the chocolate.

3. In a nonstick skillet, heat the oil, then sauté the onion until limp and translucent, about 8 minutes. Add the garlic and cook a few more minutes, stirring frequently.

4. Drain the chiles and add them to the blender along with the onion and garlic, sesame seeds, almonds, tomatoes, all the spices, salt, and a few turns of pepper. Puree until smooth. Taste, and add more salt and chile powder if you wish to spice it up.

STORAGE: Mole can be covered and refrigerated for up to five days. The mole can also be frozen for up to three months in a freezer bag. I recommend dividing a batch in half and freezing some since this recipe makes quite a bit.

NOTE: To easily peel and seed fresh tomatoes, cut an *X* in the bottom and drop in simmering water for about 15 seconds. Drain in a colander and run cool water over them to stop the cooking. Slip the skins off, slice in half crosswise, then squeeze gently to extract the seeds.

═══════════

MOLE AU POULET

CHICKEN MOLE

MAKES 4 TO 6 SERVINGS

Corn still on the cob—not those mushy, canned kernels that find their way into everything from Caesar salad to pizza around here—is unfortunately rather scarce in Paris. To me, it isn't summer without it, and if I do serve chicken mole to French friends, I accompany it with a sautéed mound of freshly shucked kernels, a less messy way to serve corn, which is a sure way to win converts. They're amazed at how much better it tastes than those from the Jolly *Géant Vert,* another American who's taken up residence in France.

The word *sauté* in French comes from the verb *sauter,* or "to jump," which refers to the action of tossing things around in a pan. In addition to a pat of butter and chopped cilantro, some bright flecks of *piment d'Espelette,* the famed Basque chile powder, give the corn a bit of a lift.

1 chicken, cut into 8 pieces, or 4 legs and 4 thighs

1 tablespoon coarse salt

2 bay leaves

1/2 batch (about 2 cups, 500 ml) Chocolate Mole (page 58)

A few toasted sesame seeds

1. Put the chicken in a large pot and cover with water. Add salt and bay leaves. Cover and bring to a boil; then reduce the heat and simmer for 20 minutes. Turn off the heat and let rest 20 minutes.

2. Transfer the chicken to a platter. Reserve the cooking liquid. When cool enough to handle, remove and discard the skin.

3. While the chicken cools, preheat the oven to 350°F (180°C).

4. Arrange the chicken pieces in a baking dish just big enough to hold them all; they should rest against each other with little or no space between them.

5. Add some of the cooking liquid to the mole. I find 1/2 cup (125 ml) of liquid is just right, but depending on your mole, it may take more or less. The sauce is best when it's the consistency of runny chocolate pudding. (If making rice to serve alongside, use the cooking liquid in place of water; it's delicious.)

6. Spoon the mole over the chicken and bake for 30 to 40 minutes, until the chicken is heated through.

7. Sprinkle the top with sesame seeds and serve.

PALETTE DE PORC CARAMELISEE

CARNITAS

MAKES 8 SERVINGS

The first time I ate at a "Tex-Mex" restaurant in Paris, I scanned the menu, excited to see a burrito on it. Remembering the "tummy torpedoes" we all gorged on in San Francisco, I asked the waitress if the burritos were large. "Oh yes, they're *huge*!" she replied, her eyes widening to emphasize their girth, as if she'd never seen anything so gigantic in her life.

"Great!" I thought.

When she brought my rolled-up burrito to the table, in the center of an over-sized plate was a little pellet of food, roughly the size of a wine cork. I could have eaten six of them. Since Mexican food isn't especially well represented in Paris, I like to show friends how good it can be, and carnitas are the perfect introduction, since it doesn't matter whether you're from here or there: who doesn't love caramelized pork?

4 to 5 pounds (2 to 2^1/2 kg) boneless pork shoulder,
    cut into 5-inch (13-cm) chunks, trimmed of excess fat
1 tablespoon coarse sea salt
2 tablespoons vegetable oil
Water
1 cinnamon stick
1 teaspoon chile powder (preferably ancho)
2 bay leaves
^{1}/4 teaspoon ground cumin
3 garlic cloves, peeled and thinly sliced

1. Rub the pieces of pork all over with salt.

2. Preheat the oven to 350°F (175°C) degrees.

3. Heat the oil in a large roasting pan set on the stovetop. Add the pieces of pork in a single layer and cook until very well browned, letting them get nice and dark before flipping them over. If your pan is too small to cook the pork in a single layer, cook it in two batches.

4. Once all the pork is browned, remove it from the pot and blot any excess fat with a paper towel. Pour in about a cup of water, scraping the bottom of the pan with a flat-edged utensil to release all the tasty brown bits.

5. Return the pork to the pan and add enough water so the pieces are about two-thirds submerged. Add the cinnamon stick and stir in the chile powder, bay leaves, cumin, and garlic.

7. Braise in the oven for 3^1/2 hours, turning the pork a few times during cooking, until much of the liquid is evaporated and the pork is falling apart. Remove the pan from the oven, lift the pork pieces out of the liquid, and set them on a platter or in a bowl.

8. Once the pork is cool enough to handle, shred it into bite-size (about 2-inch/7-cm) pieces. Discard any obvious big chunks of fat, if you wish.

9. Return the pork to the roasting pan and cook in the oven, turning occasionally, until the liquid has evaporated and the pork is crispy and caramelized. The exact length of time will be determined by how crispy you like the pork. It will take at least 1 hour, but probably more.

SERVING: Carnitas ideally should be served with a stack of warm tortillas, bowls of salsa, stewed beans, guacamole, and other Mexican accompaniments so guests can make their own tacos. If I've run out of tortillas, I serve it with rice.

STORAGE: Carnitas can be made up to three days in advance and kept in the refrigerator. Rewarm gently in a low oven.

VARIATION: If you wish to make pork mole, in step 8, once you've shredded the meat, mix in half a batch of mole (page 58), adding any pork juices to make it liquidy. Then rewarm in the oven for 30 minutes, turning the pork pieces once or twice.

MY CLE TO SUCCESS

If you haven't been to Paris in a while, one thing you can't help but notice is the startling number of banks that have opened in the past few years. Whenever a business closes, especially on a prominent corner, the construction crews arrive the next morning and gut the interior; shortly thereafter, a generic Société Générale, Crédit Lyonnais, or BNP Paribas opens its gleaming double doors.

Banks in France wield a tremendous amount of power, and if you live here, the bank-issued *clé* (key) RIB is just as vital as your government-issued identity card. The RIB (*relevé d'identité bancaire*) is a flimsy three-inch square of paper generated by your bank with a gazillion numbers on it. It proves to everyone that you've got a bank account. Which in turns proves you're a person worthy of things like gas, electricity, and telephone service.

And you need an electric bill to get your visa.

But you can't get a visa without an electric bill.

And you can't get electricity unless you have a RIB.

But you can't open a bank account, and get a RIB, without a visa.

And you can't get a visa without an electric bill.

Of all the French paradoxes I encountered, this is the one that had me closest to tears for weeks on end. My troubles began when I was compiling the paperwork required for my *carte de séjour,* a long-term visa, which had to include proof of residence. (Which is another paradox: to get a visa to live here, you need to prove you already live here.) So I needed to open a bank account. Except every single bank I visited refused to open an account for me, since I didn't have a visa. Even the post office, which acts like a bank in France and is known for being incredibly lenient, denied me the privilege of letting them hold my money.

Something Americans don't understand is that the person sitting at the desk or behind the counter in France has the inalienable right to say *non* for whatever reason he, or usually she, wants. Unlike in America, where everyone's taught to say yes, in France, *oui* means more work. And if more work sounds as appealing to you as it does to them, you're beginning to understand a bit of the logic around here.

Not looking forward to deportation, and getting desperate, I was offered an introduction to a banker by a rather well-to-do friend, who accompanied me to her branch in the place de l'Opéra. I brought along a box of La Maison du Chocolat chocolates, which the *bancaire* gladly accepted, after which, she directed me back to a branch of their bank back in my neighborhood. (One bonus of Paris being laid out in a big spiral is that it makes it easy to get back to the point you started from.)

Back in the Bastille, I spent the next two weeks making appointments at various banks, getting all dressed up in tie and jacket, then arriving with my thick dossier of paperwork only to be turned away by the less-than-interested *directeur d'agence*. One by one, I was systematically banished from their branches. With my visa hearing in just a couple of days, I started to panic and could feel my eyes welling after each grueling day of rejections.

Then it hit me. I realized I held something that few Frenchwomen would be able to resist.

So I confidently marched into one of the last banks in my neighborhood I'd yet to visit, without the requisite appointment. I strode through the imposing double doors, almost unable to breathe because of my firmly knotted tie, but was told I'd have to wait.

When my name was finally called, I entered the office of a sternly coiffed *Parisienne*, just like all the others I'd seen, who didn't seem particularly interested in me or my thick dossier. I sat still, trying not to squirm or say much, while she perused each sheet of paper in my carefully organized folder, flipping through it with a look that I had come to know all too well. When she was done, she sighed, frowned in my direction, and as she parted her lips, ready to speak, I stopped her. This time I was ready.

I reached into my bag and on cue I pulled it out: a copy of my first cookbook, one filled with dessert recipes. Even more important, it was complete with full-color photos. I handed it across the desk to her with an explanation that this was my *métier*.

You would have thought I'd told her Johnny Depp was dumping Vanessa Paradis and was on his way over, ready to take her away from this drudgery on his private yacht, to spend the summer sailing the Côte d'Azur. She became visibly flushed as she started flipping through the pages, admiring the sleek gâteau Marjolaine layered with ribbons of shiny chocolate ganache and nutty praline. She grazed her hands over the pictures of buttery cakes glazed with pinwheels of maple-caramelized pears, and sighed with pleasure at the trembling soufflés, oozing chunks of dark chocolate.

She was so excited that she called in her coworkers, who clustered around her desk with a chorus of "*Oh la la, monsieur!*" as they turned the pages, each causing more of a fuss than the previous one. (When I wrote the book, I was worried that I was paying too much for the photos. I now know for sure that it was money well spent.)

After the commotion died down and the women all went back to their respective cubicles, she turned to her computer keyboard, still so excited she was practically bouncing off her seat, looked over at me, and asked, "*Quelle est votre adresse, monsieur?*"

The moment her manicured fingers started tapping away on the keyboard, I realized that my first triumph in France had nothing to do with my fiscal fitness, but instead hinged on my culinary qualifications. I'd found my *clé* to success around here. And the future was looking a little bit sweeter for me.

=======

MOUSSE AU CHOCOLAT I

CHOCOLATE MOUSSE I

MAKES 4 TO 6 SERVINGS

Some people think of *mousse au chocolat* as something fancy, when in fact, it's a very typical, everyday French dessert. This one was made for me by Marion Lévy, who lives in the Marais, but spends many of her winters skiing in Méribel. One night after we tackled the slopes she put together this incredibly simple *mousse au chocolat*, which I thought would be delicious with a shot of Chartreuse in it, similar to the *chocolat vert* (hot chocolate with a shot of the regional herbal liqueur) served in the châlets that kept me warm and happy trying to keep up with her on the slopes.

When I whipped it up at home, I brought some to my Parisian neighbors with the warning there were uncooked eggs in it. They looked at each other, then at me, completely perplexed, and asked, "How *else* would you make chocolate mousse?" If you're concerned about raw eggs, use pasteurized ones, checking to be sure that the whites will be suitable for whipping.

Or move to France, where no one seems to worry about it.

7 ounces (200 g) bittersweet or semisweet chocolate, finely chopped

3 tablespoons (45 ml) water

2 tablespoons (30 ml) Chartreuse (or another favorite liqueur)

4 large eggs, at room temperature, separated

Pinch of coarse salt

1. In a medium-sized bowl set over a pan of barely simmering water, begin melting the chocolate with the water and Chartreuse, making sure not to let it get too hot. Take the bowl off the heat when the chocolate is almost completely melted, then stir gently until smooth. Set aside.

2. In a clean, dry bowl, whip the egg whites with the salt until they form stiff peaks when you lift the whip. They should still be smooth and creamy, not grainy.

3. Stir the egg yolks into the chocolate, then fold one-third of the whites into the chocolate to lighten it up.

4. Fold the remaining egg whites into the chocolate just until there are no visible streaks of whites. Cover the bowl with plastic wrap and chill for at least 3 hours. (You can also divide the mousse into individual custard cups, ramekins, or goblets before chilling.)

SERVING: Although you can serve *mousse au chocolat* with whipped cream, I prefer it just as is. For some reason, to me, *mousse au chocolat* is best enjoyed straight from the serving bowl, with friends and family sharing communally. You can also freeze it and serve it frozen. Dip a spoon or ice cream scoop in very hot water for easy scooping.

STORAGE: *Mousse au chocolat* will keep in the refrigerator for up to five days. It can also be frozen for up to one month.

VARIATIONS: You can use another favorite liqueur, such as Grand Marnier, rum, or Armagnac, or omit it altogether, substituting coffee or water for the Chartreuse.

MOUSSE AU CHOCOLAT II

CHOCOLATE MOUSSE II

MAKES 4 TO 6 SERVINGS

For those concerned about raw eggs, here's an alternative recipe for *mousse au chocolat*. As in the previous recipe, you can swap another liqueur, or espresso, for the Chartreuse.

8 ounces (225 g) bittersweet or semisweet chocolate,
     finely chopped
4 tablespoons (60 g) salted butter, diced
3 tablespoons (45 ml) Chartreuse
1/4 cup (60 ml) water
3/4 cup (180 ml) heavy cream

1. In a medium-sized bowl set over a pan of barely simmering water, heat the chocolate, butter, Chartreuse, and water until melted and smooth. Remove from heat.

2. In a separate bowl, beat the cream with a whisk until it's thickened and forms soft, droopy peaks when you lift the whisk.

3. Fold about one-third of the cream into the chocolate mixture to lighten it up, then fold in the remaining cream. Cover and chill for at least 3 hours. (For storage and serving tips, see preceding recipe.)

CHOUQUETTES AUX PEPITES DE CHOCOLAT

CHOCOLATE CHIP CREAM PUFFS

MAKES ABOUT 25 PUFFS

Whenever I'm having a difficult day, my remedy is to treat myself to a small sack of *chouquettes,* which bakeries sell in little paper bags. Ten *chouquettes* per bag seems to be the magic number, which coincides with exactly how many I need to eat before I feel better.

When I stopped at Aux Péchés Normands, a bakery in the tenth arrondissement, I discovered *chouquettes* studded with chocolate chips, so I now toss a handful in mine whenever I make them at home. The only problem with making them myself is that I can't make just ten, and I always end up eating the whole tray.

Pearl sugar is the key to the irresistible appeal of *chouquettes.* The large, irregular chunks of sugar provide a toothsome crunch that makes them as popular with adults as they are with children, who often get one as a reward from the baker when stopping by with their parents for the obligatory dinnertime baguette.

Shaping the mounds of dough is easiest to do with a spring-loaded ice cream scoop, although you can use two spoons or a pastry bag with a large, plain tip.

1 cup (250 ml) water

1/2 teaspoon coarse salt

2 teaspoons sugar

6 tablespoons (90 g) unsalted butter, cut into small chunks

1 cup (135 g) flour

4 large eggs, at room temperature

1/2 cup (85 g) semisweet chocolate chips

1/2 cup (60 g) pearl sugar (see Note)

1. Position a rack in the upper third of the oven. Preheat the oven to 425°F (220°C) and line a baking sheet with parchment paper or a silicone baking mat.

2. Heat the water along with the salt, sugar, and butter in a medium saucepan, stirring, until the butter is melted. Remove from heat and dump in all the flour at once. Stir rapidly until the mixture is smooth and pulls away from the sides of the pan.

3. Allow the dough to cool for 2 minutes, stirring occasionally to release the heat; then briskly beat in the eggs, one at a time, until the paste is smooth and shiny. Let cool *completely* to room temperature, then stir in the chocolate chips. If it's even slightly warm, they'll melt.

4. Drop mounds of dough, about 2 tablespoons each, on the baking sheet, evenly spaced.

5. Press pearl sugar crystals liberally over the top and sides of each mound. Use a lot and really press them in. Once the puffs expand, you'll appreciate the extra effort (and sugar).

6. Bake the *chouquettes* for 35 minutes, or until puffed and well browned. Serve warm or at room temperature.

STORAGE: *Choquettes* are best eaten the same day they're made. However, once cooled, they can be frozen in a zip-top freezer bag for up to one month. Defrost at room temperature, then warm briefly on a baking sheet in a moderate oven, until crisp.

NOTE: Pearl sugar—large, white, irregularly shaped chunks of sugar (roughly the size of small peas)—is available from King Arthur Flour (see Resources, page 271) and in some Ikea stores. Scandinavian baking supply places carry it as well. Or substitute the largest sugar crystals you can find.

WHAT THEY SAY VERSUS WHAT THEY MEAN

When they say, *"Non,"* they mean, "Convince me."

When they say, "We do not take returns," they mean, "Convince me."

When they say, "It's not broken," they mean, "Convince me."

When they say, "You need a prescription for that," they mean, "Convince me."

When they say, "The restaurant is completely full," they mean, "Convince me."

When they say, "The restaurant is completely full," they mean, "We already have enough Americans in here."

When they say, "Do you mind if I smoke?" they mean, "Do you mind if I pout and scowl for the next five minutes if you say yes?"

When they say, "It does not exist," they mean, "It does exist—just not for you."

When they walk right into you on the street and say nothing, they mean, "I'm Parisian, and you're not."

When they say, "We don't have change," they mean, "I want a tip."

When they say, "Do you want directions?" they mean, "I look forward to telling you what to do for the next five minutes."

When they say, "I'd like to practice my English," they mean, "For the next twenty minutes, I'd like to make you feel like a complete idiot while I speak picture-perfect English."

When they say, "They're up on the seventh floor," they mean, "They're right around the corner from where we're standing."

When they say, "We don't have any more," they mean, "We have lots more, but they're in the back and I don't feel like getting them."

When they say, "It's not my fault," they mean, "It is my fault, but I'm not taking the blame."

When they say, "That is not possible," they mean, "It is possible, but not for you."

When they say, "I am a Socialist," they mean, "I'm not responsible for picking up my dog's poop."

When they say, "Your package hasn't arrived," they mean, "I'm just about to go on break. Come back Monday and wait in line for forty minutes again."

When they say, "The fat's the best part!" they mean, "I'm under forty."

When they say, "The cheeses in France are the best in the world," they mean, "We are indeed a superior culture."

When they say, "We are tired of American culture," they mean, "Please don't show us Sharon Stone's vagina again."

====

GATEAU A L'ABSINTHE

ABSINTHE CAKE

ONE 9-INCH (23-CM) LOAF CAKE

If you're a recipe writer, there are no better taste testers than the French. When I made this cake for the first time, I brought it to Luc-Santiago Rodriguez, who runs a tiny absinthe-only shop in the Marais, Le Vert d'Absinthe, which is certainly one of the most unusual shops in all of Paris—and perhaps the world.

He's serious about absinthe, and the next day there was a message in my inbox from him telling me that the particular absinthe I used in the cake wasn't the best, and I should try another one that he carries. Although absinthe is now flowing freely in America (see Resources, page 271), I'm not going to recommend any specific brand. If you come to Paris, stop in; the bottle of turf-green Duplais he suggested was just perfect. (He bristled when I told him I was going to advise readers who didn't have absinthe on hand to use another anise-based liqueur. So if you go, don't tell Luc-Santiago I told you that.)

I love this cake when it's made with pistachio flour, also known as pistachio powder or meal, which gives it a lovely green color similar to *la fée verte*, the green fairy that allegedly one sees if too much absinthe is consumed. Almond powder or cornmeal can be substituted.

For the cake

$^3/_4$ teaspoon anise seeds

1$^1/_4$ cups (175 g) all-purpose flour

$^1/_2$ cup (55 g) pistachio or almond flour or $^1/_2$ cup (70 g) stone-ground yellow cornmeal

2 teaspoons baking powder (preferably aluminum-free)

$^1/_4$ teaspoon salt

8 tablespoons (120 g) unsalted butter, at room temperature

1 cup (200 g) sugar

2 large eggs, at room temperature

1/4 cup (60 ml) whole milk

1/4 cup (60 ml) absinthe

Grated zest from 1 orange, preferably unsprayed

For the absinthe glaze

3 tablespoons (45 g) sugar

1/4 cup (60 ml) absinthe

1. Preheat the oven to 350°F (175°C). Butter a 9-inch (23-cm) loaf pan, then line the bottom with parchment paper.

2. Crush the anise seeds using a mortar and pestle, or in a freezer bag with a hammer, until relatively fine. Whisk together the white flour, nut flour or cornmeal, baking powder, salt, and anise seeds. Set aside.

3. In the bowl of a standing electric mixer or by hand, beat the butter and sugar until light and fluffy. Add the eggs one at a time, until completely incorporated.

4. Combine the milk and absinthe with a bit of zest.

5. Stir half of the dry ingredients into the butter mixture, then add the milk and absinthe.

6. By hand, stir in the other half of the dry ingredients until just smooth (do not overmix). Smooth the batter into the prepared pan and bake for 45 to 50 minutes, until a toothpick inserted into the center comes out clean.

7. Remove the cake from the oven and let cool 30 minutes.

8. To glaze the cake with absinthe, use a toothpick and poke 50 holes in the cake. In a small bowl, gently stir the sugar and absinthe until just mixed, making sure the sugar doesn't dissolve. (You can add a bit of orange zest here too if you like.)

9. Remove the cake from the pan, peel off the parchment paper, and set the cake on a cooling rack over a baking sheet.

10. Baste the cake with the absinthe glaze over the top and sides. Continue until all the glaze is used up.

If you want to go somewhere in Paris and sip absinthe, on one end of the scale is the Hôtel Royal Fromentin, up near Sacré Coeur in Montmarte, where artists got a cheap buzz before it was banned. If you're looking for something more unusual, check out Cantada II, a goth bar with a menu of absinthe. But consider yourself warned: skip the *cuisine médiévale*—one bite and you'll understand why people in the Middle Ages didn't live very long.

LINES ARE FOR OTHER PEOPLE

In Paris, there are only two reasons you can cut in front of others waiting in line:

1. Because you're old, frail, or have a physical disability that prevents you from standing for long periods of time.

2. Because you don't think you should you have to wait in line behind anybody else.

Aside from our ability to form ourselves into nice straight lines in service-oriented situations, one of the most endearing traits of Americans is our ability to be self-deprecating and laugh at our foibles. Late-night talk show hosts make fun of current events, celebrities, politicians, and American culture in general. Few are spared and everyone has a good laugh. It's a cultural quirk I miss.

The French have a pretty good sense of humor, too, which may explain the popularity of Sharon Stone films here, but they tend to get a wee bit touchy when criticized by outsiders. And while they're masters of the art of argument, when really trapped, sometimes they'll say something so bizarre or illogical—that the danger from secondhand smoke is a myth, for instance, or that snipping off the ends of green beans is a simple way to remove radioactive matter—that there's just no comeback possible. I've had lots of spirited discussions with locals defending the behavior of their fellow Parisians, but the only two things they can't justify are the dog doo on the streets and line jumping.

I'm not touching the dog doo, but I've tried to understand why Parisians are such fanatical line jumpers. I've been told it's "because we are a Latin culture." Yet I've seen scant evidence of any other aspects of Latin culture inserting themselves into Parisian daily life, except for the occasional honcho peeing in a corner. And how Latin can they be if you can't even find a decent-sized burrito around here?

Parisians are always in a big hurry, but are especially frantic if they're behind you. They're desperate to be where they rightfully feel they belong: in front of you. It's a whole other story when you're behind *them*, especially when it's their turn: suddenly they seem to have all the time in the world.

Line cutting is rampant in Paris. So much so, that there's a word for it: *risquillage,* or "taking the risk." And believe me, anyone who has the temerity to slide in front of me is definitely taking a risk.

Although I lived for years in San Francisco and have seen many public displays of close, intimate physical behavior, I still find it disconcerting to have an unseen stranger pressed smack-dab up against my backside, gently nudging me forward, while I'm waiting patiently for stamps at *La Poste.* Or to have someone inching beside me in line at the supermarket with the slim hope that they're going to be able to wedge themselves within the five centimeters of space between me and the metal railing.

What are they possibly thinking? I doubt it's because Parisians have trouble keeping their hands off me. The only possible way anyone could slide around me, though, would be by transforming himself into Elasto-Man. And being a San Franciscan, I'm also no stranger to seeing people contort themselves in unusual positions in public places either, but that's one feat I'd be pretty shocked to see at my local Franprix supermarket.

In fairness to Parisians, five centimeters of space is equivalent to five *feet* of space in America. Leaving the slightest area open in front of you is seen as justification to slide right in there, so unless you're standing genitals-to-backside to the person in front of you, you may as well put up a sign pointing in front of you that says, "Please, step ahead of me."

There was a hilarious series of television ads for the newspaper *Le Parisien,* all portrayals of Parisians at their worst. (They're definitely worth catching at video-sharing sites: search *"le parisien publicité."*) In one, you hear the sound of a zipper going up from behind one of the automatic sidewalk toilets in Paris. A moment after, a well-dressed man emerges and steps over the stream he just created, which is leading right into the bottom of a woman's market basket, now resting in a pool of *pipi.* He strides up next to her and her basket, gives her a brief nod of acknowledgment, then blithely crosses the street without a care.

Another presents two confused Japanese tourists wielding a guidebook, searching for the Eiffel Tower. A Parisian gently helps them out by pointing them back down the street they came from. They thank him, nodding and bowing profusely, before heading off. As they turn and depart, the helpful fellow turns and rounds the corner, the Eiffel Tower looming just above.

But my favorite is the scenario that takes place in a supermarket, where a little old lady is shuffling down the aisle toward the bored cashier, clutching a tiny bottle of water. Just as she's about to put her small purchase on the belt, she's broadsided by a harried woman who waves her away with a weak smile of insincere apology (which is *such* a Parisian touch, brava to the actress on nailing that one!) before unloading the contents of her overheaped grocery cart onto the belt.

Just when you think she's done, as *la grand-mère* is about to set down her bottle, the woman waves her back as her husband barges in with another armload of things. The tagline for all of the ads: "*Le Parisien: il vaut mieux l'avoir en journal*" or "The Parisian: it's better to have one as a newspaper." Chalk one up for the Parisian sense of humor.

"Oh, were you waiting in line?" more than one person has said to me when I've busted them for trying to cut in. "No, not really," I want to come back with, "I was just standing here in the supermarket with a basketful of items at the register, since I had nothing else to do today."

One *dame* who stepped right in front of me at the busy Ladurée on the Champs-Elysées actually turned to me when I spoke up, and said, "Is there *really* a line?"

To clarify it for her, I pointed out the ten people in single file in front of me and the twenty people waiting behind. I don't know how her definition of "a line" differs from mine, but I gave her plenty of time to ponder that as she skulked back to the end of it.

Many expats develop certain techniques to avoid strangers pressed up against them or trying to scoot in front. One that seems to be the most popular is to wear a small backpack. Those fall into the dreaded fanny pack category for me, so my chosen weapon to defend my turf around town is something that's easier to wield: the shopping basket.

My basket is wider than I am, with an imposing handle that I can spin to block anyone coming at me from any angle. When navigating a busy market, I hold it in front of me as I walk, like the prow of a battleship, to clear the way. That doesn't always work, as Parisians don't like to move or back up for anyone, no matter what. So sometimes I hide my basket behind me, then heave it forward at the last moment; the element of surprise gives them no time to plan a counteroffensive, and when the coast is suddenly clear, I make a break for it. It's best used, though, when waiting in line, since it makes a movable barricade that I can manipulate and position, halting even the most tenacious *risquilleur* in his or her tracks.

Unless you're pretty courageous or your French is exceptional, don't try anger. I caused an incident when a woman abruptly cut in front of me in line at Tati, our low-end department store. When she refused to budge, I muttered *"salope,"* which, although technically the same word Americans use for a female dog, in France, it's the equivalent of the c-word for women. I suppose that's the price I pay for an imperfect French vocabulary. As she let loose on me, loud enough for everyone on the same floor to hurry over to check out the commotion, I certainly learned a few other new, and not very nice, words that day.

I don't recommend humor, either, which Parisians don't seem to get. I once turned around and told the Frenchman of *un certain âge*, old enough to be my grandfather, who was nudging me forward from behind, *"Pardon? But don't you think you ought to buy me a drink first?"* My humor was wasted on him, and he just blankly looked at me. Or maybe he was too cheap to spring for the drink.

Even more fun when people start to push me from behind, as they inevitably like to do. I'll slowly start backing up . . . taking a little step . . . hesitating a moment . . . then taking another backward. There's no sound more satisfying than listening to the grumbling of people collapsing together behind me like a squashed accordion. You can keep your visits to the Louvre or the Eiffel Tower—this is one of my favorite things to do in Paris!

Since wheeled shopping carts are the favored weapon of those fragile little old ladies (who you'll find aren't really so fragile if you happen to get in their way), Parisians have developed an instinctive fear of *le chariot de marché*. I've taken a cue from them and transformed mine into a demarcation line between me and others. If they want to cross it, they risk an inadvertent roll across the foot, followed by a *very* sincere *"Oh! Excusez-*

moi!" But at least I have the courtesy to feign regret: those women would bulldoze a blind, legless invalid if he were in their path.

After living here a while, I didn't see any reason why I should have to wait in line behind anyone else either. So I trained my eye on Romain, who's the pro. I watched him at work, sliding between everyone waiting patiently for their onions or Camembert, and soon joined the ranks of *les risquilleurs* myself. I now cut in line with impunity with no regard for others. And can I tell you how much time I've saved? So with all the free time I seem to have now, there's nothing to keep me from passing on my tips to others.

First off, you need to know *exactly* what you want to buy. When you've barged in front of others, it's not the time for uncertainty. If you falter or hesitate or have a question, you're sunk.

Knowing the vendor helps a lot. But being French, they'll want to chat with you. Be prepared with a few quick words, but don't go overboard. Here, the typical "*Ça va?*" which can translate into either "Hey!" or "How's it going?" does nicely. The worst is if they ask you a question that requires a thoughtful response, like, "That ice cream you brought us last week was delicious. How did you make it?" or "Can you move your basket since it's blocking all the others?"

Whether you know the person or not, be sure to fix your gaze squarely on the merchant and don't make eye contact with anyone else. Just the vendor. If you glance at the others, like that *salope* you blindsided for the last bunch of radishes she was lurching toward, you may incite another international incident.

Have correct change. If you're buying a head of lettuce and hand the fellow a fifty-euro note, you're going to be stuck there for a few uncomfortable minutes while he rifles through his pockets, gathering and unwrinkling assorted bills and fishing for coins. You want to get in and out of there before the people in line have a chance to figure out they've been had.

But mostly it's all about *l'attitude*. Do not for one minute think that you don't belong in front of those other people. I mean, who do they think they are? Don't they know that you have more important things to do than wait behind them in line?

So if you come to Paris and you want to wait your turn patiently, that's your choice. Should you see a man barreling through the market, cutting a wide swath with a wicker basket, jangling a bunch of change in his hand, don't say I didn't warn you. Unless you'd prefer to have me nudging you from behind. Just don't expect me to buy you a drink first.

═══════════

TRAVERS DE PORC

PORK RIBS

MAKES 6 SERVINGS

Although you'll often see *travers de porc* (pork ribs) for sale at the markets, if you see them in a restaurant, they're rarely grilled or barbecued, the way we cook them in America. I don't think too many restaurants here have barbeque pits, but if anyone knows of one, please let me know!

On my first day at cooking school at Lenôtre years ago, as we all sat down to eat in the cafeteria, another student (from Denmark) commented, "Aren't you going to put ketchup on everything, like all Americans do?"

I pointed out, sarcastically, that, unlike his country, America is a large and very diverse place, and we don't all eat the same thing.

Americans do have a reputation for being ketchup lovers, although the French seem to enjoy it, too. And now you can find big plastic bottles in French (and probably Danish) supermarkets with Old Glory waving in the background on the label.

I'm not all that enamored of ketchup myself, but it does give the ribs I roast in my oven a close-to-down-home taste. Ribs are one of the few foods you'll see Parisians picking up and eating with their hands. Heck, I caught one licking his fingers when he thought I wasn't looking!

$2/3$ cup (160 ml) soy sauce (regular or low-salt)

$1/3$ cup (80 ml) ketchup

8 garlic cloves, peeled and finely minced

1-inch (3-cm) piece of fresh ginger, peeled and finely minced

2 teaspoons chile powder or Asian chile paste

2 tablespoons molasses

2 tablespoons dark rum

$1/2$ cup (125 ml) orange juice

2 teaspoons Dijon mustard

Freshly ground black pepper

4 pounds (2 kg) pork ribs, trimmed of excess fat,
    cut into 6-inch (15-cm) sections

1. Preheat the oven to 325°F (160°C).

2. In a large roasting pan, mix the soy sauce, ketchup, garlic, ginger, chile powder, molasses, rum, orange juice, mustard, and pepper.

3. Add the ribs and slather the marinade over both sides thoroughly. Cover and bake for 2 hours. While they're baking, turn the ribs a few times in the marinade.

4. Uncover and continue to cook, turning the ribs at 15-minute intervals, for an additional 1 to 1 1/2 hours, until the juices have reduced and thickened and the meat easily pulls away from the bones. The exact time depends on how quickly the liquid reduces and how lean the ribs are.

SERVING: Cut the racks into individual ribs and serve.

STORAGE: Pork ribs are just as good the next day. Cut them into riblets before reheating them in a covered baking dish, making sure there's just enough liquid to cover the bottom of the dish.

VARIATIONS: Feel free to play around with the seasonings. Add a handful of chopped fresh ginger or, a big pinch of ground allspice, or replace the orange juice with rosé or even beer.

═══════════

SALADE DE CHOUX AUX CACAHUETES

PEANUT SLAW

MAKES 6 SERVINGS

Peanuts are a popular snack with drinks in cafés across Paris, but most of the peanut butter around here is found in the homes of Americans. However, Africans and Indians like it as well, and I buy jars of it up near La Chapelle, the lively Indian quarter behind the Gare du Nord.

Resist the temptation to use delicate Napa or leafy Savoy cabbage, both of which quickly get soggy from the peanut dressing. I use a mix of firm green and red cabbage, which I slice as thin as possible. Tossing the salad together at the last minute is essential to preserve the crunch of the cabbage, although the sauce can be made a few hours in advance and mixed with the cabbage and other ingredients right before serving.

1/4 cup (65 g) smooth peanut butter

1 garlic clove, peeled and finely chopped

2 tablespoons peanut or vegetable oil

3 tablespoons freshly squeezed lemon or lime juice, or more to taste

1 tablespoon soy sauce

1 tablespoon water

1/2 cup (65 g) roasted, unsalted peanuts

1 small bunch radishes, trimmed and thinly sliced

1 carrot, peeled and coarsely shredded

1/2 bunch fresh flat-leaf parsley, cilantro, or chives, chopped

6 cups (500 g) shredded green or red cabbage

Coarse salt

1. In a large bowl, mix the peanut butter, garlic, peanut oil, lemon juice, soy sauce, and water until smooth.

2. Toss in the peanuts, radishes, carrot, parsley, and cabbage, mixing until everything's coated. Taste, then add a bit of salt and another squeeze of lemon juice, if necessary.

VARIATIONS: Substitute toasted almonds or cashews for the peanuts or swap 1 tablespoon of dark sesame oil for 1 tablespoon of the peanut oil, adding a tablespoon of toasted sesame seeds to the salad.

HOT CHOCOLATE TO DIE FOR

If you're one of those people who come to Paris craving a cup of the famous rich and thick hot chocolate served up around the city, you're not alone. Many visitors get a lost, misty-eyed look when describing the ultrathick, steamy *chocolat chaud* that glops and blurts as it's poured into dainty white cups in places like Angelina and Café de Flore, which serve it forth with great pomp and ceremony.

Me? I can barely swallow the sludge.

You need to clamp my mouth closed and massage my neck to get that hyperthick stuff down the hatch—like forcing a dog to swallow a pill. That throat-clogging liquid hits my tummy with a thud and refuses to budge for the rest of the day. I just don't get its appeal.

Seriously, if I had a *pistole* of chocolate for everyone who asks me where they can find the "best" hot chocolate in Paris, I'd be able to enrobe the Arc de Triomphe. And I've learned to stay away from that kind of question, since a guest once asked what "the best chocolate shop in Paris" was. Because I replied that I couldn't easily name any one in particular as "the best," a message was posted on an online bulletin board about what a jerk I was for not giving a definitive answer.

But how can I! It's like going into a wine shop and asking the clerk, "What's your best wine?"

Each chocolate shop in Paris is unique, so I'd never recommend one as "the best." I tend to think of them all as my children, each having various and lovable quirks. Nevertheless, we Americans love our lists and even more, we love superlatives; the higher up something is, the more we like it. When the rest of the world wonders why America never adopted the metric system, it's because it's not very exciting for us to say, "Oh my God, the temperature's about to hit 37 degrees!" when we could gasp, "Oh my God, the temperature's about to hit 100!" And don't get me started on that silly "wind-chill factor," which allows us to use even more superlatives.

∽

How did all this hot chocolate madness get started around here anyway? Most credit Spain's Anne of Austria, who married France's Louis XIII, and brought chocolate into France in 1615 in the form of plump, aromatic cacao beans as part of her dowry. Back then, there was no high-tech machinery to pulverize and mold chocolate into smooth tablets, so the cocoa beans were ground, heated, and whirled up into hot chocolate, which was so rare and pricey that it could be sipped only by the fashionable elite.

Since those French royals lived lavishly, to keep them in high style, they sold chocolate to the yearning masses, and soon, almost anyone could get their hands on the stuff. The Marquis de Sade used hot chocolate to hide poison, Madame de Pompadour drank it to keep up with Louis XV's hyperactive libido (the recipe is on the Château de Versailles Web site, in case you're interested), and the randy Madame du Barry made her lovers drink the brew to keep up with her by keeping it up.

Not everyone embraced this magical elixir and although Madame de Sévigné was delighted with chocolate's "regulatory" effects on her digestive system, she warned that drinking too much could cause adverse reactions: she reported to her daughter that another Parisienne, the Marquise de Coëtlogon, drank so much chocolate that when she gave birth, the child was "as black as the devil."

Four centuries later, you can find evidence of the past at Debauve & Gallet, a former pharmacy that's now an aloof (and outrageously expensive) chocolate shop that still dispenses flat disks of *chocolat de santé*— chocolate for health. Studies continue to this day offering proof that eating and drinking chocolate may be healthy, but most of the folks in Paris aren't downing cups to improve their health. And from what I've seen around here, everyone's libidos seems to be pretty healthy, too.

Nowadays there's no shortage of places in town to indulge, and just about any café will whip you up a cup of *le chocolat chaud.* However, in most instances, it's buyer beware: often it's slipped from a powdery packet into the cup. If you're not in a place that specializes in chocolate, look for the words *à la ancienne* scribbled on the menu or blackboard, which means the hot chocolate is made the old-fashioned way. Like Darty, though, there's no guarantee of 100 percent *satisfait*, and I've sampled a few "old-fashioned" cups where the only thing *ancienne* about them was how old the mix tasted.

One day, I stopped in for a snack at one of my favorite dives in Paris. The feeling inside the place is a close equivalent to a diner, although there's no long counter or, being France, no bottomless cups of anything. Like diner waitresses, the uniformed women who work there are efficient, perfunctory, and agreeable. Judging from their muscular calves and forearms, I wouldn't mess with them, though.

That afternoon, I had one of the most satisfying experiences of my life. It was particularly cold and even though, like most Parisians, I had wrapped and artistically double-knotted my scarf all the way up and around my neck, I couldn't shake the chill that kept me shivering-cold. So I ordered a *petit chocolat chaud*. After the waitress set the clunky little cup in front of me, I blew away the cloud of steam that rose from the surface, peered at the dark brew inside, and cautiously brought the cup to my lips.

It took a moment for my brain to process what had just happened: everything I ever thought about hot chocolate was suddenly banished, dragged into the trash icon in the corner of my brain, and deleted for good. It was quite simply the best hot chocolate I've ever had, and the only one I've ever truly, madly fallen in love with.

Each day at Pâtisserie Viennoise, this extraordinary hot chocolate is whipped up fresh in the underground kitchen in a giant pot, then poured into a massive urn and measured out all day long in two sizes: *petit* and *grand*. For me, *petit* is exactly the right amount of this intensely chocolatey drink. Looking around, I'm clearly in the minority, since no one seems to have any problems finishing the larger mugs topped with a completely unreasonable amount of billowy whipped cream teetering dangerously over the edge.

Don't expect to find anything gilded around here or served on dainty little doilies. The two rooms are dark and a tad shabby with photocopied prints on the walls, and there are sizable chips in the mocha-brown moldings. But the delicious *chocolat chaud* costs just a couple of euros, so you don't suffer sticker shock when *l'addition* arrives. And if you absolutely have to have a doily underneath your cup, bring your own.

So where is Pâtisserie Viennoise?

To get to it, you'll need to brave the most hazardous street in Paris: la rue de l'Ecole de Médecine (which, fortunately, means there's a medical school nearby), in the fifth arrondissement. If it weren't for the amazing hot chocolate, I'd avoid this street entirely, since the buses speed down this narrow alley, barely missing the limbs of pedestrians, who cower as they move along on sidewalks so narrow that if you exhale at the wrong time, you can actually feel the bus graze your cheek as it rockets past. As much as I've always wanted to enjoy lingering over the lovely Viennese strudels and pastries on display in the window, when I make it to the front door, I hop inside as soon as I can, propelled forward by the whoosh of the #86 bus behind me as the driver floors it forward, barely grazing one of my other cheeks.

Once you're safely inside Pâtisserie Viennoise, slip off your coat and wedge yourself into any place you can find. If you come midday, you have to order something to eat. They won't just let you sip a *chocolat chaud* while harried Parisians wait around on their lunch breaks, eyeing your table while you enjoy your two-buck cup. You're welcome to stand at the few square centimeters of space they call a counter and have a quick fix if you arrive during mealtime, which is usually where you'll find me, even if there are tables available. It provides a great overview of the waitresses in action, one of my other favorite forms of entertainment in Paris. But when they come barreling around the corner with their hands full of tottering cups and saucers, stay out of their way; they'll run you down with as much determination as the #86 bus outside.

If you don't really want to overdose on whipped cream, do not order a hot chocolate *Viennois*. The rule here is to top each cup with a lofty puff that's equal in size to, or larger than, the cup itself. Consider yourself fortunate if it hasn't toppled off and oozed in a billowy blob melting down the sides of the cup and pooling up in the saucer by the time it reaches your table. I'm a purist, and always ask for mine *sans Chantilly*. When I do I always detect a deep wrinkle of disappointment crossing the waitress's brow.

And being a purist, I like really bitter chocolate. To someone who hasn't met a chocolate that's too bitter for him, this hot chocolate is my Waterloo. After a couple of sips, I wuss out and begin unwrapping one of the cubes of sugar perched alongside, and *fais un canard*, as they say; make it like a duck and dunk it in.

One day, while trying to sleuth out their recipe, I asked if they used unsweetened chocolate, and the waitress behind the counter promptly replied, *"Non"*—nor do they add cocoa powder, which I asked about too. She wasn't giving up the secret, yet did confide that it's cooked for a while on the stovetop, which she attempted to demonstrate by moving her right arm in a very large circular motion, large enough for me to know I don't have a pot that big. (Or muscles like hers.) And that was that; she just smiled and went back to work.

When I've reached the bottom of my cup, fully sated, I head toward the door without any feeling of overindulgence, but fortified enough to handle the fiercest of Parisian winter weather. With a warm glow, I slip on my jacket, re-macramé my scarf around my neck, drop a few coins in the dish by the register, and leave. As I exit, I'm always careful to make a sharp ninety-degree turn just after I'm out the door so I don't inadvertently meet my maker. (Or my hot chocolate maker, although I'd sure like to meet him to pick his brain.)

Come to think of it, I don't think a nice, steaming cup of *chocolat chaud* made just the way I like it would be such a bad last supper. Maybe from here on out, I'll start to accept the overload of whipped cream they're always pushing on me: if it's my time to go, at least I'll go a very happy man. And then I can say, in all honesty, that I've finally found the best hot chocolate in Paris, one that's truly "to die for."

═══════════════

LE CHOCOLAT CHAUD

HOT CHOCOLATE

MAKES 4 TO 6 CUPS

If you can't make it to Pâtisserie Viennoise, you'll be missing out on not just the most fabulous cup of *chocolat chaud* in Paris, but a pretty formidable range of

Viennese desserts, like Sacher torte, filled with apricots and glazed in shiny chocolate; flaky rectangles of strudel bursting from an overload of cinnamon-baked apples; and hearty rounds of savory, bacon-studded Tyrolean bread. And perhaps a close call with death.

Luckily, my version of Parisian hot chocolate is easy to make safely at home, and you can use either regular or low-fat milk. But do use a top-notch chocolate. Since the recipe has so few ingredients, the quality of the chocolate really does make a difference.

2 cups (500 ml) whole or low-fat milk

5 ounces (140 g) semisweet or bittersweet chocolate,
    finely chopped

Pinch of coarse salt

1. In a medium saucepan, warm the milk, chocolate, and salt. Heat until it begins to boil. (It will probably boil up quite a bit at first, so keep an eye on it.)

2. Lower the heat to the barest simmer and cook the mixture, whisking frequently, for 3 minutes. If you want a thicker consistency, cook it another 1 to 2 minutes.

SERVING: Pour into cups and serve *nature,* or with a giant mound of slightly sweetened whipped cream. Sugar can be added, to taste.

STORAGE: *Le chocolate chaud* can be made in advance and stored in the refrigerator for up to five days. Rewarm over low heat in a saucepan or microwave oven.

A FISH OUT OF WATER

I'm scared of fish. Terrified of them.

Even dead, they have those unblinking, glistening, glazed-over eyes that stare off into the distance, but always seem to be looking at me. When I see them lying there, I'm convinced that their slippery bodies are somehow going to miraculously spring back to life and take a chomp out of me.

For reasons unknown, I'm not afraid of snakes, spiders, alligators, lizards—or shellfish, for that matter. Dead or alive. But what really scares me, even more than scaly fish, are those shape-shifting, squiggly, vile creatures from the deep—squid.

It's a fear deeply rooted from the time my sister chased me around the house when I was six with a Marineland booklet spread open to the double-page larger-than-life centerfold of a giant octopus unfurling its tentacles around some innocent rock. I was sure she'd never find me hiding under my bed. But she did, and tossed that terrifying tome, spread wide-open, under there with me. It's a trauma I haven't recovered from to this very day.

Forty years later, yes, I'm still haunted by those evil encephalopods, and I think all of them deserve a fast death in hot oil—breaded first—then drowned in spicy sauce. That's the fate those ugly suckers deserve.

You can imagine my reaction during my first week of work in the kitchen at Chez Panisse, eager to do my best, when a huge plastic tub brimming to the very top with gloopy, gooshy squid was thrust into my hands, which I was expected to clean. Even though I was just one week into my two-week trial period, there was no way I was touching any of them. Conjure up your worst nightmare, and that's mine. In a panic, I had a sudden urge to go to the restroom, where I stayed until I was sure the project had been handed off to someone else. Thankfully, later I moved on to the pastry department, which was tentacle-free, and I was off the hook forever. Or so I thought.

At the markets in Paris where the *poissonnières* proudly display the daily catch of seafood on mounds of cracked ice, I find myself scared, but oddly attracted to, those slippery little devils lying in a soggy, cold heap whenever I pass them. I get a smug satisfaction knowing they're awaiting their fate for all the psychological harm they've caused me over the years. (Somehow I gave my sister a pass.) I knew they were dead but felt oddly drawn to them, peering over at the tangled pile, *almost* wanting to touch one to find out what it feels like.

Funny how we're often fascinated by what we're most afraid of. Who hasn't peered from a giant skyscraper or bridge wondering what it would be like to tumble off the edge? Or what it would be like to go to your local fish market and tell the friendly, ruggedly handsome young men there that you want to work with them gutting fish all day?

One of my favorite places to buy fish, called Pêche Paris, is at the marché d'Aligre. Brightly lit so you can inspect everything, the seafood at Pêche Paris passes even the closest scrutiny for freshness. Its ice-blue countertops are brimming with the pick of the *pêcheur:* tangerine-colored chunks of salmon, spiky, cross-eyed *rascasse*, silvery little sardines, delicate fillets of crimson *rouget*, and slender sole française, as flat and lithe as an Hermès calfskin glove.

When I was writing a book on frozen desserts, my freezer quickly filled up, and I needed to jettison several batches of ice cream at a time to make room for the next couple of batches waiting to be churned up. I correctly assumed that Pêche Paris had a big ice chest, and the young fellows who worked there, with their only-in-France waistlines, could handle eating much more ice cream than a certain American, who foolishly squandered his enviable adolescent waistline on chocolate. When the guys saw me coming, they'd drop everything to say hello, eager to see what flavors I brought them that week.

I believe in taking advantage of my decision to live in a foreign country by making myself open to new adventures whenever the opportunity arises. So one day, while I was talking with my fish boys, I asked if I could work there. Of course they were stunned. I mean, who in their right mind wants to handle ice-cold, icky fish all day, then head home all wet with fish juices clinging to your arms and sticky little scales clinging to your hair and eyelashes? Aside from the fact that I would be dangerously close to the squid, even more frightening was that they told me to come the following Wednesday at 5:30 a.m. And let me tell you, there's nothing scarier than I am at 5:30 a.m. A giant octopus doesn't even come close. As anyone who's worked with me can attest, I'm distinctly unpleasant in the morning. Waking up when it's pitch dark in the dead of winter, trudging over to the marché d'Aligre, and hefting dead fish all morning suddenly didn't seem so appealing, the more I thought about it. But since I had asked and they had said yes, it was too late to back out.

On my first day I managed to arrive just two minutes late. The French may have a reputation for being laissez-faire about things like punctuality, but when it comes to work, that reputation isn't always well deserved. The fish boys were already in full swing under the blazing, harsh lights, shoveling ice, thwacking off fish heads, and ripping out their bloody guts.

We rifled through a pile of tall rubber boots to find a pair that would fit, which I slid on, and someone handed me a thick blue floor-length rubber apron. I'd been completely waterproofed, and hefting all those fat carp and slithery conger eels around, I soon saw why this was necessary.

Because I've worked in restaurants for almost half of my life, I've learned there are three things you need to do to survive in any food service environment. The first is never to lie about your experience or skill level. There's no use bragging about something you can't do. You'll be busted for it almost immediately, and it's more endearing to be eager to learn new skills than to screw up.

The second thing that is that you need to know how to move in a kitchen. That's how I got my first restaurant job in college. I had no experience, but the head chef said I knew how to move. And I got hired.

And last, you must have the willingness to do anything. I can't tell you how many interns I trained who rolled their eyes when I asked them to juice a case of lemons or pit a flat of cherries. You would have thought I asked them to clean the bottom of my work shoes with their tongues. At Chez Panisse, even Alice and the head chefs take out the garbage, and in a restaurant kitchen, if you're above doing any sort of work (except cleaning squid, of course) you're not part of the team.

As I started working at the fish market, I realized it had been at least twenty years since I had tackled a new job. Working at home by myself, I'd forgotten that feeling of inadequacy and having to prove myself as "the new guy." So I was careful, since there's nothing worse than messing up something big on your first day to make you feel really horrible.

The first job they gave me was prepping a case of *dorade*, a task that consisted of using a jagged metal scraper to briskly rub the scales off each chubby fish, lopping off the head with scissors, slicing open the belly, and wrenching out the soggy mass of oozing organs with my hands. If you don't think about what you're doing, it's fine: you just cut, slash, and yank. If you stop and think about it, you gag. Especially at 6:03 a.m.

There's a reason fishmongers are not called fish "butchers"—you don't want to hack away at them. Each fillet needs to be clean and neatly trimmed. No one wants to get home and unwrap a piece of fish that looks like it's been on the losing end of a tug-of-war with a cat.

Once I finished cleaning the small fish, I graduated to the bigger ones, which were slapped down in front of me, making me extra-appreciative of the apron and boot combo. Aside from one whole salmon that looked like it was the victim of a serial killer with a penchant for fish that swam up-stream, I didn't do so badly. My weakness was that I wasn't so quick, which is to be expected when dealing with something new and unfamiliar. And those fish were tricky little fellas: unlike blocks of chocolate and cups of sugar, which stay put, fish slide around as you're working on them. Fil-leting one is like trying to change a tire on a moving car.

I also learned how to shuck scallops quickly and neatly, the correct way to skin and slice an eel, the delicate art of peeling the thin skin off sole, the ease of deboning a sardine with a slip of my thumb, and how not to grimace when people inquired about squid. Which whenever I passed, I looked at longingly, imagining myself running my hands over their slippery bodies, fondling those fleshy tentacles. But I just couldn't bring myself to do it.

The hardest work wasn't at the fish market, though, it was when I got home after work. (As a courtesy to others, I walked home instead of tak-ing the Métro.) After my first day, as soon as I closed the door behind me, I dove into the bathtub for a good soak, thinking that would wash off the smell. Unfortunately, I discovered that hot water just seals in the fish essences even deeper. I tried scrubbing my hands with industrial-strength soap and holding my hands under running water while rubbing them with a stainless steel spoon, which usually works, but was no match for the pow-erful smell of fish.

I was reminded of the film *Atlantic City,* where Susan Sarandon comes home every night, cuts a few lemons in half, then rubs them over her arms and hands while her voyeuristic neighbor (Burt Lancaster) watches las-civiously from across the way. So I followed suit. Unfortunately, all that left me with were two hands that felt as if they'd been immersed in battery acid.

After a couple of weeks at the *poissonnerie,* I started to feel I was getting the hang of things and was doing a decent enough job for them to let me stay on as many weeks as I wanted. Not that it was glamorous, but being there, hanging out with guys who should have been modeling for Dolce & Gabbana, having coffee in the café with the market workers, really made me feel I was blending in with the French. Surrounded by piles of dead fish, their entrails permanently lodged underneath my fingernails, the floor slippery with sea water, and flaky, translucent scales littered in my hair and eyelashes, I somehow managed to keep stoking a warm and fuzzy glow inside for what I was doing.

So imagine my surprise when one morning as I headed to the changing room to don my rubber boots and apron, Thiebaut took me aside and said they didn't need me anymore. At least that's what I think he said. He mentioned something about *les droits,* which in my predawn French, I believe meant something about French law, which is very strict about who works where. There's a chance, too, that I could have been fired. But I'd like to believe it had something to do with my lack of working papers.

Dejected, I went home and climbed back into my still-warm bed, a bit depressed. I curled up under the covers and pulled my pillow beneath my head. The only thing perking me up was that my hands smelled, well . . . they didn't smell like anything.

I thought back on one morning when I was in the shop a few minutes before we opened, alone with the fish. I had walked by a big pile of squid on ice and I suddenly plunged my hand right in and moved it around, fondling the cool, glossy heads with my fingers, trying to avoid the tentacles (I didn't get *that* crazy), and in that moment, I overcame my biggest fear in the world, one I'd been dragging around all my life.

By the next day, I didn't feel so bad about not being asked to return. (My editor keeps crossing out "not asked to return" and replacing it with "fired," but I'm sticking to my story.) In fact, I was a bit relieved to be fired—I mean, not asked to return—since that meant I'd no longer spend six sleepless nights of the week panicking about waking up at an ungodly hour on the seventh.

I'm glad to have had the experience of working among some of the handsomest *poissonniers* in Paris, too, and I still stop by at least once a week and buy my fish from them. But I'm still going to stay away from the squid—unless no one's looking.

═══════════

SARDINES AUX OIGNONS ET RAISINS SECS A LA MODE DE VENISE

VENETIAN-STYLE SARDINES WITH ONIONS AND RAISINS

MAKES 8 SERVINGS

Fresh sardines are one of the few fish that were never intimidating to me. I guess because they're so diminutive, they don't look like they could do much damage.

This idea for pickling fish in a sweet-and-sour brine goes back to the time when fish needed to be preserved, so they were pickled lightly in vinegar and sugar, which are both preservatives—not to be confused with *préservatifs*. So choose your word carefully: You'll get you some funny looks if you tell your French fish merchant that you're going to store your fish in *préservatifs*, which in French are condoms.

Vegetable oil, for frying

$1/4$ cup (35 g) flour

$3/4$ teaspoon coarse salt, plus more for seasoning the flour

Freshly ground black pepper

1 pound (450 g) cleaned fresh sardines (see Note)

1 pound (450 g) red or white onions, peeled, halved, and thinly sliced

2 tablespoons olive oil

1 tablespoon turbinado or granulated sugar

Big pinch of red pepper flakes

1/3 cup (40 g) pine nuts

1/2 cup (125 ml) white wine vinegar

1/3 cup (80 ml) dry white wine

2 bay leaves

1/4 cup (35 g) golden raisins

1. Pour vegetable oil in a large heavy-duty skillet (not nonstick) to a depth of about 1/4 inch (1 cm) and heat until shimmering hot.

2. While the oil is heating, put the flour in a shallow pie plate or similar dish and season with salt and pepper. Dredge both sides of each sardine in the flour and shake off any excess.

3. Fry the sardines, as many as will fit in the pan in a single layer, starting flesh side down. Cook for about a minute on each side, until lightly browned. Remove each one as soon as it's done with a slotted spoon and drain in a single layer on paper towels. Repeat with the remaining sardines.

4. Once all the sardines are cooked, pour off any excess oil, reduce the heat to very low, and add the onions, olive oil, salt, sugar, and red pepper to the pan.

5. Cook, stirring occasionally, until the onions are wilted and meltingly soft, 20 to 30 minutes.

6. While the onions are cooking, toast the pine nuts in a 325°F (160°C) oven for about 6 minutes, checking and stirring them frequently so they don't burn.

7. When the onions are cooked, stir in the vinegar, wine, bay leaves, raisins, and pine nuts. Remove from heat and let cool.

8. In a deep nonreactive bowl or baking dish just large enough to hold the fish snugly, alternately layer the sardines and onions, making sure to end with a solid layer of onions on top. Pour the marinade over the fish, then cover and refrigerate.

SERVING: I serve the sardines with a basket of sturdy bread, like *pain au levain* (sourdough) or a hearty rye, along with a mound of good butter. I like to butter a slice of bread, then drape a sardine across the top. Make sure there's a little dish of coarse sea salt, or *fleur de sel,* handy to sprinkle on top. This makes a great do-ahead meal, served with a big leafy salad.

STORAGE: The sardines can be refrigerated for up to two days. They're best served at room temperature.

NOTE: Most fishmongers sell sardines already cleaned. If you can't find fresh sardines, use any little fillets of fish that aren't too meaty, such as perch, sole, or sand dabs. You can also use red wine vinegar if you can't easily locate white wine vinegar, which for some reason is almost impossible to find in Paris.

THE FRENCH SECURITY BLANKET

What are the absolute last words you want to hear your host say when you're invited for dinner? How about, "We had some fish that was about to go bad. So we're having fish for dinner."

The French are notoriously famous for their love of fresh food, which abounds in the outdoor markets, where locals line up (well, sometimes) to select what's best and freshest that particular day. But they're equally famous for another trait, and that's not letting *anything* go to waste. After living in Paris for a while, when there was no longer any room even to slip an envelope into my snug apartment,

I asked around for places to donate used items, like clothes that were no longer in fashion—or more likely, that I could no longer fit into. But I was met with blank stares. Romain edified me, *"Non,* Daveed," he said, wagging his finger in front of my face. *"Les Français ne jettent rien."* ("The French throw away *nothing.")*

I fit in well, since I can't bear to throw away things either. Like those perfectly good designer pants that were such a bargain at 60 percent off, even though they felt just a bit snug at the time. In the years since I bought them, sometimes when I'm getting ready to go out, I'll try them on. Yet neither I, nor the waistband, seem to want to change. I reason to myself that parachute pants with more pleats than a Broadway theater curtain will eventually come back in style, so back in the closet they go for a few more years, even though space is lacking in my tiny French closet.

Space is equally in short supply in French refrigerators, which means that things aren't kept in there as much as I think they should. I've been a guest at people's homes and seen them leave beef stew or, worse, beef stock, unrefrigerated, on the counter, overnight. Even for a couple of days. (Stock is such as perfect medium for growing bacteria that science labs use it for that purpose.) I spent a week on vacation with a family who kept bouillon in a jar next to the stove. One by one, everyone came down with a wicked case of *le gastro*—except me, who wisely begged off the bowls of soup that were offered that week.

Somehow, no one ever makes the connection around here between getting sick and how food is handled. It's something I, and my digestive tract, have had to adjust to.

Having worked in professional kitchens, I know a thing or two about food preparation and sanitation. But I've learned to keep my cool and look the other way when the woman at the *charcuterie* lifts a dripping-wet pork loin out of the case, then proceeds to handle the slice of pâté I plan to make a sandwich with for lunch. "Maybe the alcohol will kill the pathogens," I think hopefully, pouring myself a glass of wine, even though I know it's not true. I don't usually drink much at lunch, but when I do, I gauge the amount of wine I drink in direct proportion to the attention to hygiene I witness during the food prep, so sometimes I have no choice.

At home, with such a scarcity of space, I've had to become a little more lenient about food storage than I know I should be. As I unload my market basket, I evaluate each item, then ask myself, "Do I *really* need to refrigerate this?"

At *chez Dave*, mustard, cheese, and anything pickled, preserved, or *confit'd* goes in the "perhaps" category, whereas milk, meat, and most *charcuterie* get priority access to my demi-fridge. Vegetables are on a "case-by-case" basis: if I'm not going to use them within the next twenty-four to forty-eight hours, in they go. Bulky, space-hogging root vegetables are an exception: for them, the refrigerator is *interdit*.

Meat, pork, poultry, and fresh fish, of course, get chilled. Sausages? Yes to fresh sausages—not always for *saucisses sèches*. Milk and unfermented dairy products go right in the minute I get home, since I refuse to buy into the belief of some French folks that keeping opened milk in the cupboard, even if it's sterilized, is a wise idea. To me, that's just asking for trouble. On the other hand, anyone who buys sterilized milk deserves what's coming to them.

Unfortunately when you're a guest in someone's home for the weekend, you can't always keep on top of these things. And the fish *du jour* might be from a *jour* last week. It also means you'll have the opportunity to get well acquainted with another less-than-savory fixture in every French household: *la serpillière*.

What is *la serpillière*, you ask? Even if you haven't set foot in a French person's home, if you've walked the streets of Paris, you've certainly stepped over those soggy, wadded-up rags curled up in the gutter directing water. I know, I know. It seems silly and archaic that a nation with rocketlike high-speed trains, that pioneered supersonic air transport, and was the first to implement an efficient system of cyber communication still litters their streets with foul rags—as well as dragging them through their kitchens and wadding them up in the crevices of their bathrooms.

The French love those skanky, damp gray rags, and they tow them from room to room in their homes like a security blanket. Admittedly, it's been a while since Paris was a big muddy marsh and water needed to be controlled and redirected. A few hundred years later, which would be today, most of the water stays right where it belongs: in the Seine. And with groundbreaking innovations like shower curtains, mops, and sponges, you'd think there wouldn't be any need to drag sopping-wet towels around the house. But apparently, there is.

Although I've come to love the precision of the "hose" that the French favor for taking a shower, I can't fathom why many homes and hotels in Europe don't provide curtains for their showers. All it takes is a split-second of absentmindedly reaching for the soap to misdirect the spray and you've soaked the floor, the toilet, the toilet paper, and your toiletries. I don't know about you, but the last activity I want to do when I hop buck-naked out of the shower is get on my hands and knees and start mopping the bathroom floor.

And since a holder for the hose isn't always provided, I haven't figured out where to put it down while soaping up. Perhaps you're supposed to turn it off while lathering, but in my punky handheld shower, it takes at least five minutes for the hot water to reach the nozzle from the hot water heater, which may—or may not—come roaring to life. (Unfortunately, it's much more dependable in the summer than in the winter.) So I was a big spender and sprang for a shower curtain, and boy, am I glad I did. After a shower, I can't tell you the thrill I get stepping into a dry bathroom and toweling off. What a concept! Maybe I'll start bringing them as hostess gifts when invited to people's homes.

I suppose not installing a shower curtain reinforces the French *fidélité* to *la serpillière*, similar to the oversized French ID cards, which are mandatory for all to carry but don't fit into men's billfolds. Men have no choice but to carry man-purses—it's like there's a government-issued decree requiring French men to look gay. And when I've questioned the no-shower-curtain logic, my French friends defensively ask how we sop up water in America.

"With a mop. One that has a nice, long wooden handle."

This is also a country where it's *interdit* for men to wear anything but a skimpy, religion-baring Speedo in public pools *"pour l'hygiène, monsieur!"* If someone could explain why strapping on a slingshot-style swimsuit is so much more hygienic than a square-cut swimsuit with two extra centimeters of fabric—and why I, who have less hair on my head than many of the men have on their backs, have to wear a bathing cap—I'm all ears. I don't understand how anyone can be concerned about the hygiene of a few extra centimeters of spandex in a swimsuit when all those *serpillières* are out there at large, infecting the general population.

So next time you're in France, if you really want to pick up something that's truly French as a souvenir, skip the box of luscious *macarons* from Ladurée, the snow globes of the Eiffel Tower, or the Mona Lisa T-shirts on the rue de Rivoli. Bring home a *serpillière*. Which you can pick up almost anywhere.

Literally.

ROTI DE PORC MARINE A LA CASSONADE ET AU WHISKY

ROAST PORK WITH BROWN SUGAR–BOURBON GLAZE

MAKES 6 TO 8 SERVINGS

In Paris, if you want pork you head to the *charcuterie*. For beef, it's off to *le boucher*. And for chicken, you need to visit the *volailler*. They maintain it's *nécessaire* to keep all meat, pork, lamb, and poultry separate *pour l'hygiène*, which I don't quite understand since raw meat and poultry all require the same careful handling procedures.

Brining the pork is optional, but this easy step, which was inspired by the instructions in *The Zuni Cookbook* by Judy Rodgers, gives a bit of leeway to those of us who must shop on specific days at our local outdoor market, as well as ensures a moist pork loin. Feel free to adjust or substitute any seasonings and spices in the brine, but keep the salt, sugar, and water amounts the same.

The brining and marinating can be done a day or so in advance; then you simply roast the pork for about an hour. Although *le whisky* may sound like an odd ingredient in French cuisine, it's one of the most popular apéritifs in Paris, so I keep a bottle on hand. And when invited for dinner in someone else's home, if watching the food prep, I often need a glass or two as well.

For the brine

5 cups (1¼ L) water

2 tablespoons coarse salt

½ cup (120 g) packed dark brown sugar

10 allspice berries, crushed

2 bay leaves, crumbled

A few thyme branches or 1 teaspoon dried thyme

2½ pounds (1¼ kg) boneless pork roast

For the glaze

¼ cup (80 g) strained apricot jam

¼ cup (60 ml) bourbon

3 tablespoons (45 g) dark brown sugar

1 tablespoon mild-flavored molasses

1. Make a brine by heating 1 cup (250 ml) of the water with the salt, sugar, allspice, bay leaves, and thyme. Once the sugar and salt are dissolved, remove from heat. Pour into a large bowl or plastic container. Add 1 quart (1 L) water and chill thoroughly.

2. When the brine is cold, submerge the pork and top with a small plate to keep it submerged. Cover and refrigerate for 2 to 4 days.

3. To make the glaze, mix the jam, bourbon, sugar, and molasses in a small saucepan. Heat to a low boil and cook for 2 minutes. Let cool.

4. Remove the pork from the brine, dry it well with a paper towel, and place in a sturdy zip-top freezer bag. Add the marinade, seal the top, and knead it gently to distribute the glaze. Let rest in the refrigerator for at least 8 hours or overnight, turning it occasionally to distribute the marinade.

5. To cook the pork, preheat the oven to 375°F (190°C).

6. Lift the pork from the marinade and place in a baking dish that's just large enough to hold it. Add water until it's barely 1/2 inch (1 cm) deep. Pour the remaining marinade into a bowl and reserve.

7. Roast the pork for 45 minutes to 1 hour (depending on the thickness of the pork), brushing at regular intervals with the reserved marinade and adding a small amount of water to the pan if it's evaporating.

8. The pork is done when an instant-read thermometer inserted into the center reads 140°F (60°C). Remove from the oven, cover snugly with foil, and let rest 15 minutes before slicing.

SERVING: If you want to serve this with *Oignons aigres-doux* (page 181), add them to the baking dish during the last twenty minutes of baking to heat them through.

===

OVEN-ROASTED FIGS

MAKES 4 SERVINGS

During fresh fig season, I love to serve pork with oven-roasted figs; they're very simple to make. Choose black or green figs that are just ripe, but not too squishy. These can be baked at the same time as the pork, but they are much better if baked a day or even a few hours in advance and allowed to rest, during which time the juices thicken to a smooth, syrupy consistency. The figs are luscious with just honey and sugar, but a few sprigs of thyme, some lemon zest, and a shot of *pastis* are all delicious additions.

10 to 12 (about 1 pound/500 g) fresh ripe black or green figs
$1^1/2$ tablespoons honey
2 to 3 tablespoons dark brown sugar

1. Preheat the oven to 375°F (190°C).

2. Stem and quarter the figs. Place in a baking dish that will hold them in single layer and spoon the honey over them, then crumble the sugar over the top.

3. Toss together gently, cover tightly with foil, and bake for 15 minutes.

4. Remove the foil, gently turn the figs in the syrup, and cook uncovered for 15 minutes, or until tender.

HAVING THE BOURSES TO GIVE MYSELF A SHOT

Aside from real estate prices and an unshakable fixation that French people hate us, there's nothing that fascinates Americans more than the French health care system. I've heard Americans proclaim, "People die in France waiting to get a doctor's appointment!"

Well, no, you don't. Which I can personally attest to, since I'm still alive. When I want an appointment with my doctor, I get one within a day or two, although for specialists, the wait can be a harrowingly long week or two. And when it's time for your visit, in many cases, the doctors themselves greet you at the door. No one's in a rush and there's no insurance company between you and your doctor waiting to deny your claim. If you get sick in France, people say, "How are you feeling?" instead of, "How's your insurance?"

The medical care that I've received here has been great. The only uncomfortable moments I've experienced were because doctors don't think twice about prescribing treatments that aren't always taken orally. I had a bad cough that I couldn't shake and when I stopped by the pharmacy with my prescription, I was handed a box of bullet-shaped, waxy pellets. I questioned the wisdom of placing the remedy in the end opposite from where the problem was, but the pharmacist looked at me like I was crazy to think that cough medicine might go anywhere else. So I let it drop. The medicine did indeed work, but take it from me; I don't recommend dosing yourself prior to heading to a yoga class, especially if that day you'll be concentrating on inversions.

Still, most Americans simply can't get over their skepticism about the excellence of the French health care system and how well it works. Oddly, it's one of the few things around here that does.

A few brainwashed individuals in America tried to convince me that the system in the States is better than the system in France; "I don't want some government official making medical decisions for me." I wouldn't want the government making medical decisions for me either. Or worse, a for-profit HMO. I want my doctor to make those decisions, like they do in France. There are no claims to be denied or accepted, and if you start using terms like "preexisting conditions" and "usual and customary charges," French people look at you like you're from Mars. Doctors are free to make decisions based on what they think is best for the patient.

The World Health Organization calls the French health care system "the best in the world," and French people have the third-highest life expectancy on the planet (Americans are a bit further down—we're twenty-fourth). Perhaps the French live longer since they don't have to worry about medical bills, or have to cope with the stress of spending hours on the phone with their health insurance company fighting for coverage.

Much of that longevity gets attributed to the baffling contradiction that even though the French eat a diet notoriously high in saturated fats, three times what Americans consume, they have fewer coronary problems. Frenchwomen have the second-highest life expectancy in the world (bested only by their Japanese counterparts), for which they especially deserve kudos considering that between 33 and 48 percent of the French (depending on their sex) smoke. And if you've ever had the pleasure of sitting next to a group of teenage girls who slap their cell phones and cigarettes on the café table and start fumbling for their lighters even before they're seated, you'll know which sex falls closer to the 48 percent end.

A few other advantages of the French health care system: doctors still make house calls, and each neighborhood has nurses who will give you a shot, change bandages, and remove stitches. (They make house calls, too.) Doctors give you their cell phone numbers—gladly—and you can dial SOS Médecins at any time of the day or night and they'll come racing over, within an hour, to cure what ails you. Prescriptions rarely cost more than €10 and after giving birth, women not only get in-home help with child care, but are eligible for a complimentary *rééducation du périnée*.

Even better, at least for me, is that pharmacists have a lot of leeway, and mine will give me any prescription drug I want, *sans ordonnance*, because I bring him ice cream. Now that's my kinda system!

Still, all is not perfect in the land of the single-payer system. There are a couple of downsides (aside from a proliferation of medicines that are taken upended), which I found out when I had surgery in Paris.

For one thing, I didn't realize I was going to be so do-it-yourself. I was given a list of things to bring to the clinic: bandages, surgical tape, painkillers, antiseptic, and gauze. I was surprised needle and thread weren't on the list. They don't ask you to bring a gown either, but you might want to if you're bashful. And pack a bar of soap and a towel if you plan on taking a shower. Clean sheets, beds, and pillows, however, are provided.

Although I wasn't expected to do anything but lie there during my surgery, I was expected to be able to administer to myself whatever medications were prescribed afterward. When I went to fill the doctor's prescription for a blood thinner, the pharmacist handed me a box of very long hypodermic needles with a booklet showing how and where to jab myself. He was quite surprised when I freaked.

This being France, of course everyone behind the counter, as well as the other customers, had an opinion, offering tips and techniques. "Oh, it's very easy. It's not going to be hard at all. Stop being so scared," everyone chimed in, without one iota of sympathy.

And after three or four times of bouncing the needle off my stomach, I somehow managed to *pique* myself, at last. (In retrospect, it might have helped if I'd kept my eyes open.) Once I got the hang of it, though, my doctor went and upped my dosage, which required a needle twice as wide and long. And he wasn't at all concerned that I almost fainted when he showed me the new hypodermic I had to use.

The bedside manner of French doctors can leave a lot to be desired, too. Don't expect anyone to hold your hand, look you in the eye, and tell you, "Don't worry, everything's going to be okay."

I hobbled into the doctor's office the day after I had my leg surgery, white-knuckling my cane. Painful jolts shot up and down my legs, and each step felt as if I were being Tasered. "You look like an old man!" he said, laughing. Since I couldn't move a step without wanting to crumble to the floor, thanks to the kilometers of stitches running up and down my leg, I thought it would have been nice if he'd shown a bit of compassion. But we're paying for doctors to treat us, not hold our hands. Or our hypodermics.

⌒

Fortunately, I managed to live in France for a few years before having my first full-blown medical emergency: one Friday night I thought I was having a heart attack. I was getting ready to go to a Thanksgiving dinner, which we Americans have to celebrate on the weekend, since everyone has to work on Thursday. (After all, it's just any other day in Paris. Although a surprising number of Americans ask me if French people celebrate Thanksgiving, which I find odd. I'm not quite sure why anyone might think someone in another country would be interested in celebrating the discovery of America.)

All day long I'd been having racing pains in my chest while baking my heart out (this time, I was afraid,—literally). Fearing the worst, I thought I should head to the emergency room, since I wanted to make good on my promise to master all fourteen French verb tenses before I die. And I hadn't quite reached that goal yet.

Shortly after I'd moved to Paris, my friend Lewis had handed me a little slip of paper and advised, "David, if you ever have to go to the hospital here, tell them, 'Take me to the American Hospital.' " Since I was American, I figured that I would indeed be better off with my compatriots at our very own hospital. Unfortunately, our hospital is in Neuilly-sur-Seine, a suburb on the edge of Paris. Which also happens to be the absolute farthest point in the city from where this American lives.

Certain I was dying, I did the first thing any normal person would do in that situation: I turned on my computer and checked my e-mail for one last time. Then I clicked over to the American Hospital Web site to get directions, and the good news was that the site prominently noted that they have free parking. Well, that clinched it, so I gave them a call. The Frenchwoman on the phone managed to sound typically blasé in spite of my agitated state. She purred softly into the phone, in measured French, that I should come right in.

But before she hung up, her not-so-soft tone of voice abruptly changed, and she added in textbook-perfect English, "and we are *not* a public hospital. Bring your checkbook. Or cash."

I packed an overnight bag, as well as my checkbook, and Romain and I began the trek across Paris. In the best of circumstances, the drive might take about thirty minutes. On a Friday night, all bets are off. I suppose I could have taken the Métro, but since I was dying, I didn't want to spend my last few hours below ground, suffering in a crowded, hot, stuffy subway car.

Plus there was free parking. And whose dying wish isn't free parking?

With my heart a-pounding, it didn't exactly calm me down to see traffic blocking all lanes when we hit the boulevard and that everything was at a complete standstill. Cars were barely inching from one stoplight to the next, and being Parisian, every driver thought that if he leaned on his horn, all the cars would eagerly move aside to let him pass.

Then, suddenly, the worst thing that could happen to anyone in Paris happened. I had to go to the bathroom. I certainly didn't want my mother's worst fears realized—to have her son arrive at the emergency room with less-than-pristine undies, so I made Romain pull out of traffic when I spotted one of the automatic toilets, and I sprinted out of the Citroën.

HORS SERVICE, said the circular red glow of the sign.

Zut!

I hopped back in the car, crossed my legs, and we meandered a few more blocks until I spotted another one. I sprinted toward it. **HORS SERVICE** as well. *Merde!*

"Hmm, should I just use *la belle France*? Or should I wait to find another one?" I pondered, while doing a little dance of agony on the sidewalk that perplexed the locals. I got back in the car and gave it one more chance. Luckily the third time was a charm and the next one worked fine. My mother will continue to rest in peace.

When we finally arrived at the hospital, we found that parking was not free and the hourly rate almost tipped me into full-on cardiac arrest. Good thing they told me to bring my checkbook. At the time, I had private health insurance from a company in the States. Romain was really surprised when I balked; "Don't they reimburse you for parking?"

(And people continue to ask me why I live in France.)

Due to my Yankee thrift (a gift from my mother), we looked for a place on the street. My heart attack could wait.

Once parked and inside an examination room, waiting to see the doctor, Romain was once again surprised, this time by the fact that the room had a price list in big block letters hanging on the wall.

The first doctor to see me turned out to be, as advertised, American. We chatted and joked around a bit in our native tongue before she got on with the serious questions. Romain, who doesn't speak English, wondered why the doctor and I were laughing it up like long-lost friends. French doctors don't laugh with their patients, I guess. Only *at* their patients.

Once she left, the French male nurse came in, ordered me to strip down, and strapped me into a chair, giving me a twinge of nostalgia for San Francisco. (Was this my life passing before my eyes?) He pasted little sticky things, which for some reason they store in the freezer, over my bare chest and legs. Then I understood why he had secured me to the chair. After a bunch of knobs were turned and buzzers went off, the main cardiologist arrived, who spoke very little English. Actually, she spoke none at all, which kind of negates the idea of an American Hospital. Especially at these prices.

Reading the printout, she announced that all was well and it was probably anxiety, and I could breathe a sigh of relief that I was going to live many more years. They released the straps and I was free to go. The well-dressed cashier in his remarkably fashionable suit and tie was also obviously relieved that I was going to live when I tore off a sizable check and handed it over, an amount that made Romain's eyes almost tumble out of their sockets. Good thing we were in a hospital, although I'm not sure if this one takes French people. Unless they brought their checkbook.

After that experience, when a few months later my doctor recommended the aforementioned leg surgery, I decided I'd go where the French go: *à la clinique française.*

I arrived early in the morning, shaved as directed, belly to toe, and walked into my assigned room. My roommate looked up from his book, *Gay Vinci Code*, and gave me a big "*Bonjour!*" then went back to his literature. His legs had been shaved, too, and when he pulled his nose out of his book, we began exchanging *épilation* tips. The worst part, I said, was being scratchy "down there," so he shared that I should have used *la crème* instead of *le rasoir* to avoid the inevitable after-itch. And I must admit, without hospital gowns, it was hard not to appreciate how much better his legs looked compared with my own stubbly limbs. Why do Frenchmen, even in hospitals, *always* manage to look so much better than me?

An added benefit was that I increased my French lexicon of anatomical parts, which is good to know if you need medical care. For example, if you use the word *rognons* to describe your kidneys, an entire hospital room of French doctors, nurses, and a roommate will break out in fits of laughter at your expense. Only animals have *rognons*—humans have *reins*. And there's something like six different words for neck, depending on whether you're talking about the front, back, or the whole thing. I also learned that *les bourses* is a scrotum. Which is also the word for the French stock exchange. But I'd like to know how one gets differentiated from the other, since I'd like to avoid a crash to either.

Not only did I learn that the French don't shy away from nudity or that the hospital food in France is just as bad as ours, but I learned about *le bâton de compassion*—what I came to know and love as my "sympathy rod." When I left the clinic, I had to hobble around with a cane. Although my doctor didn't offer much of a shoulder to cry on (I was tempted to give him a little stock market crash of his own with it), walking around Paris with that stick changed everything. People became incredibly courteous, and like Moses parting the Red Sea, I could part the crowds on the most jam-packed Métro or markets without Parisians ramming right into me the way they usually do. *Quel paradis!*

I hated to hang it up a few weeks later, when I went back to navigating the streets and sidewalks of Paris on my own. The upside is that I'm now in the French health care system, and if something happens to me, I don't have to worry about anything. Except maybe having to do another clean sweep of body hair. But thankfully, I've gotten a second opinion on that.

PAIN D'EPICES AU CHOCOLAT

CHOCOLATE SPICE BREAD

ONE 9-INCH (23-CM) ROUND CAKE

Pain d'épices is a honey-rich spice bread often made in big slabs, sometimes sold by weight. Mine is a nontraditional version, and since it's my own invention, I get to call the shots. I can't resist bucking tradition and adding a dose of dark chocolate. Don't expect a light, airy cake; *pain d'épices* is meant to be dense and packed with flavor. This is made a bit differently from other versions and has a more compact crumb, with an intense, full-on chocolate flavor.

I serve wedges all by themselves, which are good with dark coffee, or with slices of fresh or poached pears.

7 tablespoons (100 g) unsalted butter, cut into pieces,
   plus more for the pan

7 ounces (200 g) bittersweet or semisweet chocolate,
   coarsely chopped

1¼ cups (160 g) flour

3 tablespoons (25 g) unsweetened cocoa powder

1 teaspoon baking powder (preferably aluminum-free)

¾ teaspoon ground cinnamon

½ teaspoon ground ginger

½ teaspoon ground cloves

¼ teaspoon coarse salt

½ teaspoon whole anise seeds

2 large eggs, at room temperature

2 large egg yolks

¼ cup (80 g) honey

⅔ cup (130 g) sugar

1. Preheat the oven to 350°F (180°C). Butter a 9-inch (23-cm) round cake pan, line the bottom with a piece of parchment paper, and butter that as well. Dust the insides of the pan with a bit of flour or cocoa powder, and tap out any excess.

2. In double boiler or a large, heatproof bowl set over a pan of simmering water, melt the chocolate and butter together, stirring until smooth. Let cool to room temperature.

3. In another bowl, sift the flour, cocoa, baking powder, cinnamon, ginger, cloves, and salt. Add the anise seeds.

4. In the bowl of a standing electric mixer or with a handheld mixer, whip the eggs, yolks, honey, and sugar until thick and mousselike, about 5 minutes on high speed.

5. Fold half of the whipped eggs into the chocolate and butter. Then fold in the remaining egg mixture.

6. Add the dry ingredients one-third at a time, using a spoon to sprinkle them over the batter and folding until the dry ingredients are just combined.

7. Scrape the batter into the prepared pan and bake for 30 to 35 minutes, until the cake feels barely set in the center, but still moist.

8. Remove from the oven and let cool for 15 minutes. Tap the cake out of the pan and cool completely on a rack. Wrap the cake in plastic and let stand at room temperature for 24 hours to let the flavors meld.

STORAGE: Well-wrapped, this cake will keep for about one week at room temperature, or one month in the freezer.

MY FRENCH PARADOX

Americans became obsessed with the French paradox when a report aired on *60 Minutes* in 1991, which explored the question of why the French eat lots and lots of rich, fatty foods but have very low rates of cardiovascular disease. The impact was so profound that red wine sales in the U.S. soared by nearly 50 percent for weeks afterward.

They may indeed have lower rates of heart disease than we do, but that doesn't keep them from being obsessed with their cardiovascular health. While Americans are famous for trying an endless string of wacky diets, French people are equally apt to beg off cheese or dessert because, they'll tell you, they're terrified of *le cholestérol*. Most are stunned when I tell them I'm not taking anticholesterol medication. Indeed, it's surprising to the French to come across *anyone* who isn't on any medication of some sort. That's another reason the French home bathroom is off-limits: it's usually crammed-full with every kind of pill and remedy you can imagine.

After my health scare, which had prompted the trip to the American Hospital, my general practitioner referred me to a French cardiologist to get my heart checked out. Whenever I've stepped into a doctor's office in France, it's invariably pitch black and I find myself having to squint to see anything. And this cardiologist's room was no exception. The French seem to like being in the dark, which probably explains the explosion of fancy eyeglass boutiques that are in a race with the banks to take over any and all storefronts as soon as they become vacant in Paris.

Undressed and ready for my cardiogram, I felt my way over to the examination table, worried how I would be able to find my clothes afterward. (Now I know why everyone wears that nautical clothing with all those reflective patches.) The gruff doctor hooked me up to a machine that beeped and blipped while reading my vitals. When we were done, he looked at the printout, grudgingly nodded, and told me everything seemed to be just fine. So I hopped off the table, groped around until I located my clothes, and got dressed. We found our way back to his desk, where I sat down across from him, and he began to question me about my health and lifestyle.

"*Vous êtes sportif?*" he asked.

"*Oui, bien sûr!*" I told him. "I do yoga three or four times a week."

"Yoga?" he said, recoiling. "That's not exercise. That's a philosophy!"

While he himself didn't look like he'd had any firsthand experience with exercise, I suppose he might have been partially right. When I'm standing on my head, with every muscle in my arms and back quivering to support the weight of the rest of me, I do question why I ate that generous, melting block of foie gras with the perfectly sublime glass of Sauternes on Saturday night, or why I couldn't say no to a scoop of *glàce à la vanille* with that *gâteau au chocolat noir* after lunch.

Then he asked about my meals. *Gulp.* Aside from the occasional in-dulgence, I eat pretty well. I like a good steak if I go out, but tend to cook mostly leaner meats, like pork and poultry, at home. I avoid squid, at all costs, but try to eat a good amount of fresh fruits and vegetables. After dinner, I usually take a bite of cheese before dessert. (I somehow omit any mention of the *pistoles* of chocolate I snitch from my stash all day.)

At this point, the doctor began a diatribe about Americans and why we're all fat: "There's something in your genetic composition that makes all Americans fat. They're not quite sure what it is, but it's in your nature. You Americans are just prone to being fat."

Even though the light was dim, I could make out, paradoxically, that his expansive French waistline was at least three times larger than my Amer-ican one. Still, I just nodded in agreement, thanking him for the lecture on diet and exercise. I wanted to return the favor and give him a few pointers in exchange, but I've learned it's just easier to nod rhythmically in agree-ment and let French people, doctors or not, finish their commentary.

There are lots of things that don't seem to make sense around here: the waiter who tells you that there's no mineral water when a slew of bottles is lined up in plain sight behind the bar, the teller at your bank who tells you they have no change that day, or why it's perfectly okay on the Métro to stick your finger in your nose but it's not okay to stick a sandwich in your mouth.

I'm learning not to let these paradoxes bother me, since I don't really need to see anyone for diet or exercise tips. Especially from someone more than twice my size. Plus I'm concerned about my eyesight. But at least I know there are plenty of fabulous eyeglasses in Paris, should I ever need them. I'm just worried that if I go to my bank to withdraw some money to buy a pair, they'll tell me they're out of cash that day. And everyone knows stress isn't good for your heart.

====

TAPENADE AUX FIGUES

FIG-OLIVE TAPENADE

MAKES 6 TO 8 SERVINGS

It can be stressful entertaining Parisians. Manners dictate guests arrive at least twenty minutes late, as a courtesy to the host who's doing last-minute preparations, but I have some friends who think nothing of arriving an hour or more after the appointed time. It makes having people over nerve-racking, since it's hard to come up with a workable timetable.

To deal with latecomers, Parisians have *l'heure de l'apéro*, which is the hour between when people are requested to come and when they actually do. So hosts offer nibbles to go along with apéritifs, which are more popular than cocktails. Thankfully, most dips and spreads can be made well in advance, so harried hosts can enjoy drinks with their friends.

One of the first things I wanted to stock my Parisian kitchen with was one of those gorgeous Provençal marble mortar and pestles. The kind that are well worn from years of use—and huge! It's seems I'm not the only one who wants one: I searched everywhere in Paris, and if you're lucky enough to find one, it's likely to cost hundreds of euros. Dejected, I sulked for months until I found an inexpensive mortar and pestle in the thirteenth arrondissement, the Chinatown of Paris, for less than fifteen euros. Nothing to complain about there, except lugging it home on the Métro during rush hour.

I use dark kalamata olives or olives from Nyon, which I get from my pal Jacques, whom you can find manning his stall, Le Soleil Provençal, at the Richard Lenoir market. He stocks the best, and biggest, selection of olives from Provence I've ever tasted outside of the region itself.

My favorite recipe is Carrie Brown's Fig and Olive Tapenade, which she serves up at the Jimtown Store in Healdsburg, California. Her recipe uses dried figs, which means less pitting and cuts the saltiness of the tapenade. I like tapenade with pita bread points that have been brushed with spiced oil, then toasted until crisp (page 126). Ice-cold rosé or *vin d'orange* are lovely accompaniments, too.

1/2 cup (85 g) stemmed and quartered dried Black Mission figs

1 cup (250 ml) water

1 cup (170 g) black olives, rinsed and pitted

1 garlic clove, peeled

2 teaspoons capers, rinsed and drained

2 anchovy fillets (see Note)

2 teaspoons whole-grain mustard

1 teaspoon finely chopped fresh rosemary or thyme

11/2 tablespoons lemon juice

1/4 cup (60 ml) extra virgin olive oil

Coarse salt and freshly ground black pepper

1. In a small saucepan, simmer the figs in the water with the lid askew for 10 to 20 minutes, until very tender. Drain.

2. If using a mortar and pestle, mash the olives with the garlic, capers, anchovies, mustard, and rosemary. (Sometimes I chop the olives first, which means less pounding later.) Pound in the figs. Once they are broken up, stir in the lemon juice and olive oil. Season with salt and pepper.

3. If using a food processor, pulse the olives, figs, garlic, capers, anchovies, mustard, rosemary, and lemon juice to create a thick paste. Pulse in the olive oil until you've achieved a chunky-smooth paste. Don't overdo it; good tapenade should be slightly rough. Season with salt and pepper, if necessary.

SERVING: Serve with pita toasts (recipe follows) or crackers, or smear it on grilled chicken breast or tuna steaks for a main course.

STORAGE: Fig-Olive Tapenade can be made up to two weeks in advance and stored in the refrigerator. It's actually better served at least a day after it's made.

NOTE: If you don't think you like anchovies, next time you're in France, try the French anchovies from Collioure, a town on the Mediterranean justifiably famous for its anchovies. At home, it's worth tracking down a good source of anchovies (see Resources, page 271); oil- or salt-packed are both fine to use. If using salted anchovies, soak them in warm water for about ten minutes, then rinse them well, rubbing out any bones with your thumbs. If you're still not convinced, simply omit them.

PAIN LIBANAIS GRILLE

Pita Toasts

MAKES 2 SERVINGS PER PITA ROUND

All of the Arab markets in Paris sell puffy rounds of pita bread, which is sometimes called *pain libanais,* or Lebanese bread. It's slightly thinner than its American counterpart, more delicate, and it crisps up beautifully in the oven if cut into triangles, served crackerlike with lots of different spreads. Whatever the thickness of the pita bread that's available where you live, the important thing is to bake the triangles until they're golden brown and crispy; no one anywhere likes a soggy chip.

You can use regular or whole wheat pita bread, and feel free to add some herbs to the oil. Finely chopped oregano or thyme (fresh or dried), a generous pinch of chile powder, or some *za'atar*—a mix of herbs, sesame, and salt, which Arabic spice markets sell ready-mixed—are all excellent additions.

Whole wheat or plain pita rounds
Olive oil
Coarse salt

1. Preheat the oven to 375°F (190°C).

2. Generously brush the pitas with olive oil on both sides, but not so much that it's dripping off. You'll need about 1 tablespoon of oil per pita.

3. Cut the pita rounds into six or eight equal triangles, depending on

ıt the triangles. Arrange them in
: with salt, and bake for 8 to 10
ıg baking, until the triangles are
hick, you may want to flip them
ing. Pita chips can be made a day
ıt container at room temperature.

that I

ed the

ong as

iation

ong as

that

pre-

want

ı my

need

LES BOUSCULEURS

Since everyone always asks, I should let you all know don't know how long I'm going to live in Paris. I trash other half of my round-trip ticket years ago, and as l I have the fortitude to suffer through the annual humi known as my "visa hearing," I'm staying put for as l I can.

But if you really want to know, there is somethin often makes me think of leaving. It's something tha vents me from doing all the wonderful things that I to do in Paris, and some days I pine away alone i apartment, afraid to go out because of it. If I do to go out, I quickly do what I need to get done, then rush straight home.

What is it that makes me often wish I hadn't tossed the unused half of my round-trip ticket? It's *les bousculeurs.*

Paris is a city of *bousculeurs,* a word few people recognize and a French term I assumed I'd made up (which I have a tendency to do) until I located the verb in my *dictionnaire français.* There it was; right there between *bour-soufler*—the verb "to bloat"—and *bouse*—"cow manure." And it's about as enjoyable to experience as both of them.

Bousculer: Pousser brusquement en tous sens.

To push abruptly in all directions.

At first I thought it was just something specific to the French. I'd moved to a foreign country and, naturally, the streets and sidewalks had a different rhythm and flow from what I was used to. Paris is far more compact than most American cities and space is at a premium, so naturally there's bound to be a bit of bumping into each other. Or so I thought. Then I visited Lyon, the second-largest city in France. Going from one place to another was a breeze, and not one person rammed right into me as if I weren't there.

So when people say to me, "It must be so fun to live in Paris! What do you do all day?" I don't think "Avoid people" is quite the answer they're expecting. But it's true. You know those knuckleheads who step off the escalator before you, then just stand there looking around, oblivious to anyone else who might need to pass? Imagine living in a city with two million people like that, thinking only of themselves, and you get the drift of what I'm up against here.

A short walk to the *boulangerie* turns into an annoying game of people-pinball, where I'm dodging folks right and left as they come at me. Who's going to move first? If I dodge to the right to avoid them, they'll veer in the same direction I do. If I veer to the left, suddenly that's where they want to be, too. I sometimes play around with their minds, feigning I'm going in one direction, then at the last second, cutting across to another. But they always outfox me, and I invariably find myself swerving out of their way at the last minute. It's exhausting, as well as humiliating. I actually had a couple laugh at my misfortune just after they cut me off on a crosswalk, landing me in the gutter.

Sometimes if someone's coming at me, I'll take refuge behind one of those immovable traffic barriers, which Parisians have nicknamed *bittes* (pricks). Other times I'll back myself up against a stone wall and stand there, just to see what they'll do. Believe it or not, Parisians will still take it upon themselves to walk right up to me and expect me to move. It's like a show of power. I'm sure if I fainted on the sidewalk, they'd stop in front of where I fell, wait, then expect me to get out of their way when I came to.

~

If there is a positive side to this, it's that it helps to answer another question I'm frequently asked. "How do you eat all those chocolates and pastries and stay so thin?" That's easily explained: I walk twice as far as necessary, putting in twice the mileage as I should, steering myself around everyone else.

Parisians have one glaring flaw: they're selfish. If you're scrambling for a pencil and paper to write me a hostile letter, don't bother. It's a quote from Romain, who was born and raised in Paris. "Parisians are *horrible*," he says. "They only care about themselves and no one else. They're *très, très impolis.*" And that's coming from the most Parisian person I know. A journalist friend, Julie Getzlaff, interviewed Parisians about what they disliked most about their city, and almost everyone said, "le comportement des gens"—the behavior of people. Even Parisians describe themselves as *"désagréables"* and *"impolis."*

I quickly got over the idea that it was my fault and that it was I who wasn't moving correctly. I'd spent twenty years working in very cramped restaurant kitchens maneuvering among lots of people, all of us rushing around dodging scalding-hot pans and holding sharp objects. But did I crash into people? *Pas du tout.*

There was something I wasn't understanding here. Fed up with being on the losing end of too many urban jousting matches, I tried to come up with a few possible explanations for their behavior.

1. Paris has few straight lines, so you can't expect Parisians to walk straight. They haven't been trained properly.

True. Although I scraped by at the bottom of my class in high school geometry, I do remember the Euclidian definition of parallel lines, which means they never intersect. Too bad Euclid never had to walk in Paris. Or maybe he did, but got fed up and split before he came up with that theory.

2. Because they think, "We're a Latin culture."

False. Parisians use this line to justify all sorts of bad behavior, from cutting in front of me in line, to short-changing people, to public urination. I don't know what being a "Latin culture" has to do with anything, but thank goodness I don't live in the Latin Quarter: I'd be hungry, poor, and stepping over a lot of dubious puddles.

3. Parisians are too busy thinking about important, interesting things, and can't be bothered to think about where they're going.

True and false. Finance Minister Christine Lagarde suggested that French people should "stop thinking so much," presumably in an effort to stimulate them into action. (Or maybe she had the same fellow paint her apartment that I did.) Fortunately, I don't think many Parisians got that memo, since I didn't notice any changes around town after she made her pronouncement.

If people are thinking too much around here, it clearly isn't about where they're going.

The first bit of the *bousculeur* puzzle fell into place for me when I was racing out of my apartment building one morning, emerging from the big wooden doors and out onto the busy sidewalk. In my haste, I crashed into a woman, who stepped back and apologized—to me! "*Oh, désolée, monsieur.*" "That's odd," I thought. No, not because a Parisian actually accepted blame for something that was obviously her fault. But because *I'd* run into *her*, yet she apologized to me. Maybe I needed to learn to go with a different flow.

I recalled the panic of my first driving lessons in Paris. Somewhere out there is a list of traumas; losing a partner, getting divorced, being fired, and moving are right up there in the Top 10. For some reason, driving in Paris isn't on that list. I don't know why.

Romain, my driving instructor, sat in the passenger seat wearing dark sunglasses, impassively, with a cigarette dangling from his mustached lips.

I, on the other side of the emergency brake, was a mess—a jangle of nerves, white-knuckling the steering wheel and sitting ramrod straight with my face glued up against the windshield. In Paris, if you're stopped at a red light and don't floor it a nanosecond after the light changes to green, an explosion of horns will erupt behind you. So the moment I stepped on the gas, I found myself immersed in my first-ever Parisian *rond-point*, the traffic circle that wraps around the very busy place de la Bastille. Sheer mayhem ensued. Cars came at me from all sides, honking and swerving toward me from every which way, floating in and out of my path with no semblance of order.

I held my place while we all played a game of stop-and-go. The rules seemed to be for each player to drive at the highest rate of speed possible, get within a millimeter of another car, then slam on the brakes and stop short at the absolutely last possible moment, then lean on the horn. By the time I emerged from the other side, I understood why everyone here smokes. I needed a cigarette too.

Behind the wheel anything goes in Paris. Unlike in America, people don't really seem to mind if you do stupid or unpredictable things while driving, things that would be punishable by road rage in America. You can do whatever you want while driving here, as long as you're not drinking coffee, which is unheard of, or talking on your cell phone, which is a heavily ticketable offense. *"Très, très dangereux,"* Romain warns me. But he doesn't seem to think there's a problem with taking his eyes off the road for thirty seconds to fumble through his jacket pocket in the back seat for his lighter while the car goes sailing across three lanes of traffic—and I silently say a prayer, thanking God for French health insurance.

So I'm learning a new way of thinking around here. It's not about doing what's right to keep the flow of traffic moving, it's about doing what's right for *you*. I've attempted to explain "Don't block the box" laws (which make it a violation to block an intersection after the light changes) to Parisians, who look at me like I'm insane. "How else are you going to get in front of others if you don't cut them off?" I can hear them thinking.

You also can't think in linear terms (which applies to more than just walking around). Paris isn't structured as a grid, like most other major cities, so it takes a bit more savvy to get around in linear fashion. Back in the 1850s, Baron Haussmann tried to change the way Parisians moved by reorganizing the city into grand boulevards, which cut though Paris in straight paths. But if you talk to Parisians a hundred and fifty years later, they're still really miffed about it. They just refuse to be herded into straight lines.

Defeated, I gave up. There's no way I'm going to change two million people. They'd won and I had no recourse but to simply become one of them, since I didn't want to be responsible for adding "sidewalk rage" to the French lexicon.

Now I never, ever back up for anyone. *Ever.* You'll never get any kind of respect around here if you're going to pull that kind of behavior. I do have to watch it when I head back to the States, though. I've been in a few situations where it wasn't clearly understood that people were expected to move for me. And I've had to do a bit of apologizing and backpedaling as a result. For safety's sake—notably mine—it's something I'm glad that I haven't completely forgotten. I don't know if my insurance covers a broken nose if I'm abroad. And I'm not exactly anxious to find out.

==========

TOMATO AND SOURDOUGH BREAD SALAD

MAKES 8 SERVINGS

One major reason I live in Paris is that I can visit Poilâne any time I want. Of all the *boulangeries* in Paris, Poilâne is certainly the most famous, and if I'm willing to brave the city sidewalks of the Left Bank, my reward is a rustic wedge of their world-famous *pain au levain* cut from the large loaves of sourdough lined up in the bakery, with a cursive *P* inscribed in the crust.

Since I'm a regular, they often invite me to pop in downstairs to see the wood-fired ovens in action. Before I head down, a saleswoman always hollers something down to the bakers. For years I didn't know what they were saying. But after racing down the stone steps one time a little too quickly and finding a half-dressed young man wearing only ragged cotton shorts scrambling to get his T-shirt over his head, I realized she was hollering: "*Habillez-vous!*" ("Put some clothes on!")

If you're ever invited downstairs, do try to descend as quickly as possible. The giant loaves of bread baking in the oven are great to see, but they aren't the only attraction down there.

    4 cups (about 750 g) roughly torn 1-inch (3-cm) pieces of levain
        (sourdough) bread
    1 teaspoon Dijon mustard
    1¼ teaspoons coarse salt, plus more to taste
    Freshly ground black pepper
    2 to 3 garlic cloves, peeled and finely minced
    6 tablespoons (90 ml) red wine vinegar, plus more to taste
    ⅔ cup (160 ml) extra virgin olive oil, plus more to taste
    8 medium tomatoes (1½ pounds/750 g)

1 large cucumber, peeled, halved lengthwise, and seeded

$^3/_4$ cup (150 g) pitted black olives (I prefer kalamata)

1 red onion, peeled and diced

1 packed cup (80 g) mixed coarsely chopped fresh basil, mint,
   and flat-leaf parsley

$^1/_2$ pound (250 g) feta cheese

1. Preheat the oven to 400°F (200°C). Spread the bread pieces on a baking sheet and toast until deep golden brown, about 15 minutes, stirring once or twice as they're toasting. Set aside to cool.

2. In a large bowl, whisk together the mustard, salt, pepper to taste, garlic, vinegar, and olive oil.

3. Remove the stems from the tomatoes, slice in half, and squeeze out the juice. Cut them into 1-inch (3-cm) pieces. Cut the cucumber into 1/2-inch (2-cm) pieces.

4. Add the tomatoes and cucumber to the bowl with the dressing. Mix in the olives, onion, and herbs and toss well. Taste, and add more salt, oil, and vinegar to your liking. (I like this salad somewhat vinegary, but feel free to use additional olive oil if you wish.)

5. Crumble the feta over the top in large chunks and toss briefly. Let stand 1 to 2 hours before serving.

SERVING: Some people like bread salads served right away, and some prefer to let them sit for a while. Whatever you choose, I think they're best served the day they're made.

=====

MACARONS AU CHOCOLAT

CHOCOLATE MACAROONS

MAKES 15 COOKIES

If you're old enough, you might remember the television commercial where two people collide. One's eating a chocolate bar and the other's snacking on peanut butter. After they've recovered, they realize they've mingled two tastes, which in turn created one great candy bar.

Since few Parisians like peanut butter, I can't imagine peanut butter–filled cookies being much of a success over here. But they sure love cookies filled with dark chocolate.

Anyone in search of chocolate eventually makes the pilgrimage to Ladurée, the world-famous tea salon just off the place de la Madeleine. Pressed against the window, you'll find everyone from tourists to normally blasé Parisians looking to see what flavors they're featuring that month. Someday, I'd love to see chocolate and chunky peanut butter—but I'm not holding my breath. Still, I'm always content to walk out with a little box of *chocolat amer*, the darkest of their famous chocolate *macarons*.

Not many people know that this chic *salon de thé* was the first public drinking spot in Paris where women could mingle with their friends without male companions and not be considered "loose" or "for sale." Nowadays the only things sold loose at Ladurée are the *macarons*, which are lined up individually by flavor, and find their way into gilded boxes as fast as the salespeople can package them.

For the cookies

1 cup (100 g) powdered sugar

$1/2$ cup almond flour (about 2 ounces/55 g sliced blanched almonds, pulverized; see Note)

3 tablespoons (25 g) unsweetened Dutch-process
   cocoa powder

2 large egg whites, at room temperature

5 tablespoons (65 g) granulated sugar

For the chocolate filling

1/2 cup (125 ml) heavy cream

2 teaspoons light corn syrup

4 ounces (120 g) bittersweet or semisweet chocolate,
   finely chopped

1 tablespoon (15 g) salted or unsalted butter,
   cut into small pieces.

1. Preheat the oven to 375°F (190°C). Line two baking sheets with parchment paper and have ready a pastry bag with a plain tip (about 1/2 inch/2 cm).

2. To make the cookies, grind together the powdered sugar, almond powder or sliced almonds, and cocoa in a blender or food processor until there are no lumps and all the dry ingredients are fine and powdery.

3. In the bowl of a standing electric mixer or by hand, beat the egg whites until they begin to rise and hold their shape. Gradually beat in the granulated sugar until very stiff and firm, about 2 minutes.

4. Carefully fold the dry ingredients into the beaten egg whites in 2 or 3 batches with a flexible rubber spatula. When the mixture is just smooth and there are no streaks of egg white, stop folding and scrape the batter into the pastry bag.

5. Pipe the batter onto the baking sheets in 1-inch (3-cm) circles (about 1 tablespoon of batter each), evenly spaced 1 inch (3 cm) apart. Rap the baking sheet a few times firmly on the countertop to flatten the cookies a bit, then bake them for 15 to 18 minutes, until they feel slightly firm. Let cool completely.

6. To make the chocolate filling, heat the cream and corn syrup in a small saucepan. When the cream just begins to boil at the edges, remove from heat and add the chocolate. Let sit 1 minute, then stir until smooth. Stir in the butter. Let cool to room temperature before using.

7. To assemble the macaroons, spread a bit of chocolate filling on the inside (the flat side) of one cookie, then sandwich it together with another one. I tend to overfill mine, but you might not be so generous, so you may not use all the filling.

SERVING: Let the macaroons stand at least one day, in an airtight container at room temperature, before serving to meld the flavors.

STORAGE: Keep in an airtight container for up to five days or freeze. If you freeze them, defrost them in the unopened container to avoid condensation, which will make the macaroons soggy.

NOTE: Some almond flours can be a bit chunky, so I recommend pulverizing them to ensure they're as fine as possible.

NE TOUCHEZ PAS!

Everything in Paris is here for a specific purpose. Even if I haven't figured out exactly what mine is yet.

Each and every church, boulevard, lamppost, monument, department store, bridge, pastry shop, park bench, café table, sewer cover, hospital, and garbage can—everything in the city is carefully placed where it is, as a result of much thought and reflection. A team of thirty people moves about under the cover of darkness each night, constantly adjusting, focusing, and softening the lights to give Paris and its monuments that extraspecial glow. The lime-green brooms the street sweepers use are chosen for style over efficiency. And you won't find any frumpy, beignet-eating cops in Paris: they're all given well-tailored uniforms to wear. Sometimes I'm a little embarrassed when I see them; I never imagined that I'd come across a policeman with a much better sense of style than I have.

And, of course, the food is stunning in Paris as well. Store windows are lined with bursting puffs of yeasty brioche, neat cubes of sugary *pâtes de fruits*, and rows and rows of unctuous chocolates filled with everything from creamy *ganache* to whipped *mousse au caramel*. The outdoor markets tempt with tight clusters of dewy grapes, lush, ruby-red strawberries, and mounds of plump Burlat cherries with their perky stems. All are just begging to be scooped up and brought home. And what about those bins of sun-dappled apricots, fresh from Provence, their sunny orange skin promising sweet, succulent juices? Or the tiny *mirabelles*, those sweet little plums that you can't wait to get home and stew into the most marvelous jam you've ever tasted? They all look so tempting too, don't they?

Well, *ne touchez pas!* Don't touch them!

Things in Paris are arranged just so, and great pains are taken to make sure they stay there to remain in the most pristine condition possible. And that means keep your grubby hands off them.

In a city where window-dressing is an art, you'll find a note of apology in any *vitrine* left uncompleted: "*Excusez-nous, vitrine en cours de réalisation.*" ("Excuse us, window under production"—which is also a clever way of skirting the law requiring that prices be displayed in windows.)

During my first trip to Paris, I remember seeing a nice-looking shirt in a window, and I stepped inside to try it on. After a few minutes of parading around in front of the mirror, I told the salesperson I liked it, but wanted to think about it. "*Pourquoi, monsieur?* It looks so good on you!" She was right, it did look good on me. After I went through the trouble of trying it on and she went through the bother of carefully taking it off the shelf and unfolding it, she just couldn't fathom why I didn't buy it. I slunk out of there, embarrassed beyond belief.

I learned that once you've touched anything, you're pretty much committed to buying it. So be careful what you put your hands on. Whether it's an ordinary orange or an orange Kelly bag, once you've made that first move, the next step is to take the relationship to the next level. So a warning to those who have trouble with commitment: if you don't want to get involved, keep your hands to yourself. Because like most relationships, once things reach a certain point, waffling is no longer an option, and you're going to get stuck for life.

There's a lot of justifiable griping about the lack of a Customer Is King attitude, or any sort of "customer service" at all, in Paris. If I have to go into a store for a service issue, I spend hours practicing my speech in my head before leaving the house, occasionally making notes and looking up any specific vocabulary that might be thrown at me, so I'm ready for anything.

I almost didn't win over a salesclerk who wouldn't let me exchange a broken ice cream scoop, since I had the temerity to open the package and use it. I begged and tried to convince her that if I hadn't opened the package to use it, I'd never have known that it was broken, which she didn't understand.

So I tried a different tactic. After I got up off my hands and knees, I told her that I was a *glacier,* and either she felt sorry for me, or was impressed by someone who made ice cream professionally. Only then did she hand me a new one off the shelf.

(Which broke the first time I used it, too. But I've since learned, to preserve my fragile sanity, that when something breaks, it's simply better just to toss it and buy a new one elsewhere.)

Since no one's under any obligation to help you, you need to prove you're worthy of receiving their attention. It's nearly impossible to fire anyone in France, so why *should* they help you? You need to make them *want* to help you. Believe me, it's worth it. There's something truly wonderful to be said for French service when it's bestowed upon you.

Believe it or not, most French people do want to be helpful. A lot of shopkeepers and merchants are rightly proud of what they are offering. It's just that *le marketing* is a cultural no-no and many feel odd, or *très commercial,* if they try to push something (behavior I've also heard described as *très américain*). Handing out samples is considered *vulgaire,* and if you come from a capitalist country, you need to forget that vendors should be eager to make a sale. Here, if a vendor has high-quality products, it's up to the client to be worthy of their wares. Losing a sale is nothing compared to loss of pride.

To get good service, I've perfected my own special blend of politesse with a soupçon of obsequious groveling. First, I use all the proper salutations when entering a shop—"*Bonjour, madame*" or "*monsieur.*" Then, whatever I'm inspecting for purchase, whether a bar of chocolate or a bar of soap, I consider it with a bit of reserve and disdain—as though I'm wondering if that soap is really worthy of my skin. This puts the staff on high alert, right where you want them. Still, I never touch anything, whether it's tomatoes, chocolate, flowers, shirts, bread, soap, newspapers, suits, peaches, or shoelaces, without first getting permission.

The most baffling cross-cultural divide occurs at *la fromagerie.* Or to be more specific: why don't they let you sample the cheese?

There's no cheese shop in America that doesn't encourage you to take a taste before you buy. Whether confronted with the walnut-crusted cheese balls chopped into little tidbits at Hickory Farms in the mall, or a wispy shaving of Red Hawk cheese at Cowgirl Creamery in San Francisco, we've become accustomed—some feel it's our right—to being offered a bite before deciding. And to take all the time we want, tasting as many as possible.

Much to the disappointment of visitors, shopkeepers in Paris are rather meager on samples. (I used to think they were just being stingy until I was almost crushed to death at the Salon du Chocolat in Paris, and now I can't say I blame them.) You're expected to rely on the expertise of the *fromager,* who's the master of his or her subject, to suggest a cheese that you'll like. They're experts and can deduce from your responses to their questions— like when you'll be serving it or what you'll be serving before it—what cheese is best for you. Then you're supposed to rely on their judgment and buy what they suggest. While this may seem like a funny arrangement, in all my time living in Paris, I've never been steered wrong. The secret is to trust your *fromager* and you'll be amply rewarded for your loyalty.

Julia Child wrote in *My Life in France,* "If a tourist enters a food stall thinking he's going to be cheated, the salesman will sense this and obligingly cheat him. But if a Frenchman senses that a visitor is delighted to be in his store, and takes a genuine interest in what is for sale, then he'll just open up like a flower."

When I brought guests on market tours, standing among the blooming flowers and salespeople, they'd inevitably ask, "Why don't they give out samples? Wouldn't they sell more cheese if they did?" They never understood my response: "They don't care if they sell more cheese. It doesn't matter." It's something I wouldn't have understood before I moved here either. Now, of course, it makes perfect sense.

There is an exception to the rule, a lone *fromager* who stands out in front of his shop on the Île Saint-Louis, offering nibbles. Even when the normally tranquil Île Saint-Louis turns into a tourist stampede on Sunday afternoons, he's out there with a bounteous *plateau de fromages—mon Dieu!—*giving them away! In an unscientific poll I conducted, nearly 100 percent of the tasters headed into the store to buy some cheese afterward. After I took a bite of an eyes-to-the-skies-good Comté he handed me, I went home with a slab, too.

Perhaps this is the wave of the future in Paris. After all, *le marketing* is a relatively new concept around here, but it's starting to take off. "Yes! I speak Wall Street English!" say the young, smiling French people, pumping their fists in the air in the ads for a "business" language school, which are plastered across Paris. They may be reaching for the skies, but they're not touching it. They know better than that. After all, they're in Paris.

===

CAKE AUX LARDONS ET FROMAGE BLEU

BACON AND BLUE CHEESE CAKE

ONE 9-INCH (23-CM) LOAF CAKE

In my opinion, the French don't do *"cuisine branchée,"* or trendy food, very well. For some reason, most of the experimental cuisine I've had in Paris comes off as precious or contrived. And don't get me started on the subject of square plates with a line of sauce in one corner and a dusting of ground cumin on the other.

One trend I do like, though, is *le cake* (pronounced "kek"). A departure from their sweet American counterparts, these savory quick breads are welcome served as an hors d'oeuvre before dinner, thinly sliced, with glasses of cool Muscadet or a snappy Sauvignon Blanc. Midafternoon, I hack off a slice or two for *le snack.* At that hour, unless you live in Paris, a glass of wine is optional. But for me, after a long day, it's sometimes *obligatoire.*

Two hints: To make the blue cheese easier to crumble, leave it unwrapped on a plate in the refrigerator to dry a bit a day ahead. The second tip is to reserve the bacon fat and use that to grease the pan, which will add aromatic smokiness to the cake.

Butter or bacon fat for preparing the pan

1^1/2 cups (210 g) flour

2 teaspoons baking powder (preferably aluminum-free)

1 teaspoon chile powder

^{1}/2 teaspoon coarse salt

4 large eggs, at room temperature

^{1}/4 cup (60 ml) olive oil (if possible, use one that's very fruity)

^{1}/2 cup (120 g) plain whole-milk yogurt

1^1/2 teaspoons Dijon mustard

^{1}/2 small bunch chives, finely chopped (about ^{1}/4 cup) or scallions

5 ounces (140 g) blue cheese or Roquefort, well crumbled

2 ounces (60 g) grated Parmesan

8 strips of bacon (about 5 ounces/150 g), cooked until crisp,
   then crumbled into pea-sized pieces

1. Preheat the oven to 350°F (180°C). Grease a 9-inch (23-cm) loaf pan with butter and line the bottom with a piece of parchment paper.

2. In a large mixing bowl, whisk together the flour, baking powder, chile powder, and salt.

3. In a separate bowl, whisk together the eggs, olive oil, yogurt, mustard, and chives until smooth.

4. Make a well in the center of the dry ingredients and use a rubber spatula to stir in the wet mixture, stirring just until the wet ingredients are almost incorporated. (A bit of flour should still be visible.) Don't overmix.

5. Fold in the blue cheese, Parmesan, and bacon bits until everything's just moistened. Scrape the batter into the prepared loaf pan.

6. Bake for 50 to 60 minutes, until the top is golden brown and the cake springs back when you gently touch the center.

7. Let the cake cool for 5 minutes, then tilt it out onto a wire rack. Peel off the parchment and let cool before slicing.

STORAGE: The cake can be wrapped in plastic and kept at room temperature for up to three days. It can also be frozen, well wrapped, for up to two months.

VARIATION: For a *cake au chèvre et aux olives* (Chèvre and Olive Cake) substitute 6 ounces (170 g) crumbled goat cheese, such as a Bucheron or Montrachet (or one that's neither too aged nor too soft) for the blue cheese and omit the bacon and Dijon mustard. Add 1/4 cup (40g) finely chopped pitted green or black olives in step 6 as well.

JEANNE

Even though I live in a small apartment, I'm not especially good at keeping it tidy. I'm fairly neat and organized, which is essential when living and working in the same space. But I'd rather spend my time baking brownies than scrubbing sinks, if you can believe it.

Jeanne is my housecleaner, and she comes every other week (except during her eleven-week summer vacation). The first time we met, she strode in the front door for her interview, and immediately said to me, *"Je ne suis pas une voleuse, monsieur"*—"I am not a thief." And I was sure she was telling the truth, since she was better dressed than I.

She arrived wearing a silk scarf tied impeccably around her neck and strode through my door in elegant leather pumps. The flowery lilt of French perfume wafted toward me as she entered, and her hair was so neatly coiffed and sprayed into place that a mistral, the violent wind that sweeps through Provence, wouldn't have been able to budge it. Being from San Francisco, I did the brief Adam's-apple check and yes, indeed, Jeanne was the real thing.

But lest you think Jeanne was dainty and sweet, think again. The first time she came to clean, she kicked off those fancy pumps, put on some slippers, and padded off in search of the *eau de Javel*, that universally loved liquid developed here in 1789 that's still dear to the French to this day. In fact, they're still beaming with so much pride they've named a Métro stop after it, "Javel." Imagine if there was a subway stop in your city called "bleach." It's one of the few Métro stops in Paris I've never been to—but I presume it's the cleanest.

Because my apartment is basically just two small rooms, you'd think it would be simple to clean. When we first met, Jeanne said it would take her two hours to do it, which sounded like a long time. But since it takes me about two weeks to work up the energy to unearth and untangle all those cords and hoses on my *aspirateur* (and I always manage to find something more interesting to do in Paris than vacuuming), I went along with it. During her first visit I left and went to the movies.

When the film was over and two hours had passed, I figured she'd have finished up and it was safe to return. But when I turned the key in the lock, the door swung open and there she was, still padding around, engulfed in bleach fumes. Although she'd been there way past her estimated time of departure, she was cleaning around the buttons on my fax machine like a madwoman . . . but hadn't yet made it to the kitchen or the bathroom.

I hung around and tried to stay out of her way, and when she finished, I suggested that the next time she came, it might be better if she started in the "critical areas," namely the bathroom and kitchen—instead of detailing *le fax*. Jeanne slipped back into her pumps, neatly folded her rubber gloves, and finally left a good four hours after she had arrived.

Since our first encounter, we've been together for years and Jeanne's become a fixture in my life. So much so that I've slipped from using the more formal *vous* to the friendlier *tu* with her. Although she still uses *vous*, I guess she feels pretty comfortable with me, since each time she arrives, she scrutinizes my face very deeply and tells me she's worried about my health. She says I should be eating more red meat, a diagnosis that she brings home by vigorously punching her fist in the air. I want to tell her, thanks—now could she just clean the toilet? But I'm worried about that well-manicured right-hand jab, so I don't say a word.

I've finally got her down to cleaning my tiny place in just under three hours, a feat that's taken me years to accomplish. I can't tell her outright to leave, so I come home and feign surprise each time that she's still there, praying that she might get the hint. That's after I've sat through *War and Peace*, stopped somewhere afterward for a glass of wine, then wandered aimlessly in the freezing rain until I thought, "Of course, she *must* be finished by now" hoping to be allowed back into my home again. But no matter what time I return, there she is, bleach in hand, scrubbing the rubber bumpers under the base of my KitchenAid mixer.

I'm not complaining. True to her word, nothing's gone missing and I'm happy with the great cleaning job she does—in spite of the small fortune I'm spending on *eau de Javel*. My next task is to convince her that I participate in this newfangled thing called "recycling." Still, I can't imagine life without Jeanne, and I'd miss our bi-weekly sessions of her doling out health advice and me wishing she'd concentrate her energy on the kitchen floor instead of the plastic holes behind my alarm clock.

Oddly, one day I came home and she'd already left, which was a first. There was a note that she was missing a sock and if I found it to please let her know. I looked under the shelves, where there was not a speck of dust. I moved a few boxes around and saw the walls and corners had been scrubbed and polished. I lifted up the sofa, and the carpet looked as fresh as that day I installed it. But no sock.

Feeling the need to stop in the bathroom, something struck me as odd: I looked around and noticed that it hadn't been cleaned—at all.

I couldn't imagine what she'd been doing and how someone could spend half a day cleaning a two-room apartment but forget the bathroom. Yet I was happy to forgive her. Because when you're all alone in a foreign country, it's nice to have someone looking after you. And I think it's a good idea to keep her on my side. Especially with that right hook.

BOUCHEES CHOCOLAT AU YAOURT

CHOCOLATE YOGURT SNACK CAKES

MAKES 12 INDIVIDUAL CAKES

I often wonder what Jeanne does during all that time she spends in my apartment. Sometimes I think that as soon as I leave she slips off her slippers and socks and curls up on the sofa, watching television and snacking on chocolates. I suppose if I installed a hidden camera, I could find out for sure, as well as finally finding her long-lost sock.

The recipe for these moist little chocolate cakes comes from my friend Meg Cutts, the mother of two young boys, who I'm sure knows a thing or two about cleaning house—and lost socks.

The French call things that don't neatly fit into any other dessert category *bouchées* (mouthfuls), and these little cakes certainly fit that description.

7 ounces (200 g) bittersweet or semisweet chocolate,
    coarsely chopped

$1/2$ cup (125 ml) vegetable oil

$1/2$ cup (125 ml) plain whole-milk yogurt

1 cup (200 g) sugar

3 large eggs, at room temperature

1 teaspoon vanilla extract

$1/2$ teaspoon almond extract

1^{1}/2 cups (200 g) flour

1^{1}/2 teaspoons baking powder (preferably aluminum-free)

^{1}/2 teaspoon coarse salt

1. Preheat the oven to 350°F (180°C). Line a 12-cup muffin tin with paper cupcake liners or lightly butter the pan.

2. In a heatproof bowl set over simmering water, melt the chocolate with 1/4 cup (60 ml) of the oil. Once melted and smooth, remove from heat.

3. In another bowl, mix the remaining 1/4 cup (65 ml) oil with the yogurt, sugar, eggs, and vanilla and almond extracts.

4. In a large bowl, whisk the flour, baking powder, and salt.

5. Make a well in the center of the flour mixture and add the yogurt mixture. Stir lightly a couple of times, then add the melted chocolate, and stir just until smooth.

6. Divide the batter among the muffin cups and bake for 25 minutes, or until they feel barely set in the middle.

7. Remove from the oven and cool on a wire rack before serving.

SERVING: Even though the French never take their coffee until after dessert, I make an exception and like to serve it with these cakes, to adults, of course. Kids will probably appreciate a glass of milk instead.

STORAGE: The cakes can be stored in an airtight container, at room temperature, for up to four days.

TOO MANY WAYS TO SAY THE SAME THING

Somewhere in the city of Paris there exists a shop dedicated to anything you might ever want, no matter how strange or obscure. I've visited shops in Paris that manage to subsist by offering one and only one thing, such as lightbulbs, vanilla, taxidermied animals, handmade umbrellas, fresh-pressed nut oils, antique medical equipment (which is kinda scary), horsemeat (which is very scary), antique doorknobs, organ meats, vintage musical instruments, new and used rat traps (the used ones still have the rats in them), vintage little black dresses (at more than modern-day prices), beer, fishing lures, and American paramilitary gear. I've been to a place that stocks nothing but five bottles of perfume, a latex clothing boutique where a fetish-minded friend insisted I try on an outfit (taking it off was another epilation lesson, and a rather painful one, I might add), and the tiniest shop in Paris: the sports nutrition store on the rue Quincampaux, which always seems to be empty.

But the most unusual shopping experience I've had in Paris was just a couple of blocks from the working-class place de la République. With a doctor's note in my hand, I knew I was at the right place when I stood facing an expansive *vitrine* that was a mad jumble of plastic limbs pointing in a myriad of directions, each sporting the latest and greatest in orthopedic hosiery.

Stepping inside, I handed over my doctor's *ordonnance* and accompanied the no-nonsense woman of *un certain âge* to the back of the shop to the changing room, in preparation for my fitting of over-the-knee socks that I was told would make the hours I spend on my feet a pleasure, rather than the problem they had become.

Before she closed the curtain, the saleswoman instructed me to take off every stitch of clothing, including *mon slip.* Then she handed me two flimsy paper towels before snapping the curtain shut. French people are pretty lax about public displays of body parts and don't shy away from nudity, which I'm now used to. Chalking it up to the French penchant for *naturisme,* I stripped off everything, including *mon slip,* and covered my bases on both sides, with the flimsy paper towels, which barely did the trick: French paper towels aren't exactly Brawny-size.

On the other side of the curtain, she asked if I was ready. "*Vous êtes prêt, monsieur?*" to which I replied, clutching the two wispy squares of paper, "*Oui, madame.*"

Pulling back the curtain, she walked in, her rubber-gloved hands outstretched like a surgeon. She stopped, took one look at me, from top to bottom, pausing in the middle, and let out a gasp so loud I thought it might have been her last breath, ever.

Thinking about it later I realized she must have said, "*Déshabillez-vous. Enlevez tous vos vêtements* sauf *le slip,*" instructing me to take off everything *but* my underwear. Funny, I don't remember hearing that. (And I'm still not clear on what the paper towels were for.)

I don't know which of us was more embarrassed by my inadequate command of the French language, although since I was standing in a booth with someone's grandmother, clutching a couple of squares of paper for dear life, I'd say it was me. Unfortunately, that wouldn't be the last time I was caught with my pants down when it comes to my understanding of the language.

It's entirely possible to get by in France without speaking much French, thanks to the Internet, CNN, international bookstores and newsstands, and the very eager English-speaking waiters who have learned that if they charm a table of flummoxed American tourists, they'll get a nice tip. But if you want to live here and be a part of French life, and do more than barely cover your butt, learning French is essential.

When people ask, "How long did it take you to become fluent in French?" I respond, "Become fluent? Even the French aren't fluent in French." To prove it, there's an annual Dicos d'Or, a dictation contest where French people compete against each other to see who can best comprehend and write down what's spoken to them—*in their own language!*

To alleviate some of the confusion, there exists the Académie Française. Within those hallowed, plush chambers on the Left Bank, the definitive dictionary of the French language was started in 1635. And to this day, forty *immortels* (a name that demonstrates the reverence they inspire) regularly meet and discuss what words should be spoken in France, a decision that can take decades. American dictionaries are updated far more frequently to include new, important words, like *muffin top* (the overhang from low-slung jeans), *prehab* (intervention for junior celebs), and *designer baby* (none of which I've been able to translate, or even explain, in French).

The biggest problem these days for *les immortels,* whose average age is a ripe seventy-eight, is trying to prevent the insidious encroachment of the English language from contaminating the sacred French vocabulary. Nevertheless, words like *relooking* (makeover), *le fast food,* and *très People* have jumped the line and are heard in everyday speech, government-sanctioned or not.

Most of the words arrive via *les teenagers,* which is evident when you consider some of the un-French words that have become part of *la langue populaire: nonstop, le weekend, le star système, l' happy hour, le feeling, le jet-set, le shopping, le "must"* (always in quotes), *le snack, le gadget,* and the latest rage that's sweeping all of Paris—*le scrapbooking.*

There's so much concern about the encroachment of *franglais* into the French vocabulary that the government has issued *les quotas musicaux,* which mandates that only a strictly limited percentage of music played on the radio in France can be non-French. Listen for a short while to French radio, and you might start off by enjoying a heart-wrenching serenade by Edith Piaf, followed by an ear-splitting blast from Iron Maiden, leading into a jaunty chant from French tennis star Yannick Noah, whose successful recording career, if you've ever heard him, is one of the more unfortunate consequences of *les quotas musicaux.*

The French take their language very, very seriously, and I can't remember a dinner party where an argument about some aspect of the language didn't at some point break out and was not resolved until someone went to a bookshelf and pulled out a copy of Larousse, an important fixture in every French household.

Especially vexing is that seemingly ordinary words that one might innocently translate from English to French, like *populaire* ("I'm popular!"), take on drastically different, less-than-complimentary meanings when translated. Calling someone *populaire* means they're from the lower classes.

Similarly, complimenting the beauty of something—*"C'est joli!"*—can have frightening consequences. I made the grave mistake of telling a clerk at Moisan bakery what I thought was a compliment—that the magnificent tray of golden-rimmed madeleines she was putting on display were indeed *très jolies*. "*Elles ne sont pas jolies, monsieur! Elles sont délicieuses!*" She screeched back, "They're not beautiful! They're delicious!" before walking away in a huff. After that, I avoided the bakery for a full year. Which was unfortunate, as it was one of my favorite places to buy bread. But after monitoring the situation safely from the other side of the window week after week, only when I deduced she no longer worked there did I dare step inside again to try the madeleines.

After I took my first bite, I took smug satisfaction that I was right: they were, indeed, beautiful. And I stopped wondering what happened to her and figured she must have been fired for lying because they weren't, as she claimed, all that delicious.

I give Parisians a lot of credit for taking pity on me as we mutually struggle to understand each other. Even after living here for over six years, more often than not, I still don't have a clue as to what people are saying to me. I have become a *César*-worthy actor and perfected an award-winning look of comprehension, avoiding the deer-caught-in-the-headlights look when someone barrages me in rapid-fire French. But what can they expect? I mean, in all honesty, how can one begin to master any language that's so difficult, it lists six different ways to say "because"? *Puisque, comme, à cause de, car, grâce à*, and *à force de* all mean "because." The difference between them comes down to because of *what*?

Look at the banquet of choices for a chicken breast: *poitrine de poulet, blanc de poulet, émincé de poulet, escalope de poulet*, and *suprême de poulet*. And a jug of wine can be a *carafe, pichet, pot, décanter, cruche*, or *fillette*, which is also a young girl. So be careful where you are when you order one.

A can of soda is a *canette*, not to be confused with *canette*, a young female duck (not be to confused with a young male duck, which is a *caneton*). And a can of vegetables is a *boîte de conserve*, but if you're going out to a nightclub, you're going to *sortir en boîte*, so let's hope that after a night out on the town, you don't come home a vegetable.

If you want chicken, you go to a *volailler*. But if you want beef, head to the *boucherie*. Is it pork you're after? Stop off at the nearest *charcuterie*, because the *boucher* might not have it. Pork is not meat, it's pork. But lamb *is* meat, and you can find that at the *boucherie*. Like innards? Those can be found at the *triperie*, which I'll let you find on your own.

Rabbits fall inexplicably in to the same category as our feathery friends found at the *volailler*. And in case you're looking, horsemeat is normally found at the *boucherie chevaline*, although it can sometimes be found at the regular *boucherie*, too. But not necessarily vice versa. And if anyone can tell me the difference between a *saucisson sec* and a *saucisse sèche*, I owe you a dried sausage. Or a freshly dried one.

∽

My most unnerving mangling of the French language was at Sur les Quais, a fantastic *épicerie*, where I was explaining to out-of-towners the different flavors of jam made by Christine Ferber, a famed *confiseuse*. (Yes, there's a gender-specific word for a female who specializes in cooking sugar.)

I was translating the lineup of flavors for each *pot de conserve*, to the best of my abilities, for someone. (An empty jar is *un bocal*, but putting jam into it turns it into *un pot*.) When I mentioned there were jars of red currant jam, *confiture de groseilles*, my guest perked up, "Oh yes! That's what I'd like."

So I asked the salesclerk for a jar of *confiture de groseilles*, which is pronounced "gro-zay." But with my less-than-stellar command of the language, I asked for "*confiture de grosses selles*" (which I pronounced as "gross sells"). The saleswoman's jaw nearly hit the counter: I'd ordered turd jam . . . make that big-turd jam.

At this point, I realized that I needed to seek professional help, an assessment that salesclerk probably shared, and enrolled in a French class.

Paris is rife with schools that advertise in the freebie expat papers distributed around town, promising to help us all "learn French—the easy way!" Flip through the pages or search the Internet and you'll find everything from classes that meet in a park where the admissions procedure consists of "finding the guy with the bowler hat" to another that lures potential pupils with an ad showing two ruby-red lips pursed in an undeniably French manner, poised and ready to give pleasure to the Eiffel Tower.

I wasn't sure that was the kind of French I needed to learn—maybe later. Right now, I needed to get serious, and I chose a school located up near Père Lachaise cemetery, affiliated with the Ministry of Culture. It promised supervision *"rigoureuse,"* and for a world-class *procrastinateur* like me, they were speaking my language.

As I opened the creaking door of the school, I was confident I was on my way to becoming a true Parisian, excited by the possibility of joining an international coterie of expats and locals engaged in lively debates on Proust and Existentialism, all the while mastering the merits of the *plus-que-parfait de l'Indicatif* over the *plus-que-parfait du subjonctif.*

I stepped into a grand courtyard jam-packed with Korean teenagers playing Ping-Pong. Most of them were sucking on rank-smelling Gauloises, furiously texting messages back and forth between friends standing a few feet away, and gulping inky vending-machine coffee from plastic cups. This was not the intellectual environment I had envisioned.

The upside was that I developed my first Parisian crush *d'amour* on a special someone. It was Laurent, my French teacher. He wasn't anything particularly special, but like the best French lovers, he was patient and careful, tending to my needs. He taught me how to wrap my lips around complex verbs, and most of all, took pity on me for all my embarrassing Americanisms.

But like most things in Paris, just when you think you've got it all figured out and things are going smoothly, something happens and you're thrown for a loop: one day, in walked a new teacher and *poof,* dreamy Laurent was gone. Our new professor strutted through the door, hugely muscled, looking like a living, breathing Michelin man—as *gonflé* as those puffy breads at La Brioche d'Or. For once, I can aptly apply the cliché: both resembled pastries on steroids.

Unlike lovely Laurent, this *mec* didn't care how much any of us were struggling, and as the days progressed, I was sure he was determined to belittle me—which frankly, wasn't all that much of a challenge—as much as possible in front of my classmates.

On his first day, I made the common mistake most Anglophones make and pronounced every letter of every word: if there's a letter there, it just seems logical to pronounce it. I'm sorry!

For that infraction, Monsieur No-Neck came strutting over to where I was sitting, stopped in front of me with his hands curled into tight fists by his side, and proceeded to shout at me for a full five minutes in front of the class. My Korean classmates were cringing in their seats, clutching their electronic translators in fear of this Gallic Godzilla, breathing his fiery wrath on me.

And that, I vowed, would be my last French class there. I later ran into one of my classmates, who told me shortly thereafter the professor walked over to the wall and punched his fist right through it. "Yikes, that could've been me," I thought to myself. It probably would have been, had I stayed.

My eagerness and enthusiasm for learning French was diminishing rapidly, yet I did dabble in some of the other schools around Paris. As I went from one school to the next, however, I soon became sympathetic to the urge to punch someone out: in the classes I attended, there was always one *sac à douche* whom I dubbed "the corrector." No matter what their skill level in French was, whether or not their comprehension was any better than mine (it was usually worse), these people felt they were doing me a favor by constantly correcting me when I spoke up.

I got to the point where I could spot "the corrector" types the moment I began a new class, and could see them out of the corner of my eye practically wetting themselves in anticipation that I'd make a mistake so they could chime in with the right answer. No matter how hard I tried to block them from my peripheral vision, I could see them almost leaping out of their seats, their heads volleying back and forth, from me to the teacher, as if watching a tennis match at Roland Garros, hoping, *praying*, that I'd make a mistake so they could fill the enormous gap in my intelligence with their words of wisdom.

So before I put my fist through something, or someone, I gave up on French classes altogether and decided my best teachers were going to be the Parisians themselves—whether they liked it or not. It's a task not all of them seem to appreciate very much.

My greatest gaffe in French at a social event occurred at a chic dinner party with people I didn't know. I had just returned from a trip to Italy and was describing how terrific it was. I'd climbed high in the mountains of Piedmont to see Oropa, the magnificently situated sanctuary famous for its Madonna Nera, a black Virgin Mary who inspires cultlike worshippers. It's an inspiring spot, no matter what your faith, and pilgrims and tourists flock there from all over the world to head up the winding mountain road, then up a formidable number of stairs to see her. (The hot chocolate and pastries they serve in the adjacent *caffè* are additional incentive to make the trek, too.)

Hoping to impress everyone with my highly cultured and richly detailed description of the lovely lady herself, I contributed my account: "Up in the mountains in Italy, *il y a une verge noir. C'est magnifique!* People come from all over the world to worship it. They kneel before it and pray to it."

As I'm talking, rambling on and on and on in my impeccable French, I notice everyone looking uncomfortable and glancing around at one another, taking a renewed interest in what's on their plate, rather than what's coming out of my mouth. But like a high-speed TGV train, I keep going, picking up speed: "You drive up this long, winding road and when you open the door, you see it and it's really, truly *incroyable*. It's surely one of the most famous *verges* in the world."

I fail to notice anyone getting as worked up as me about this icon, until Romain leans over, "Don't you mean the *Vierge Noire*, the Black *Virgin*?"

"Uh, yes. Isn't that what I was talking about?"

"Daveed, a *verge* is a penis."

I know my version of the story would have received a better reception in different company, but perhaps I was a bit hasty in dropping out of French school. I'm just happy he stopped me before I went on about all the pictures I'd taken of it, from every conceivable angle.

I'm still struggling with some of the facets of the language that are foreign to *les anglophones*. Like the two-tiered system of *tu* and *vous*, depending on how formal you need to be (what happened to *égalité*?), and *la concordance*, the insidious way that the gender of the subject changes the spelling and pronunciation of not only the noun, but the adjective and verb as well. It's no wonder even French businessmen and women are shipped off to schools to improve their French.

Just like me, a lot of French people have atrocious spelling, and they cover it up with magnificent, cursive handwriting, which you'll recognize if you've ever tried to decipher a handwritten café menu scribbled on a blackboard. I've even corrected the spelling of some French people, who take it in stride. So I don't feel so bad when I make an error myself.

Needless to say, I spend a lot of time laughing, and getting laughed at. But I've made a truce with the French and their language: that neither of us fully understands the other, and neither of us probably ever will.

DINDE BRAISEE AU BEAUJOLAIS NOUVEAU ET AUX PRUNEAUX

BRAISED TURKEY IN BEAUJOLAIS NOUVEAU WITH PRUNES

MAKES 4 SERVINGS

I struggled for quite some time to get my *volailler*, Catherine, to understand me when I wanted turkey: I would pronounce *dinde* ("dand"), as "din-dee." Which may sound logical to those of us who believe that letters are there for a reason.

Another thing that's hard to comprehend is the big deal made over Beaujolais Nouveau. Each November, specifically the third Thursday of the month, Beaujolais Nouveau is released across France and the rest of the world. There's lots of clever marketing meant to spread excitement among Parisians, who don't fall for the hype and remain a bit blasé about quaffing this young wine.

I share their disdain, but fruity Beaujolais Nouveau does make a wonderful cooking wine; its robust flavor holds up well when braising turkey thighs, *les cuisses de dinde*. If unavailable, substitute another fruity red, such as Brouilly, Merlot, or Pinot Noir.

The French rarely pit prunes, or *pruneaux* (not be confused with *prunes*, which are not prunes, but fresh plums), perhaps due to the lack of lawsuits, but also because the pits are said to add a bit of flavor. You may wish to alert any non-French guests if serving prunes with pits *à la française*, or just use pitted ones.

For the prunes

8 ounces (225 g) prunes (dried plums)

$1/2$ cup (125 ml) Beaujolais Nouveau

2 tablespoons honey

1-inch (3-cm) strip orange zest

6 sprigs fresh thyme

For the turkey

1 turkey leg and thigh (about 3 pounds/$1^1/2$ kg)

1 tablespoon olive oil

Coarse salt and freshly ground black pepper

2 cups (500 ml) Beaujolais Nouveau

$1^1/2$ cups (375 ml) chicken stock or water (if using canned stock, use low-sodium)

8 sprigs fresh thyme

1 bay leaf

$1/2$ recipe Oignons aigres-doux (page 181; see Note)

1 bunch flat-leaf parsley, coarsely chopped

1. To prepare the prunes, put the fruit in a small saucepan along with the Beaujolais, 1/2 cup (125 ml) water, honey, orange zest, and thyme. Bring to a low boil and let simmer for 2 minutes. Cover, remove from heat, and set aside to plump. (Prunes can be cooked up to 5 days ahead and refrigerated.)

2. To braise the turkey, rinse the turkey pieces and wipe them dry. Heat the olive oil in a Dutch oven or large covered casserole. Add the turkey, season with salt and pepper, and cook, turning the parts only occasionally so they get nicely browned all over.

3. Meanwhile, preheat the oven to 325°F (160°C).

4. Remove the turkey from the pot and discard the oil. Return the turkey pieces to the pot and add the Beaujolais, stock, thyme, and bay leaf. Cover the pot and cook for 2 hours, turning the turkey a couple of times during braising.

5. Transfer the turkey to a plate or bowl, then simmer the liquid on the stovetop until reduced by half. In the meantime, pull the meat off the bones, trying to keep it in large chunks. Drain the prunes and discard the orange peel and thyme.

6. Once the liquid is reduced, return the turkey meat to the pot along with the onions and prunes to warm them thoroughly. Garnish with a handful of parsley.

SERVING: The red wine liquid will be screaming to be served over noodles like pappardelle, with the parsley as a colorful contrast.

STORAGE: Like most braised dishes, you can store the turkey with the sauce in the refrigerator for up to three days. Rewarm on the stovetop or in the microwave for serving.

NOTE: If you wish to use fresh boiling onions instead of the sweet-and-sour ones, add 1/2 pound (225 g) peeled boiling onions to the braising liquid during the last 45 minutes of cooking.

===

CARAMEL AU BEURRE SALE

SALTED BUTTER CARAMEL SAUCE

MAKES ABOUT 2 CUPS (500ML)

They say the best way to learn French is simply to speak it without fear. I don't know if I'm great proof of that theory, but since chefs speak the same language everywhere, I have no problem going up to another cook and striking up a conversation in any language.

On a trip to Brittany, I had the most wonderful *galette de sarrasin*, a *crêpe* made of buckwheat flour that was drenched with a copious puddle of the most sublime caramel sauce, enriched with salted butter.

In yet another quirk of the language, a *crêpe* is made from white flour only. If buckwheat is used, it's usually called a *galette*, and no one will know what you're talking about if you order a *crêpe de sarrasin*. Confusingly, sometimes buckwheat (*sarrasin*) is called *blé noir*, so if you ask for a *crêpe de blé noir*, they'll understand perfectly what you're talking about.

Got that?

Gérard Cocaign, the *crêpe*-maker at Les Chardons Bleus in Brittany—which cryptically calls itself a *crêperie*, but offers both *crêpes* and *galettes*—welcomed me in his kitchen to show me how to make this deep-amber sauce, which he finishes with a *noisette* of local butter. *Noisette* means hazelnut, but is closer in size to a walnut—so shouldn't *that* be a *noix-sette?* Next time *les immortels* meet, I think I should go; I've got a bunch of questions for them.

But no questions about how superb this sauce is: when I tasted a spoonful, I swooned. Like Gérard does, use a very large pot, since the caramel will bubble up once you add the cream. Except a pot in French is not called a *pot*, but a *casserole*. Unless it has two handles, in which case it's a *cocotte*.

2 cups (400 g) sugar

1^2/3 cups (400 ml) heavy cream

2 tablespoons (30 g) salted butter

1/4 teaspoon fleur de sel or coarse sea salt (or to taste)

1. Spread the sugar in an even layer in a large metal Dutch oven or casserole, at least 6 quarts (6 L). Set over moderate heat and cook without stirring, until the sugar near the edges just starts to liquefy.

2. Using a wooden spoon or heatproof spatula, begin gently stirring, encouraging the melted sugar around the edges toward the center and delicately stirring up any sugar melting on the bottom as well. The sugar will start to look pebbly as it cooks, but keep going; it will melt completely as it turns amber.

3. Continue to cook until the sugar turns deep brown and starts to smoke. (Don't worry about any large chunks of caramel.) The darker you can cook the sugar without burning it, the better the final sauce will taste. It's ready when it's the color of a well-worn centime, or penny, and will smell a bit smoky.

4. Remove from heat and quickly stir in about a quarter of the cream. The mixture will bubble up furiously, so you may wish to wear an oven mitt over your stirring hand. Continued to whisk in the cream, stirring as you go to make sure it's smooth. Stir in the butter and salt. Serve warm. If you like your sauce a bit thinner or less rich, add 1/4 cup (60 ml) water.

STORAGE: The sauce can be made up to one month in advance and kept refrigerated. Rewarm the caramel in a small saucepan over low heat or in a microwave.

ASK HIM FOR A CAFE AU LAIT
ONLY IF YOU WOKE UP WITH HIM

It's almost impossible to find a drinkable cup of coffee in Paris: the coffee here is among the worst I've ever had.

Before Francophiles race to chime in about how bad American coffee is, yes, I agree with you. There's a lot of bad coffee in America. The difference is there's the *possibility* of finding a good cup in the States.

Plus North Americans have an excuse: we don't share a border with Italy, that magical kingdom of coffee, where each tiny sip is a multisensory explosion of flavor. From the moment the barman puts that little cup under the spigot, until I polish off the last of the syrupy espresso that trickles out of the tiny cup, my mind can't concentrate on anything but that intense dose of masterfully extracted coffee. Ah—*il espresso perfetto.*

In a country where there's such an emphasis on fine dining, whose good food is celebrated not just here, but around the world, it's stupefying why Parisian coffee is so vile that fed-up French food writer Sophie Brissard described it as "donkey piss." The only good coffee I've found in Paris has been in places run by Italians. To them, serving bad coffee would be an insult to their entire culture. When I asked the woman at the Italian tourism office how she was able to live in Paris and subsist on the coffee served here, she looked as if I'd made her queasy just by mentioning it. "I will *not* drink coffee in France," she responded. "I only drink tea."

Grasping for some explanation, I did some research. I learned that many of the cafés are forced to buy their beans from the same supplier, described as an Auvergnat Mafia. If that's the case, I suggest the Italian Mafia take over. I'm sure they'd lean on the cafés to improve the quality of the coffee.

Speaking of beans, I don't believe for a minute that much of the coffee labeled *pur Arabica,* considered the best, actually is. If that's Arabica they're brewing, then I'm Maurice Chevalier and the lady who's the *guardienne* of my building, the one with the mustache, is Catherine Deneuve.

Then there's the term "French roast," which means the coffee is roasted until it's burnt beyond recognition. It's a process designed to cover up the awful flavors of bad beans. I avoid anything labeled "French roast."

I pulled up an online interview with a café waiter, who said if you're not looking, they'll often reuse coffee grounds. If anyone in Italy did that, they'd be tossed to the real Mafia. It's not because I'm cheap that I stand at the bar for my coffee (where it's indeed cheaper); it's because I'm distrustful. I watch the barmen like a hawk, and although I've never seen anyone reuse grounds, I've also never once seen anyone flush the funky, spent grounds out of the machine afterward, something you're supposed to do after each and every cup. From the taste of things, I doubt they even do it after each and every month.

And Parisian barmen must think the tamper is there for decoration, since they rarely use it. Every time they dump some coffee into the filter holder and twist it closed under the opening of the machine, I want to leap over the counter, waving my arms, "Stop! Stop! Press that coffee down first! Thirteen kilos worth of pressure! That's what that little round metal thing is for!"

But I keep quiet, drop a sugar cube in the murky black sludge, and sip it while grimacing, wondering if maybe donkey piss might be an improvement. If you've ever wondered what all those pensive thinkers are pondering in the cafés, that might be it, too.

Frustrated, I got myself a bulky Italian-made espresso machine and enrolled in the Università del Caffè espresso-making school at Illy Caffè in Italy. There I learned all the components for pulling a perfect espresso: how to grind the beans to a fine powder, fill the filter holder with just the right amount of ground coffee, then tamp it down with proper pressure. Each extraction that came dribbling out of the machine was chocolate-brown manna from heaven. It was so exciting I couldn't sleep at night thinking about all I'd learned. (Or, more likely, it was the nine or ten shots of espresso I downed each day.) I came home with a suitcase packed with coffee, and every time I go to Italy, I bring an empty one to restock my larder.

However, I was finding it difficult to sustain my coffee-running operation across the border. Fed up, and armed with my newly acquired knowledge— and a professional espresso maker at home—I headed up to the twentieth arrondissement, to the highly regarded Brûlerie Jordain. (I needed little encouragement to go there, since it's conveniently located just next door to Boulangerie 140, whose brick oven turns out some of the best bread in Paris.)

I told the owner, who was also the coffee roaster, my plight. "I'm looking for a coffee that's roasted and ground for espresso. I have a new, professional-quality Italian espresso machine and want to make coffee that tastes just like Italian coffee." The owner of the shop, considered one of the best places in Paris to buy coffee, wrinkled up his nose and replied—Warning: If you're Italian, please don't read the next sentence—"Why would you want your coffee to taste like *Italian* coffee?"

Good Lord. I'm not even a single bit Italian, and I'm offended. Imagine if an expert on chocolate sniffed at you, "Why would you want chocolates that taste like *Parisian* chocolates?"

So I stick with coffee imported from Italy as much as possible and try to drink my brew at home, since I don't think many Parisian waiters would look very kindly upon me if I plunked a thermos down on the table and started pouring. But maybe I should: they might get the message.

But let's say you don't have a coffee machine, or don't want to risk the wrath of an unsympathetic waiter: how do you order coffee in Paris? If you just say, "I'll have a coffee," the waiter's going to bring you a small cup of *express*. And don't correct me. In France, it's spelled with an *x*. I know, I know. They can't even get the spelling right.

It's usually the moment the waiter sets down that tiny cup of brown sludge and dashes away that most visitors recoil in surprise. Then they spend the next ten minutes trying to flag the waiter down for milk. I can see not understanding that they don't automatically bring milk the first few times, but after a while, you'd think tourists would get with the program. I mean, doesn't it sink in that milk isn't brought with coffee and you have to ask when you order it in France after it happens the tenth time? No one's keeping a master list around here of how each visitor takes his coffee.

Sharp minds figure it out eventually, though, and most people who want to down a hefty mug of milky coffee will order a café au lait, which literally translates as "coffee with milk." Just so you know, café au lait is served only at breakfast—at home—sipped with people you've spent the night with. Cafés don't serve café au lait, except trendy French-style cafés in New York and Berkeley.

An honest-to-goodness café au lait is a large, steaming-hot coffee with warm milk, and it's not served in a mug, but in a footed bowl. It's commonplace for waiters to get requests for café au lait, especially in touristy areas, so you're not likely to get any raised eyebrows the way you once might have. But what you really want to ask your waiter for is a *café crème*. Unless you're waking up next to him, which is entirely possible given their reputation.

If that happens, I can't give you much guidance—that's out of my range of expertise, but unlike making coffee, it is one skill that the French do excel at.

CAFE FRANÇAIS

Should you plan on drinking your coffee in cafés, not in strangers' homes, I'm happy to help you out.

Café express Sometimes called *café noir, café nature,* or *café normal.* This is a small, espresso-style coffee. (Calling it an espresso would raise the ire of Italians everywhere.) If you simply say you want a "café," this is what you're going to get. Every time.

Café serré A "tight" *café express,* more concentrated since it's made with less water than a *café express.*

Café allongé A *café express* made with extra water during the extraction. If you're in a café and you want to linger longer, order one of these.

Café léger A *café express* with hot water added after it's extracted. Not recommended. At all.

Café noisette *Café express* with a "hazelnut"-sized dollop of steamed milk floating on top. Recommended if you find the taste of Parisian coffee off-putting. De rigueur to order on *l'autoroute* or on trains, where the food, like coffee, will challenge anyone's perception that everything in France is delicious.

Café décaféiné Once upon a time, ordering anything decaffeinated used to give waiters the sadistic pleasure of looking down on you as a lame American. Now they all order it, too, and simply say *"un déca."*

All coffees can be ordered decaffeinated by simply saying *"déca"* at the end of your order. But if your older waiter grunts when you do, you might be up later than you'd like.

Café américain American-style coffee is sometimes called *café filtre*, which is brewed or filtered. Caution: Sometimes you'll be given watered-down *café express*. Commonly served at hotel breakfasts or at home.

Café soluble or café instantané Instant coffee. Avoid at all costs.

Café au lait *Café express* or strong brewed coffee lightened with warm milk, served in a bowl, only at home, for breakfast. Or in trendy "bistros" in America for $6.50.

Café crème A *café express* served in a cup with warm (generally sterilized) milk added. Available in *normal* or *petit,* in which case you ask for *"un petit crème."*

Cappuccino A *café express* served in a cup with lots of frothy, steamed milk. Some cafés will put it in a foofy glass mug, add a light dusting of brown powder, and charge a whole lot more than they should for it. If you really want a cappuccino, go to Italy.

Café viennois Coffee with whipped cream, a drink you'll usually find in an ice cream shop or tea salon, although some cafés will whip one up. (Although it's unlikely they'll whip up real cream for it.) If you get one in the right place, taste the whipped cream before adding it to your coffee; French whipped cream is so good, you may want to skip the coffee underneath, which will ruin it.

Café frappé or café glacé Proceed with caution: since it's not really part of the culture, this is the French interpretation of "iced coffee," and it's generally tooth-achingly sweet and served in a chintzy portion, with one half-assed ice cube bobbing on top. It will invariably be too expensive for what you get, so don't get your hopes up. You do get a cool stirrer, though.

A few more caveats: After a meal, think of coffee as a deft punctuation mark that signals the close of a meal, not an open-ended invitation to stay with refill after refill. A *café crème* is never served after lunch or dinner, although it's becoming more commonplace as an afternoon drink, since it's linger-friendly. Coffee is served only after a meal, never during, and only after dessert. You'll never get it at the same time since it's not considered *correct*. And you always want to be correct, *non?*

Last, in case you're a coffee lover and come to Paris, there's always tea, which was something I never really understood the appeal of until I moved here. Now I'm drinking it more than ever. Who would have thought that living in Paris would actually make me more Italian?

SHAKERATO

BLENDED ICED COFFEE

MAKES 2 SERVINGS

You'd think people who worked around coffee all day long would be tired of the stuff. But the employee coffee bar at Illy in Trieste was the busiest place in town. The woman behind the bar didn't have any nose rings or tattoos. In fact, she looked as if she could be someone's Italian grandmother. But boy, could she crank out those coffee drinks.

When it was my turn and she asked what I wanted, the *shakerato* on the list caught my eye. I was mostly taken with the name, which I loved, and the idea of a well-made frosty coffee drink was hard to resist.

Here I've added liqueur to give the shakerato a bit of a kick, which I saw being done in a few *caffès* in Trieste. French people love Baileys, which they pronounce "Bay-layz," but you're welcome to play around with other liqueurs. If you want to skip the liqueur altogether, replace it with a few generous squirts of chocolate syrup.

2 medium scoops vanilla or coffee ice cream, softened slightly

2 or 3 shots strong espresso, cooled

$^1/_2$ cup (125 ml) Baileys Irish Cream

A few ice cubes

Unsweetened cocoa powder or grated chocolate

1. In a cocktail shaker or blender, combine the ice cream, espresso, Baileys, and ice.

2. Shake or blend vigorously, until the ice cream has melted and is smooth.

3. Pour into short tumblers and sprinkle the tops with cocoa powder. If you use a blender, there may be fragments of ice, which I don't mind. If you do, strain them out.

════════

TARTE TATIN, POUR LE RÉGIME

CARAMELIZED APPLE TART (LOW-FAT)

MAKES 8 SERVINGS

Many French women—and men—are obsessed with *le régime,* or their diet. Although you don't see as many heavy people in France as you do elsewhere, that's changing. *Le Figaro* newspaper reported that in the past thirty years, the average Frenchman gained 11.8 pounds. (Fortunately there were no published statistics about the weight gain of American men who've moved to France.) And even though French people don't obsess as much as we do about what they eat, there are plenty of Parisians who will readily admit that they'd like to lose a few kilos.

This is my "diet" version of the classic tarte Tatin, an open-faced tart of caramelized apples on a very thin sheet of flaky pastry. Since I use apples that have lots of flavor, all that's needed is a pat of butter to add a bit of richness.

I may be hopelessly American when I say this, but a good accompaniment to tarte Tatin is a steaming cup of espresso, and I'll enjoy them together at home. But if you come to Paris, sit in a café, and order both at the same time, and you get a funny look, don't say I didn't warn you.

For the dough

$^3/_4$ cup (110 g) flour

$^1/_4$ teaspoon coarse salt

1$^1/_2$ teaspoons granulated sugar

2 tablespoons (30 g) unsalted butter, cut into $^1/_2$-inch (2-cm) cubes
    and chilled

3 tablespoons (45 ml) ice-cold water

For the apples

8 firm, tart baking apples

Juice of $^1/_2$ lemon

1 tablespoon (15 g) unsalted or salted butter

$^1/_2$ cup (120 g) packed dark brown sugar

1. To make the dough, combine the flour, salt, and sugar in a food processor, standing mixer, or pastry blender. Add the butter and mix until the butter is in pea-sized chunks. Stir in the water and mix just until the dough holds together. Shape into a disk and wrap in plastic wrap. (Dough can be made up to 3 days before using.)

2. To make the tart, quarter, peel, and core the apples. Toss the pieces with the lemon juice in a big bowl and set aside.

3. Melt the butter in a 10-inch (25-cm) cast-iron skillet. Stir in the brown sugar and remove from heat.

4. Arrange the apple quarters in the pan rounded side down, with their cored sides facing upwards. Tightly pack the apples in overlapping concentric circles. Really cram them in. It may seem like a lot, but they'll cook down, so don't worry.

5. Cook over medium heat for 20 to 25 minutes. Do not stir or move the apples while cooking, but gently press them down slightly with a spatula as they soften.

6. While the apples are cooking, preheat the oven to 400°F (200°C). Position a rack in the upper third of the oven.

7. Roll the dough on a lightly floured surface into a 12-inch (30-cm) circle. (It will be thin, but don't worry.) Drape the dough over the apples, tucking in the edges, and bake the tart on an upper rack of the oven for 35 to 40 minutes, until the dough is golden brown.

8. Remove from the oven and invert a baking sheet over the tart. Hold the skillet in place wearing an oven mitt and flip both the skillet and the baking sheet simultaneously, being careful of any hot pan juices. Lift off the skillet, loosen any apples that may have stuck, and reunite them with the tart.

SERVING: Serve tarte Tatin warm, with a scoop of vanilla ice cream or crème fraîche (page 193). At Berthillon in Paris, the famed ice cream shop, they serve a picture-perfect version in their tea salon with a scoop of caramel ice cream, which is over-the-top good.

WELCOME TO FRANPRIX!

On recent trips back to the States, I noticed something interesting had happened during my absence: supermarkets had become inviting places to shop. Seemingly overnight, grocery stores in America have gone to great lengths to make shopping there more pleasant, transforming giant steel and concrete bunkers into lush, welcoming spaces. Some now feature spas, massage therapists, and soothing music; as well as well-stocked salad and coffee bars; mood lighting; clean restrooms; florists; and fresh fruits and vegetables heaped in wicker baskets with a gentle mist falling on them, with photos of happy, dirt-free farmers smiling down from above.

Last time I went to an American supermarket, I felt so welcome and got such a warm, cozy feeling inside that I didn't want to leave. The ultra-plush seating area set amid a jungle of exotic plants and aromatherapy sprays was more comfy than home. After I did my shopping, I almost hated to interrupt the staff, luxuriating in their hot tub, to ring up my groceries.

When I think of a French supermarket, the feeling that comes to mind is "Romanian prison." My local Franprix *supermarché* is a place I step into only with great reluctance: I buy what I need and check out as soon as possible. I look forward to going there as much as having oral surgery, without anesthesia.

From the moment you cross the threshold, instead of a friendly greeting, a grim, dour security guard in an ill-fitting Dacron suit will scan you up and down, mentally frisking you. If you have any bags, you'll need to either check them on the way in or they'll certainly be rifled through, with more thoroughness than airport security, on the way out. I make sure to arrive empty-handed, since I figure it's only a matter of time before I'm pulled out of the checkout line for a full-on cavity search.

From the horrendous fluorescent lighting that makes even Frenchmen look bad, to the floor that always feels unnervingly tacky, my Franprix is grimy and poorly maintained. If something needs to be unloaded, the staff invariably stacks the crates right in the center of the aisle, blocking everything and making it impossible to get around. And if you think anyone would ever dream of moving out of the way so you can get by, you need to go back and reread *"Les Bousculeurs."*

If something gets dropped or spilled in an American supermarket, an overeager soul will breathlessly get on the loudspeaker to issue an all-points-bulletin to cordon off the area and get it cleaned up. Pronto. At my Franprix, if there's a mess, all the employees gather in a semicircle around it to watch it spread. They just stand there, watching it, waiting for something to happen. You can see them backing away and thinking to themselves, *"C'est pas ma faute . . . c'est pas ma faute . . . ,"* hoping for someone else to take the initiative. They'll toss a plastic cone nearby, shrug, then head back outside to finish their cigarettes.

And if there is anything welcoming in there, aside from the rows of inexpensive wine, I've yet to find it. While American supermarkets have caught on to the fact that if you make the supermarket experience more pleasant people will (1) want to spend more time there and (2) want to spend more money, both of those concepts have eluded the French supermarket chains. That is, with the exception of Monoprix, which also happens to be under the same ownership as the chic Galeries Lafayette department store. The only reason I can think of for the lack of improvements is that French people have been so used to going to the outdoor markets and small shops for their needs that no one gives any thought to the supermarket "experience."

There are about seventy-five outdoor markets in Paris, which take place on various days of the week. Yet only two specialize in foods cultivated in the Île-de-France, the central region of France, where Paris is located. The Raspail market on Sunday and one at Batignolles on Saturday mostly feature produce grown by the local *producteurs* themselves: organic breads, earthy greens like *puntarella* and *brocollini*, tight clusters of white-tipped radishes; you can even find *les brownies américains* at the Raspail market. (People keep asking me if I've tried them, but why on earth would I, of all people, need to buy an American brownie in Paris?)

But to find the best options for locally sourced produce in Paris, you really need to get out of the city. I have a few favorite markets, such as the one in Coulommiers—an unexciting town, but the epicenter for Brie, which is quite a treat for cheese lovers like me. But my favorite is in Provins, a small town about an hour outside of Paris. Once a week, the town center comes alive with tables and carts heaped with beautiful, locally grown fare. The farmers don't even bother pulling the weighty pumpkins off the truck since they'd surely crush their rickety tables. They just hack off a slice as you order it. I've tasted strawberries so sweet—deep red throughout—that they burst like Japanese candy in your mouth. And I bag up handfuls of itty-bitty leafy greens, all tangled together (the vendors let you help yourself—"*Comme vous voulez!*" "As you wish!"), which I was thrilled to do, being used to bossy Parisian vendors. "*C'est plus facile pour tous, monsieur,*" one told me with a smile: "It's easier for everyone."

The first time I went, I was bewildered. As I piled everything into my basket, racing from one table to the next, I asked one of the men, who had soil caked under his fingernails and whose hands were as deeply wrinkled as his leafy Savoy cabbages, "Why don't you bring this gorgeous produce into Paris?"

"*Je déteste les Parisiens,*" he said.

A lot of French people aren't fond of Parisians. But since that's where I live, and since I do like Parisians (well, most of them), I thought driving a few hours back and forth to do my shopping wouldn't help me *réduire mon empreinte* CO_2. So I'm stuck doing my shopping closer to home.

⟋

When I bemoan the state of French supermarkets, comparing them to those back in the States, people tell me, "David, that's San Francisco, which is really different from other places. You don't know what it's like outside of San Francisco."

True. Except Paris is a world capital, often called the Capital of Cuisine, and I think it's reasonable to compare it to San Francisco, and other cities, and hold it to the same standard. It's not like I'm comparing Paris to Podunk. It's Paris, for God's sake. Yes, Paris! You should walk into any food market and be knocked flat by the *qualité exceptionnelle* of everything. Not knocked flat by slipping on a broken bottle of frying oil that no one could be bothered to clean up.

If you think the quality of the produce is bad, the service scores even lower. My local supermarket closes at 9 p.m. But if you're not in the door by 8:45, you can forget it. I've tried to go at 8:46 p.m., and the staff has already barricaded the door and started turning out the lights.

So you need to be constantly thinking ahead. Which means that if you haven't bought everything you need by Friday afternoon, you're sunk until the following Tuesday. Yes, Tuesday. Since most of the supermarkets are closed on Sunday, everyone with a day job has to do all their shopping on Saturday, when the stores are pandemonium and the lines are epic. It's a day that I avoid Franprix even more than usual.

But you're probably wondering why you have to wait until Tuesday. Aren't they open Monday? I don't even bother showing up on Monday, since it takes at least until Tuesday afternoon for them to restock the shelves from the hordes that descended over the weekend. So if I realize I'm out of Tropicana Pure Premium Réveil Gourmand on Saturday morning, I shouldn't expect another gourmet wake-up call until at least Wednesday.

The final insult is the checkout, where the cashiers barely look up from what they're doing to grunt an acknowledgment in your direction. It's not that they're rude; it's that they're under strict orders not to chat with customers so they can give their full attention to the money. There's barely any interaction, and if I merit a mumbled *"Bonjour,"* it's a momentous occasion.

If something's on *promotion*, I don't even bother to toss it in my basket, since I've had too many showdowns with cashiers when the sale price doesn't ring up at the register. And no one wants to distract the manager from his nose-picking duties to do a price check. Most manufacturers have gotten wise to this tactic and just reformulate their packaging to offer 15 percent more orange juice or tuna fish rather than hope the stores honor a price reduction.

It's also not common to get help with bagging your groceries in France. (Someone left a comment on my Web site that bagging groceries in the States was "the last remainder of slavery.") But the self-service model doesn't work. Once the clerk passes your groceries over the scanner, she flings them down to the end of the counter in a careless heap. Meanwhile, the person in front of you hasn't had time to pay and pack up *his* groceries, which are scattered all over the place. So when your groceries head down the chute, off they go, mingling with the purchases of the customer ahead of you.

Soon you're simultaneously engrossed in a discussion over whose milk is whose—did you or I buy that can of *le tripe* in *sauce tomate?* (I insist it's his)—and didn't I buy the Gamay and you bought the Chinon? And I'm sure those *oursons guimauve,* the chocolate-covered marshmallows shaped like bears, are mine. But the pistachio *macaron*-flavored yogurt isn't. (though I kind of wonder what it tastes like.)

And while you're both sorting through the jumble of goods and you're praying you won't suffer permanent kidney damage from the person behind you, who's jamming you forward with her basket, more groceries start heading down the pipeline, inciting another wave of panic.

Once I actually got help from a cashier who must have been basking in her freedom after the shackles of slavery had been removed, and instead of just sitting there watching, pitched in to help me. Or maybe she was just new. When I thanked her profusely—"*Ça va, monsieur, c'est plus vite*" ("That's okay, it's faster")—I wondered if she might inform her coworkers that there was a more expedient way. But I'm not holding my breath.

Maybe I should give them a bit of a break. After all, I have to spend only a few minutes there each week, while they have to be in there all day. Sure, I'd like it better if the aisles were cleaner, the fruits and vegetables were fresher, they had more than one grocery divider per store (they must be terribly expensive in France), and the cashiers were a little friendlier. Featuring local products would be nice, too. All that would probably help lift the spirits of those who work there, plus make it a more enjoyable place to shop.

But I'll continue to shop there unless they raise the price of wine. As long as they have that going for them, it makes it a little bit easier to put up with the other indignities. After all, I do have my priorities.

===

OIGNONS AIGRES-DOUX

SWEET-AND-SOUR ONIONS

MAKES 6 TO 8 SERVINGS

It's so challenging to find good fruits and vegetables in supermarkets that many Parisians head straight to Picard, a chain of frozen-food stores. The stores are immaculately clean and brightly lit, each a beacon of hope in the bleak landscape of supermarket produce. Although I'm not the addict that many others are, I'm amazed at what you can find there: shelled fava beans, lobes of foie gras, individually frozen *macarons*, ready-to-bake *soufflés a la framboise,* precut bags of leeks, and big sacks of pitted sour cherries, of which—as someone who's pitted a heckuva lot of cherries in his lifetime—I am a great fan. They also have small peeled onions that I like to cook in a sweet-and-sour mixture of sugar and vinegar and serve alongside roast meats.

In general, though, I prefer to use regional products as much as possible, and on a trip to rural Brittany, I passed a sign for a *producteur-récoltant* with a colorful drawing of some appealing-looking apples. Slamming on the brakes, I made an unauthorized U-turn, ignoring the ire of drivers in both directions. They were undoubtedly left cursing the Citroën, whose license plate read *"département* 75" (the mark of the despised Parisian driver), that was running amok in their idyllic countryside. I followed the dirt road that led to the apple orchard of Paul Loïc, where he and his family press the most wonderful apple juice and make a fruity apple cider vinegar, which smells just like fall apples, too. It adds a lovely fruit note to these sweet-sour onions.

If you have fresh boiling onions, you can peel them by dropping them in boiling water and letting them simmer for five minutes. Drain them, and let them cool. Then slice the ends from each one and slip off the skins. You can also use small shallots. These are terrific served alongside a meaty pâté or added to a braised meat or poultry dish, like the Braised Turkey in Beaujolais Nouveau (page 160). If you like them spicy, use harissa or Asian chile paste instead of tomato paste.

This recipe was inspired by Judy Witts Francini, who teaches Italian cooking in Florence, but who has French roots.

1 pound (450 g) small boiling onions, peeled

2 tablespoons light brown sugar

$1/4$ cup (60 ml) apple cider vinegar

$1/2$ cup (125 ml) apple juice or cider or water

1 tablespoon tomato paste or $1/2$ teaspoon harissa or chile paste

$1/2$ teaspoon coarse salt

1. Put all the ingredients in a deep, nonreactive skillet, cover, and cook over moderate heat for 10 minutes.

2. Remove the cover and continue to cook the onions. During the first few minutes, you don't need to stir them, but as the liquid slowly reduces and the onions begin to caramelize, you should start stirring.

3. Keep stirring during the final minutes so they don't burn, cooking until the liquid is thick and syrupy; they're done when a thin layer of liquid remains on the bottom of the pan. Remove from heat and transfer the onions to a bowl, scraping the flavorful juices clinging to the pan as well.

STORAGE: These onions are even better the next day, and will keep in the refrigerator for up to one week.

FANCYING LE FROMAGE

Aside from the so-so supermarket fare, there are a lot of exceptional things to eat in France. Although I have a well-known weak spot for the chocolates, what's truly special are the French cheeses, which no other country or culture could ever hope to match. From Abondance to Vacherin, every round, square, or *bouton* of cheese is an expression of *terroir,* climate, and other geographical elements specific to the region where it's produced.

Each cheese is distinct and appealing in its own particular way, whether aged and earthy or ripe and runny. Although I have my favorites, I haven't tasted a cheese that didn't make me swoon. I want them all. How can one decide between a wedge of Coulommiers and a chunk of Comté? The happy tradition of the cheese course, which still concludes meals in France, gives one an opportunity to try several of them.

My friends David and Randal host wonderful dinner parties, with excellent food and well-chosen wines. It's always clear they've spent a lot of time setting a handsome table and preparing yet another fabulous dinner the moment you walk into their Latin Quarter flat. After dinner, they invariably bring out a tray arranged with the most gorgeous French cheeses, hand-selected from the exceptional *fromagerie* Laurent Dubois, each at its peak, and place it in the middle of the table. *Oh la la!*

After a recent dinner, as usual, out came a big, wide platter. On it was a sublime, oozing-ripe Camembert de Normandie wafting its sweet barnyard fragrance in my direction. Next to it was a squat, ash-rubbed cushion of chèvre, its snow-white creaminess peeking through the gray smudges blanketing the surface. I couldn't wait to lop off a slab of the nutty Comté, a top cheese in my book, made from cows who've spent their days leisurely grazing their way across mountains in the Jura. And to complete the picture of perfection, there was a wedge of cave-ripened Roquefort, mottled throughout with its much-revered fuzzy green mold. All were simply arranged on a cheese board, as they should be. No fruit or leaves or anything superfluous: just cheeses presented in their exquisite perfection.

I actually gasped when the platter was put before us. Everyone around the table fell silent to inhale the aromas, savoring the moment of being in the presence of perhaps the ripest, most perfect specimens of cheese available anywhere in the world. Then the calm was broken. With self-assurance, a guest visiting from New York grabbed the lead—and the cheese knife. "Here, I'll make this easier," he announced.

Making good on his promise, with a few deft strokes of the knife, he pounced on the cheeses and started hacking away, cutting them all into little cubes as if they were going to be served with frilled toothpicks at a gallery opening alongside jugs of Mountain Chablis. In a matter of moments, he'd managed to decimate what had taken several generations of cheesemakers to perfect. We all sat in stunned silence, horrified by the desecration; our cheese course was ruined.

⤳

The French have certainly taken their share of knocks over the years, but no one would dare complain about their ability to make cheese. I can't pass a cheese shop without taking a deep whiff of the pungent air just outside the door, or craning my neck in the doorway to see what specialties on the straw-lined counters await the lucky shoppers that day. Even if I have an overload of cheeses stockpiled at home, I usually can't resist ducking inside, and I inevitably leave with a compact little chèvre or Rocamadour, a slab of nutty Beaufort, or milky-sweet Cantal cut from a colossal wheel.

There are several fancy, very famous *fromageries* in Paris, but it's hard to go wrong in any of them: any cheese shop you set foot in will carry a carefully chosen selection of specialty and regional cheeses that will blow your mind—not to mention your wallet and your arteries.

I knew I had found the right dentist when, after my first appointment, he sat me down in his office and we had an in-depth discussion, not about brushing and flossing techniques, but about French cheeses. As he talked, he jotted down a list of cheeses from the Auvergne, the region in the center of France where he was born. And at the top of that list, which he underlined twice, was a creamy Bleu de Laqueuille that he insisted I just *had* to try. I can't imagine a better reason for choosing a dentist than one who's also well versed in regional cheeses. (It doesn't hurt that he's movie-star handsome, either.)

Not only is it worth tasting as many cheeses as possible when in France, but it's also crucial to learn the right way to cut them. The technique is pretty easy to figure out, and most of it is logic: you wouldn't eat a bagel from the inside out, or slice a round birthday cake in long slabs like a ham, would you?

Here's how to work your way around the cheese tray.

If you're presented with a solid round cheese, like a Camembert de

Normandie or a petit Reblochon, think of it as a round birthday cake (*sans* the sugary blue roses), and cut it similarly into triangular wedges, not lengthwise slices starting from one edge. If the cheese is particularly small, like Rocamadour, crottin de chèvre, or any that would fit in the palm of your hand, it's permissible to cut those small rounds lengthwise, since wedges would be Lilliputian.

For cheeses you buy in wedges that are cut from a larger round, like earthy Saint-Nectaire, hearty Tomme de Savoie, or pungent Brie de Meaux, whatever you do—even if you're getting first stab at it on a cheese platter—never lop off the pointy *nez*, the "nose," of the cheese. This is considered terribly rude and arrogant. Take a lengthwise slice off the side and include a bit of the rind from the outer edge. Once again, pretend it's a birthday cake and everyone after you should have a bit of each part. No hoarding the roses.

Large rectangular hunks of mountain cheeses, like Salers, Comté, or Cantal, can be cut in whatever way makes sense. But in general, if you're faced with a big fat slab lying on its side, simply cut across, top to bottom, creating a rectangular *bâton* of cheese with a bit of the rind on both ends. Do not cut a small square out of the middle (which if I hadn't seen another of my compatriots do, I never would have thought possible). As for the rind, it's time to answer that perennial question: Should you or shouldn't you eat it?

Jean D'Alos, an *affineur* who ripens cheese in his cool, dry *caves* buried deep below the city of Bordeaux, runs one of the finest cheese shops in France. "It's easy," he says. "There is no rule. Don't eat the rind if it's going to negatively affect the flavor of the cheese."

If the rind looks dried-out, gnarly, fuzzy, or has a musty grayish-green mold—or is teeming with mites—you're probably better off leaving it on the plate. Especially if it's moving. Hard cheeses, like Vieille Mimolette, have firm, inedible-looking, waxy rinds that are a tough chew, and you probably want to avoid them. Ash-covered or orange-hued rinds are usually okay to eat, but if the surface resembles the forest floor, like Brin d'Amour, you should rake off the leaves and twigs.

How much to take? However much you can heap on your plate! Okay, seriously, I always find it tempting to take too much when the cheese platter lands next to me. But normal decorum dictates that during round one, you can select up to three different varieties of cheese. I've been known to play the "Oops. Didn't know. Silly me!" card and take a few extras if I'm not sure I'll get another go.

If offered, or if the platter's left on the table, taking seconds is fine. Thirds are generally frowned upon. But please, whatever you do, don't even think of asking for a doggie bag. Or frilled toothpicks.

=====

SOUFFLE AU FROMAGE BLANC

FROMAGE BLANC SOUFFLE

MAKES 8 SERVINGS

I bake this stress-proof soufflé in a shallow baking dish on the upper rack of my oven, so what emerges is a vision of dark, caramelized crust, which in my opinion is the best part of any soufflé. Like the French, I like my soufflés very, very creamy in the center, erring on the side of underbaked.

If you're timid about making a soufflé, don't worry: this is spectacular served piping hot from the oven, but is equally good when it has settled. Served at room temperature, it becomes a cheesecake-like "cake." When I brought a wedge of it to Leticia, the cute-as-a-button young lady who fries up crêpes at the Richard Lenoir outdoor market, she told me it was the best thing she had ever eaten in her life. Ever! And she's had a lot of experience with desserts, let me tell you . . .

I made this with full-fat (20 percent) and lower-fat (8 percent) fromage blanc, and both were delicious, although for the smoothest result, I recommend the full-on version, if you can find it. If there's no fromage blanc where you live, you can use the variation with cottage cheese and yogurt at the end of the recipe.

8 tablespoons (120 g) unsalted butter, at room temperature,
     plus more for the baking dish

11^1/$_2$ tablespoons (165 g) sugar, plus more for the baking dish

Freshly grated zest of 1 lemon

3 tablespoons (25 g) cornstarch

4 large egg yolks

2 cups (480 g) fromage blanc

6 large egg whites (at room temperature)

Pinch of salt

1. Liberally butter a shallow 2-quart (2-L) baking dish, with sides that are at least 2^1/^{2} inches (8 cm) high. Sprinkle a few spoonfuls of sugar inside, tilt the dish to coat the bottom and sides, then tip out any excess.

2. Preheat the oven to 375°F (190°C).

3. Using a rubber spatula or an electric mixer with the paddle attachment, mash the very soft butter with the lemon zest and cornstarch until completely smooth. Beat in the egg yolks until smooth, then whisk in the fromage blanc.

4. With an electric mixer or by hand, whisk the egg whites with the salt in a clean, dry bowl (not plastic) until frothy. Increase the speed and beat until the whites begin to mound and hold their shape. While whipping, gradually add 10 tablespoons (140g) of the sugar, 1 tablespoon at a time. Once you've added all the sugar, beat until stiff.

5. Fold one-third of the beaten egg whites into the fromage blanc mixture, then fold in the remaining egg whites just until incorporated. It's okay to have some tiny bits of white; that's preferable to overfolding the batter.

6. Scrape the batter into the prepared baking dish, gently smooth the top, and sprinkle with the remaining 1^1/^{2} tablespoons (25 g) of sugar.

7. Bake on a middle rack (or slightly higher, if possible) for 30 minutes, until the top is browned and the soufflé is just set but still very jiggly in the center if you nudge it. Depending on your oven, this may take slightly less or more time. Rather than going by strict baking times, touch the center to tell when it's done. If you like your soufflé creamy in the middle, the center should feel rather soft, like runny pudding. If you like it more firm, you can bake it until a toothpick inserted into the center comes out pretty clean.

SERVING: Serve immediately, scooping portions onto serving plates or bowls, making sure to include some of the crunchy topping with each portion.

The tang of fromage blanc is a great pairing with summer berries. Toss some sliced strawberries, raspberries, or any stone fruits with a bit of sugar until juicy, then divide them among shallow bowls. Once the soufflé emerges from the oven, use a large spoon to rest a warm, fluffy mound of soufflé on top, making sure to give everyone a nice bit of the sugary crust.

Or serve the soufflé by itself. With a tipple of Armagnac or Chartreuse on each warm serving, it makes a pretty effortless dessert.

VARIATION: If fromage blanc isn't available, you can make a perfect substitute by whizzing together $1^1/2$ cups (360 g) whole-milk cottage cheese (try to find one labeled "cultured") with $1/2$ cup (120 g) whole-milk plain yogurt in a blender or food processor until it's as smooth as possible.

═══════════

GATEAU MOKA-CHOCOLAT A LA CREME FRAICHE

MOCHA–CREME FRAICHE CAKE

MAKES 12 TO 16 SERVINGS

What's passed off as crème fraîche elsewhere bears little resemblance to the unctuous, hyperthick cream you get in France. While the kind you can make at home isn't bad, I urge—no, *insist*—that if you come to Paris, you make it a point to treat yourself to a small tub of the real deal. If you don't like it, there's something wrong with you. (And call me: I'll take the rest off your hands.)

Similarly, I can't imagine anyone not liking this cake, especially serious chocolate lovers. What you might not like is trying to get perfect, clean slices out of the pan. But don't worry if you don't get pristine portions: one thing I learned eating in French households is that food is meant to be enjoyed, not examined.

I sometimes serve this cake frozen, which makes it easy to slice, and a sliver is wonderful in the heat of summer with a scoop of brightly flavored Orange Sorbet (page 191), or another favorite ice cream or sorbet, melting alongside.

12 ounces (340 g) bittersweet or semisweet chocolate, chopped

^{2}/3 cup (160 ml) brewed espresso (or very strong coffee)

^{1}/4 cup (60 g) Crème Fraîche (page 193)

5 large eggs, at room temperature

Pinch of coarse salt

^{1}/2 cup (100 g) sugar

1. Lightly butter a 9-inch (23-cm) springform pan and wrap the outside of the pan with aluminum foil, to seal it watertight. Set the cake pan inside a larger pan, such as a roasting pan, large enough to make a water bath, or *bain marie*.

2. Preheat the oven to 325°F (160°C).

3. Put the chocolate and the espresso in a large heatproof bowl. Set the bowl over a saucepan of simmering water, stirring gently until melted and smooth. Remove from heat and let cool to room temperature. Stir in the crème fraîche.

4. In a standing electric mixer, whip the eggs, salt, and sugar on high speed until they hold their shape, about 5 minutes.

5. Fold half of the whipped eggs into the chocolate mixture, then fold in the remaining eggs.

6. Scrape the batter into the prepared pan. Add warm water to the roasting pan until it reaches halfway up the outside of the springform pan, creating a water bath.

7. Bake for 50 minutes to 1 hour, until the cake is slightly firm, but still feels soft in the center.

8. Lift the cake pan from the water bath, remove the foil, and set on a cooling rack until room temperature.

SERVING: Slide a knife along the outside edge of the cake to release it from the pan. Release the outside ring of the springform pan.

Because the cake is delicate, I slice it with a thin, sharp knife dipped in very hot water and wiped clean before each slice. You can also cut wedges using a length of dental floss (unflavored, please), pulled taut and drawn across the diameter of the cake. This cake can be served at room temperature, chilled, or frozen with a scoop of ice cream or frozen yogurt—a great warm-weather dessert for summer—or with whipped cream and a spoonful of chocolate sauce.

NOTE: You can substitute water for the espresso in the recipe.

STORAGE: The cake will keep for up to five days at room temperature or refrigerated. If well wrapped, it will keep in the freezer for up to one month.

═══════════

SORBET ORANGE

ORANGE SORBET

MAKES 4 TO 6 SERVINGS

A simple sorbet is always welcome after dinner, either alongside a rich chocolate cake or with crisp cookies. For the best-tasting sorbet, use good juicing oranges or, if available, colorful blood oranges. In season, tangerine juice can be used instead.

2 cups (500 ml) freshly squeezed orange juice

$1/2$ cup (100 g) sugar

2 tablespoons Champagne or dry white wine, optional

1. Warm 1/2 cup (125 ml) of the orange juice with the sugar in a non-reactive saucepan, stirring until the sugar has completely dissolved.

2. Stir the sugar mixture into the remaining orange juice and add the Champagne, if using.

3. Chill thoroughly, then freeze in your ice cream maker according to the manufacturer's instructions.

SERVING: If left in the freezer, Orange Sorbet tends to chill rather firmly. Adding the wine helps prevent it from getting rock-hard, but you should remove it from the freezer five to ten minutes before serving; it'll be easier to scoop.

VARIATION: If you don't have an ice cream maker, you can make Orange Granita. Use just 1/4 cup (50 g) of sugar, or to taste, then pour the mixture into a shallow plastic container and put it in the freezer. Scrape it with a fork several times as it's freezing, raking it into icy crystals.

CREME FRAICHE
Cultured Cream
MAKES 1 CUP (250 ML)

Obscenely thick crème fraîche is available in every *fromagerie* in Paris, where it's often scooped from big earthenware bowls. This recipe makes a good approximation. Check the Resources (page 271) for producers of traditional crème fraîche in America.

1 cup (250 ml) heavy cream
1^1/2 tablespoons buttermilk

1. In a clean bowl, mix the cream and buttermilk.

2. Cover with a tea towel or plastic wrap and store in a warm spot for 12 hours, or until thickened and slightly tangy. Refrigerate until ready to use.

STORAGE: Crème fraîche will keep in the refrigerator for up to one week.

GREVE GRIEF

Imagine if you were the parents of a bunch of very unruly children. And every time they misbehaved or threw a temper tantrum, you caved in and gave them whatever they wanted. Now imagine them maturing as adults. What do you think they would do whenever they wanted something? Welcome to my world.

Strikes are so well known in Paris, so part of the cultural fabric, they even have a season. In early fall, then returning later in May, the strikes and *les mouvements sociaux* begin to erupt on a regular basis. The general timeline is this: signs are posted warning of an intended strike or demonstration, then the protest takes place for a few hours in the afternoon (rain or shine). Shortly afterward the disaffected group meets with government officials who—as usual—cave in to the protesters' demands, and everyone goes back to work after getting what they wanted.

The first major all-out, opened-ended *grève* after I moved to Paris was in November of 2007, and it lasted much longer than an afternoon. Like *les bousculeurs*, it was a game of playing chicken, this time with newly elected President Nicolas Sarkozy, and it was his first major challenge. He proposed changing the contracts for employees of the transit and electric and gas unions—agreements that allowed them to retire at the ripe old age of fifty, a throwback to the times when working the rails meant shoveling coal and other laborious duties. Nowadays, that argument was pretty moot—and costing France a ton of money. (While I'm sure sitting in a station selling tickets isn't the most stimulating job, I can think of worse.)

To add to the chaos, the students struck at the same time. And so did the teachers and customs officials. And postal workers and hospital workers and civil servants and tax inspectors. And newspaper and television employees. Many banks shut their doors, too, since getting to work was *pas possible*. Most of Paris just shut down.

The demonstrators, instead of sitting at home and staring at a blank television screen or rereading last week's newspapers, took part in festivities that the Associate Press reported had "a picnic atmosphere, with music, roasted sausages and balloons." Strikes in Paris are often rather convivial, aided by good food and free-flowing, cheap wine. In fact, I'm thinking I should go on strike once in a while, too.

Contrary to what a lot of people imagine, many French workers aren't part of any *syndicat* at all. In 2005, just under 10 percent of the workers here were members of a union, one of the lowest rates in Europe. The same year, 12 percent of Americans belonged to a union. Yet the unions hold a lock-hard grip in France, much stronger than elsewhere, and they certainly enjoy more widespread public support than they do in America.

I remember a few transit strikes that occurred when I lived in the Bay Area. At first, they were just a nuisance. By "at first," I mean for the first five minutes. As the day wore on, people were not just upset, they went ballistic. Streets were clogged, sidewalks mobbed, folks couldn't get to work, and by noon, people's patience with the strikers had reached a boiling point. Negotiations for a resolution soon ensued.

By contrast, the French shrug off the strikers with pursed lips and a look of resignation, as if to say, "We are French. That's what we do."

When the smoking ban was implemented at the end of 2007, I thought, "What are the smokers going to do? Take to the streets *against* something that's killing sixty thousand of their fellow citizens a year?"

Well, yes, they did. The biggest *manifestation* was four weeks before doomsday for *les fumeurs*, when ten thousand of them invaded the streets of Paris to assert their right to smoke-out everyone around them with the stinky, unhealthy fumes from their cigarettes. I'm not quite sure what they hoped to accomplish: even in France, it's hard for smokers to arouse a lot of sympathy from the general public. And since the health minister was wise and declared the ban to be not a law, but a "decree," it was impossible to reverse. But I'm glad they got what they needed to off their chests, so the rest of our chests could breathe a little easier when eating out.

Another hopeful group of strikers was the pesky motor scooter riders, protesting a crackdown on parking and driving on the sidewalk. Personally, I don't mind if scooters park on sidewalks. You can walk around them. But I do mind when riders rev them up to high speed before flying across the walkways, sending everyone scattering in multiple directions while they barrel through. One day at a crosswalk, waiting for the light to change, I felt someone jostling me from behind, even more aggressively than usual. I turned to discover it wasn't exactly a person doing the shoving, but the front wheel of a scooter that was nudging me forward. I don't know if there's ever been a demonstration for the rights of pedestrians, but I'd be happy to organize one to take back the sidewalks.

And oddly, there was also a firemen's strike where *les pompiers de Paris* lit dramatic fires as part of their protest, in the place de la Bastille, prompting the police to come and calm things down. Now that was something I never thought I'd see: police in riot gear battling firemen.

The Bastille, where I live, is best known as the site where the infamous prison was seized and ransacked by the masses, igniting the French Revolution. Two hundred and twenty years later my doorstep is still the starting point for almost all the marches and strikes that happen in Paris. Fortunately it doesn't happen all that much. Just once a day or so.

I don't need to read the paper or watch the news to find out when the strikes will be taking place; I just have to listen out my window. I know something's up when the normal cacophony of traffic slows to a halt followed by a few minutes of silence, while the police clear the streets. My whole apartment will start to quiver from the dull thud of thousands of feet heading my way. (Being from San Francisco, the first time this happened, I almost dove under a table, thinking it was an earthquake.) As the mob closes in, there's unrelenting shouting, cheering, and screeching into bullhorns, all accompanied by the smell of roasting *saucisses* and blaring music, while throngs of people march down the boulevard carrying banners, clogging the streets, and causing general havoc for the next few hours.

To make matters worse, the drivers of the cars blockaded on the side streets somehow imagine that leaning on their horns nonstop will persuade twelve thousand protesters to stop what they're doing and kindly move aside for them to pass. The upside is that I'm saving a fortune on newspapers; a glance outside is all that's necessary to keep me up-to-date on current affairs.

I was very excited the first time I saw a *manifestation*. (The French just say *manif*; since they're so frequent, there simply wouldn't be enough time in the day if they had to pronounce the whole word every time one happened.) I was absolutely entranced. "Oh look! The people are taking to the streets, shouting in French. How charming! It's going to be so much fun living here. I can't wait to see the next one!"

But when it happens the second day . . . then the third . . . then the fourth (sometimes twice a day), *les manifs* quickly lose their appeal—

especially when members of the striking *syndicats* plaster your neighborhood with solidarity and brotherhood stickers, and set up a wall of speakers, each the size of a Renault, right underneath your window, blaring music while steamed-up drivers in backed-up cars lean on their horns. My whole apartment vibrates until everyone's had their say and they pack up the grills and head home. There must be a different *syndicat* of people responsible for scraping all the stickers from the lampposts, walls, and Métro stations—workers whom the previous group don't feel the need for any *solidarité* and *fraternité* with.

The aforementioned strike in November of 2007 marked a big turning point for modern France. Nicolas Sarkozy had been elected by promising deep and tough reforms, vowing to tighten up France's notoriously generous benefits. His Napoleonic ego was infamous and he was about as stubborn and feisty as they come. Sarko (as he was quickly dubbed by the abbreviation-happy French) had stood up in a huff and bid *adieu* to Lesley Stahl during a television interview for *60 Minutes* when she asked about his wife, who had left him several times for her boyfriend in New York, before finally splitting for good. (Previously, when Sarkozy's ex-wife was asked by an interviewer where she expected to see herself in ten years' time, she replied, "Jogging in Central Park.") Just after his contentious election, the French were positively scandalized when he had the nerve to take a short vacation on—gasp—a friend's yacht. Other transgressions included his distaste for wine, mingling with American celebrities, and engaging in the unseemly practice of *le jogging*.

Jacques Chirac, the previous president, had a history of giving in. But right from the start, Sarko said he wouldn't be having any of that, and everyone knew he meant it. The strikers could bring the country to a screeching halt for all he cared, but he was even more stubborn than they.

So the strikes of '07 began. All transit came to a halt and no one could go anywhere. If you absolutely insisted on coming into Paris from the suburbs, traffic jams lasting three hours were the norm. Although everyone said this was going to be the great test of the new Vélib' free-bike program, I gave it an F, since every time I showed up at the rack, all the bikes were gone. Or claimed by crafty Parisians who had chained the communal bikes to the station with their own personal locks.

After ten days of strikes, public disapproval of the strikers was at a whopping 70 percent and Métro and bus drivers in Paris started going back to work regardless of the strike, since they weren't getting paid to stay home and do nothing. In an almost unknown show of conciliation, the union actually agreed to head to the bargaining table with the government.

While the strikers did demonstrate that they could hold the country hostage for days on end, they also proved how fed up modern French people were with the tantrums of a small minority of very well compensated workers. And a subtle yet very powerful shift in power was felt across the country: people were no longer behind the workers, regardless of whether they were right or wrong.

⌒

A Parisian friend who is a member of the Communist Party said, "The French strike because they are selfish people. It's all about 'me'; they strike for their own benefits. And if they say they're going on strike in sympathy with the other unions (like La Poste striking along with the train workers), it's only because they think they're next."

As a casual non-Communist observer, I'm not exactly sure how true that is. But since I'm around fifty, I know if I were expecting my gold watch soon, I'd be miffed, too. I'm interested in seeing what happens down the road. (And I don't mean the road in front of my apartment.) Have the French people and their government lost patience with the unions and their frequent strikes? Or will things go back to normal, leaving the rest of us to fend for ourselves on the sidewalks of Paris?

I can't say for sure. But there is a similarity between the two most recent *mouvements sociaux*: I feel a little bit healthier breathing in less secondhand smoke when dining out or sitting in a café, and I know I'm a lot safer not sharing the sidewalks with the motor scooters. I'll let Sarko duke it out with the unions over how much longer people will have to work. But could they please do it under someone else's window for a change?

=====

MELANGE DE NOIX EPICEES

SPICED NUT MIX

MAKES 4 CUPS (400G)

In advance of a strike, signs are posted at the various bus and Métro lines a few days before so we can adjust our plans accordingly. Regardless of how disruptive they are, at least the strikers are kind enough to think of others.

Similarly, when Parisians have a party in their apartment, they post a note in the lobby of their building or in the elevator, letting others know they're having a gathering that may get noisy. My neighbors are lucky since my apartment is too compact for large, rowdy gatherings. When I do have guests, we tend to be a fairly subdued crowd. So far, I haven't had any complaints.

This is my favorite party mix and I keep a small box of *bretzels d'Alsace* on hand so I can toss a batch together at the last minute. It makes an excellent nibble.

2 cups (275 g) raw nuts—any combination of pecans, almonds, peanuts, cashews, and hazelnuts

1 tablespoon (15 g) salted or unsalted butter, melted

3 tablespoons (45 g) dark brown sugar

1/2 teaspoon ground cinnamon

1 teaspoon chili powder or smoked paprika

2 tablespoons maple syrup

1/2 teaspoon unsweetened natural or Dutch-process cocoa powder

1^1/2 teaspoons coarse salt

2 cups (100 g) small pretzel twists

1. Preheat the oven to 350°F (180°C). Spread the nuts on a baking sheet and toast for 10 minutes.

2. Meanwhile, in a large bowl, mix the butter, brown sugar, cinnamon, chili powder, maple syrup, and cocoa.

3. Stir the warm nuts into the spice mixture to coat them completely, then sprinkle on the salt.

4. Mix in the pretzels, then spread the mixture on the baking sheet and bake for about 15 minutes, stirring once or twice, until the nuts are well glazed and browned. Remove from the oven and cool completely. Once cool, break up the clusters and serve.

STORAGE: The nuts can be stored in an airtight container, at room temperature, for up to five days.

THE VISITORS

The biggest thing Americans living in Paris complain about isn't the constant strikes, or tangling with French bureaucrats. Nor is it the lack of customer service or the availability of necessities, such as molasses, cranberries, organic peanut butter, and chocolate chips.

It's visitors.

At first it sounds like a lot of fun having friends arrive. You can take them to your favorite restaurants! Spend afternoons meandering through museums! Introduce them to that charming little bistro on your corner! Visit chocolate shops! Best of all, you can catch up on all the latest gossip about everyone back home.

But all too soon, the morning check of e-mails that have cascaded in during the night includes an ever-increasing number with subject lines like these: "Guess What?!" or "We're On Our Way!!" or "Remember ME??" The worst are the ones that assume I'm able to drop everything I'm doing for their impending arrival: *"In Paris . . . this weekend!"*

It's one thing when the messages are from people you know, and visits are spaced out over the course of a few months. But when word got out that I lived in Paris, I had no idea what a popular guy I was. And not just with my friends, but with friends of friends. And their friends, too.

You click to open . . . "Hi David! We're friends of your brother's friend, Tom, the guy who used to cut his hair. He said that we should look you up since we're on our way to Paris, and you'd show us around." And it gets better: " . . . and we'd love to meet up with you for dinner one night. You can help us order since two of us are vegans, but we don't eat vegetables. Oh, and my sister is deathly allergic to shellfish, and the triplets can't have gluten, dairy, or anything with DNA. We can't *wait* to have dinner with you!"

By necessity, I had to formulate a policy of getting together for a meal only if the word "invited" was included somewhere in the message. Simply "meeting up for dinner" doesn't rouse me to action. Because once committed to "meeting up," I know I've got my work cut out for me.

I'll start by translating the menu—usually twice, since one person wasn't listening the first time. Shortly thereafter, I'll have to explain that "sauce on the side" isn't an option in France and that it's going to come drenched in a lot of butter whether they ask for it or not.

Then there's explaining the inexplicable: French cuts of beef, which are different from American cuts and don't correspond. A typical French menu might have on it, say, *Pavé de boeuf grillé*. *Pavé* refers to something slablike, and *grillé* is obvious; order this and you'll get a grilled hunk of beef. In France wine lists rarely list the grape, because the French aren't so concerned with knowing the origin and genealogy of every item when they place their order, nor do they expect a narrative from the waiter of how each item is going to be prepared and presented. They just order and leave it up to the cooks in the kitchen to make their dinner. (What a concept!)

Americans are "customizers" and we want to know before ordering what cut of steak it is, how it's going to be cooked, which ranch it was raised at, how far away it was, what the cow ate, did he live a happy life, what exactly is going to go into the sauce, what's going to come alongside it (and can they change that?), whether it'll be possible to share it, and whether they can take the rest of it home. It takes great restraint for me not to yell across the table, "Just order the damn piece of meat—and eat it!"

The final straw was when one of those friends-of-friends types, whom I foolishly agreed to meet, deeply insulted a waiter at what was once my favorite café in the Marais. The charming waiter, who liked to joke around with me, said to this fellow, who ordered his drink in English, "You should try to speak a little French, after all, you are in France!" To which my gracious guest glared and shot back, "You know what? I don't even *want* to try." I would have looked a little funny trying to disappear by sliding under the table, so instead, I gulped down my drink quickly and got out of there as politely as I could. And I haven't gathered up the courage to go back. After that, I swore off guests forever.

A few years later, when Maury Rubin, owner of the superlative City Bakery in New York, wrote to tell me about a friend who was coming to Paris for a month, I decided to rethink my policy of no guests, since anyone who has Maury's seal of approval was probably all right. And I didn't want to risk being cut off from his fabulous salted croissants on my next trip to New York, either.

If you don't know City Bakery, the place just screams Manhattan and is busier than Grand Central Station. Most make a beeline for the thick hot chocolate with a plush homemade marshmallow melting on top, or one of the frisbee-sized chocolate chip cookies. As arduous as it sounds, some people manage to down both. Others wolf down a slice of French toast of such girth, it would feed a French family of four. And then there are the aforementioned salted croissants, which I learned on my last visit I can easily eat three of all by myself. Thank goodness all my friends know better than to ask me to share.

Maury's a hard-core New Yorker and opened a branch in Los Angeles, but was having difficulty adjusting to life among us West Coast types. He joked that he was going to have a trap door built and as soon as anyone uttered the word *diet*, it would open up and neatly dispatch them away.

Maury's friend turned out to be Nancy Meyers, a director and screenwriter, whose most successful film was *Something's Gotta Give*. I remember not only the film, but the midnight phone call from my friend Lewis, who lives in the nearby place des Vosges, telling me to "get down here— *right now!*" when they were filming the scenes with Jack Nicholson strolling through Paris. I hadn't moved so fast since my days in the kitchen at Chez Panisse.

So I decided to make an exception to my long-standing policy against visitors.

Shortly after Maury's matchmaking, Nancy and I were corresponding daily, and I was sending her addresses to all my favorite places for good food near the apartment she was renting on the rue Jacob: I insisted she stop at Da Rosa for *pots* of Christine Ferber's *confitures* and oval pats of handmade butter from Jean-Yves Bordier. She must get her cheese, I told her, from the cheerful crew at Fromagerie 31, and it was obligatory to pick up her daily *pain aux céréales* from Eric Kayser on the rue de l'Ancienne Comédie. And she must run, as soon as she landed, to Pierre Marcolini for chocolate-covered marshmallows even before she unpacked her suitcase. (In retrospect, she must have thought I was nuts: here I was, planning her whole vacation around things to eat.)

When we finally met in person, Nancy was laid back, and indeed, as the French say, *"très cool,"* and more than happy to indulge in all the places I recommended. She asked if I knew any good spots for seafood, but I drew a blank and could think of only one place: Le Dôme. I'd had lunch there once, and was quickly ushered past all the festive Parisians having a grand time eating their *plateaux de fruits de mer* heaped with glistening oysters, cracked crab, and lobster-length *langoustines,* to Siberia, a hideously decorated, overlit hideaway. One look around and I saw it was their repository for Americans who showed up in sweatshirts with fanny packs strapped to their sides. I was there with a pastry chef friend who had just sold her bakery for somewhere in the neighborhood of fifty-five million dollars, and we were both dressed just as nicely as the guests in the main dining room. I suggested that it would have been pleasant to sit in the gorgeous gilded dining room, but the maître d' thought otherwise.

And the next morning, after our lunch in purgatory, both of us were too weak from writhing on the bathroom floor all night, clutching our stomachs, to even think about our carefully planned Paris pastry crawl that day. But I figured since Paris was giving me a second chance at life—and I was giving myself a second chance with visitors—why not just declare a blanket pardon to all, which included giving Le Dôme another chance as well?

This time Nancy and I were led to a plush booth, and over fillets of St. Pierre with rounds of crusty, buttery pan-fried potatoes, she gave me some equally juicy Hollywood gossip while I filled her in on more tasty Paris hot spots to check out. This time, the service was *très correct,* with the handsome and assured waiters hovering over us, their long aprons wrapped around their waists and impeccably starched collars standing tall. I remarked to Nancy on how nicely we were being treated. She responded, "Well, if you really want to see star treatment, you should see what happens when I go to Le Grand Colbert."

For those of you who don't know, etched in the minds of every middle-aged woman is the scene toward the finale of *Something's Gotta Give* where Diane Keaton sits down for dinner with Keanu Reeves at Le Grand Colbert to dine on roast chicken, which she'd raved about as being the best in Paris at various points in the film. (Although it wasn't even on the menu until Nancy wrote it into the script.) I was dying to see what "star treatment" meant to not-so-easily-impressed Parisian waiters. So I called Le

Grand Colbert to make a reservation for lunch the following week. The person who picked up the phone was pleasant, if a tad reserved.

"*Bonjour, monsieur,* I'd like a reservation, *s'il vous plaît*" (which was, by the way, the first sentence I mastered in French).

"*Oui, monsieur. Pour quelle date?*"

"Tuesday."

A bit of silence as I could hear him leafing through the pages of his reservation book.

"*Oui. Eh . . . (pause) . . . à quelle heure?*"

"1 p.m.?"

"*Bon.*"

I could hear some pen scribbling in the background.

"*Combien de personnes, monsieur?*"

"*Deux.*"

A moment of silence. More writing.

"*À quel nom?*"

My moment had arrived. I took a deep breath. "Nancy Meyers." I stood back and took a mental bow. This time, there was a long silence.

"*Nan-cee May-oarz?*" he asked, his voice going up several octaves.

"*La directrice? Mais oui, monsieur! Pas de problème!*"

I'd been to Le Grand Colbert once before and, frankly, I had been skeptical. Plastic-laminated English menus in the window and a faded poster of the movie tacked up in the window weren't exactly beacons for good food. The silly pink writing on the menu was totally inappropriate for a Parisian bistro, and aside from the gently aged façade, the appeal of the place was lost on me. I was tempted to bolt to Le Grand Véfour nearby in the Palais Royal, constrained only by my credit card limit.

But step inside and *bien sûr,* Le Grand Colbert is indeed a classic *bistro parisien,* right down to the mirrored walls, starched linen napkins, waiters gliding across the room with platters of oysters, and the aged, yellowed ceiling attesting to decades of Gauloises clouding the air. The food had been fine, but, I wasn't especially eager to return.

But this time I was. And as I whizzed around the place des Victoires, with Louis XIV on horseback lording it over me and my bike, I made a pact with myself that I wouldn't have anything to drink, so I'd be on my best behavior with Nancy. I have a tendancy to mindlessly toss down whatever's put in front of me to mask my anxiety in social interactions, a problem that's especially acute if I'm around anyone famous. Water, rum, fruit juice, wine, absinthe, iced tea, kava, Champagne, or vodka all quickly disappear if I've got a glass of it in my hand.

The moment we sat down, two tall frosty flutes of Champagne were set in front of us. I grabbed mine right away, brought the thin rim of the chilled glass to my lips, and gulped down three-quarters of it. Nancy took a delicate, measured sip and put hers back on the table.

I'm always amazed how my journalist friends are masters at whipping out their notebooks and furiously jotting things down when meeting important people. I often have a hard time focusing. Trying to appear equally respectable, I'd brought my little Moleskine notebook, as Nancy told me beforehand that she was willing to answer any and all questions. I asked her about what Jack and Keanu were really like (she loved them both), why she chose Keanu Reeves (he was a star, but different enough to not be dominated by Jack's large-scale presence), how fabulous Diane Keaton is. And then she told me about Daniel Craig, which got my undivided attention.

Daniel Craig? He wasn't in *Something's Gotta Give.*

Okay, he had nothing to do with the film, or Le Grand Colbert. But he'd come to her office for a part in another film wearing a skin-tight muscle shirt, and she was willing to spill. No gossip, but she said his fabulously muscled stomach wasn't just flat—it was concave, a curve she demonstrated by gracefully shaping a vertical arc with her hand in the air, which transfixed me even more than the Belle Époque surroundings. I should have asked her to draw it in my still-empty notebook, but that would have been especially unprofessional of me.

Thankfully, my fiercely knotted tie was blocking my windpipe, which was probably a good thing.

Yet even greater than my thirst for celebrity dirt was my hunger for food, so we ordered. My Champagne was almost gone and I didn't want to embarrass myself by flagging down the waiter for more. Nancy, who hadn't adapted to the French midday spree of lunch *plus* wine, had had only a few sips. I wanted to ask, "Hey—are you gonna finish that?" But I didn't.

Turning to the questions of food and dining, I asked Nancy: Why Le Grand Colbert, and why roast chicken, especially when they didn't even have it on the menu?

For the film, she'd originally chosen Brasserie Lipp, a notoriously uptight spot on the Left Bank, part of the trilogy of all-star Parisian cafés, along with Café de Flore and Les Deux Magots. As filming time came closer, someone at the Lipp changed his mind and made the less-than-brilliant decision not to let the film be made there. So that left Nancy to scout out an equally classic Parisian bistro to shoot in. In the end, she was much happier, and the host at Le Grand Colbert reported that they were thrilled, too, because afterward, business increased permanently by 20 percent. (No report on how the folks at Brasserie Lipp felt.)

As for the chicken? Nancy herself doesn't eat meat. So when I asked, "Then why chicken?" she didn't remember how she came up with "The Most Famous Roast Chicken in the World." She just thought that a big ol' hunk of beef or massive lamb shank wasn't something that Erica Barry, the prim writer played by Diane Keaton, would rhapsodize over. Correctly anticipating a barrage of roast chicken orders, the chef afterward came up with a respectable recipe for the menu. So if you go and order their roast chicken, it may not be the absolute best version in town, but it is pretty darned good. Heck, if it's good enough for Diane, it's good enough for me.

That day Nancy and I were the only Americans in the restaurant, and we were surrounded by French business folks from the nearby *Bourse*. No one was paying any attention to the minor fuss being made over Nancy, except for the headwaiter, who at one point came by with a scrapbook of images from *Tout Peut Arriver* ("Anything Can Happen"), as the film was called in France. And sitting there with Nancy, being fawned over by the entire staff, I felt like I'd—at long last—arrived here, too.

Aside from the hyper-hygienic bathrooms, there's another touch of Americanism at Le Grand Colbert: just behind the table where the roast chicken landed in the film, there's a Hollywood-style clapboard that reads "Nancy Meyers." Proving that no matter how long you've lived in Paris or how famous you are, it's still fun to play tourist, Nancy and I took a few snapshots before we headed out into the brisk Parisian air and toward Les Halles in pursuit of a tarte Tatin pan for her at the pastry equipment store MORA, and more edible adventures in the neighborhood.

I was happy that I'd limited myself to one slender flute of Champagne, but when I got home, I realized that I had made only a few cursory remarks in my notebook, which made me a better dining companion than journalist. As a result of that lunch, I've changed my tune regarding visitors. If you want to come to Paris and meet up, we can talk. But VIP treatment is an absolute requirement. When Nancy comes back to town, I'll certainly make the time for her. If Diane happens to make the trip back, I think I can find time in my schedule for a dinner date. And if an e-mail from Daniel Craig pops up one day in my in-box, even if it's last-minute—I'm definitely available.

SAUCE AU CHOCOLAT CHAUD DE NANCY MEYERS

NANCY MEYERS'S HOT FUDGE SAUCE

MAKES 1 CUP (250 ML)

I'm not in any position to edit one of Hollywood's most successful screenwriters, so I thought I'd tread carefully reprinting Nancy's instructions. In the recipe she sent me she wrote, ". . . Toss it all in a small pot, stir, and eat immediately."

I did as I was told and have to agree with Jack Nicholson: this is one heckuva hot fudge sauce. It's very, very thick, and although I'm not one to get between a woman and her chocolate, you may want to stir a little bit of milk into the sauce at the end until it's the consistency you want. This recipe can also be doubled. But I find a little goes a long way.

3 tablespoons (45 g) unsalted butter, cut into small pieces

1/3 cup (65 g) granulated sugar

1/3 cup (70 g) firmly packed dark brown sugar

1/2 cup (50 g) unsweetened Dutch-process cocoa powder

1/3 cup (80 ml) heavy cream

Pinch of coarse salt

1. Place all ingredients in a 1-quart (1-L) heavy saucepan. Stir over low heat until the butter is melted.

2. Continue to cook over low heat, stirring without stopping and scraping the bottom and sides of the pan, 3 to 5 minutes more, until the sugar is melted and the sauce is smooth. Serve immediately.

STORAGE: The sauce can be refrigerated for up to one week. Reheat slowly in the top of a double boiler or in a microwave.

===

LE CHEESECAKE

CHEESECAKE

MAKES ONE 9-INCH (23-CM) CAKE, 12 TO 16 SERVINGS

Nancy began her Hollywood career not as a screenwriter, but as a cheesecake maker. Starting out in Tinseltown, she decided to bake and sell cheesecakes, since it was something she could do at home while she was busy typing away.

Quickly overwhelmed with orders, and with only one oven, she offered to pay her neighbors' electric bills if she could use their ovens to meet the demand, and thus a star was born. Unfortunately, she'd been sworn to secrecy and vowed never to divulge her recipe for cheesecake, even after her writing career took off. But since my career depends on sharing recipes, I'm happy to share mine.

French people love Philadelphia-brand cream cheese, and *le cheesecake*, even more than Americans, if that's possible. It doesn't matter where you live, though, the rules for baking a great cheesecake aren't constrained by cultural allegiances: make sure your cream cheese is at room temperature, don't overwhip the filling, and be careful not to overbake it.

For the crust

4 tablespoons (60 g) unsalted butter, melted, plus more for greasing the pan

1 1/4 cups (100 g) graham cracker (or gingersnap) crumbs (about 9 crackers)
    pulverized

2 tablespoons sugar

For the cheesecake

2 pounds (900 g) cream cheese, at room temperature

1 1/4 (250 g) cups sugar

Grated zest of 1/2 lemon, preferably unsprayed

3/4 teaspoon vanilla extract

4 large eggs, at room temperature

2 tablespoons flour

1/2 cup (120 g) plain whole-milk yogurt

1. For the crust, lightly butter the bottom and sides of a 9-inch (23-cm) springform pan. Preheat the oven to 375°F (190°C) and position the rack in the upper third of the oven.

2. Mix the graham cracker crumbs in a small bowl with the sugar and the melted butter until the crumbs are moist. Press the crumbs into a flat layer in the bottom and slightly up the sides of the pan. (You can use the flat bottom of a glass to get it even.)

3. Bake the crust for 12 minutes, until golden brown. Set the pan aside on a cooling rack while you prepare the batter. Turn the oven up to 500°F (260°C).

4. For the batter, begin by creaming the cream cheese and sugar for about 1 minute at low speed in a standing electric mixer, or by hand. Beat only until the batter shows so signs of lumps. Add the lemon zest and vanilla.

5. Stir in the eggs one at a time, scraping the sides of the bowl as necessary to incorporate the cream cheese. Add the flour.

6. Mix in the yogurt until completely blended but do not overbeat.

7. Pour the batter over the crust and bake for 11 minutes.

8. Keeping the oven door closed, turn the oven down to 200°F (100°C) and continue to bake the cheesecake for 40 minutes, until it jiggles slightly in a 3- to 4-inch (7 to 10-cm) circle in the center when you gently shake the pan; it will appear to be *just* ready to set in the center. Do not overbake.

9. Remove from the oven and cool on a wire rack until room temperature.

SERVING: Refrigerate the cheesecake for at least 3 hours before serving. Slice with a sharp knife dipped in warm water for best results.

STORAGE: You can refrigerate the cheesecake for up to five days. Cheesecake lovers are divided; some prefer to eat theirs chilled, while others insist on room temperature. Cheesecake freezes well for up to two months, if well wrapped in plastic, then wrapped snugly with foil. Let thaw with the plastic wrap and foil intact to avoid condensation forming on the cheesecake.

HAVING IT ALL

There's no shortage of wide-eyed newbies, like me, who've moved to Paris, expecting to be able to find all the things just like we're used to back home. There are even a couple of shops that cater to homesick Americans who are willing to pay the price just to savor the taste of microwave popcorn, canned soups, bacon bits, and I Can't Believe It's Not Butter.

Since I write recipes primarily for Americans, part of my job is to track down the equivalents of familiar ingredients here. After my arrival, I spent months searching out some of the things that I use most, hoping to find a place where they were sold in bulk, since it's not uncommon for me to blitz through a ten-pound tablet of *chocolat noir* in a week. Sometimes I even bake with it.

I was spending *beaucoup d'euros* breaking up those fancy tablets of chocolate into little pieces and was certain that when I moved to a culinary wonderland like Paris, I'd be able to find chocolate in jumbo slabs as well as larger sacks of cocoa powder so I wouldn't have to rip open all those undersized pouches sold in supermarkets.

In other cases I had to find substitutes. I figured it would be nearly impossible to find corn syrup here, something I use sparingly, but is an essential ingredient for certain candies. And I knew professionals worldwide used glucose, which would be a good substitute. Since Paris is the pastry capital of the world, I suspected glucose was lurking somewhere in one of the twenty arrondissements. I just had to find out which one of them it was.

Upon my arrival, I'd stocked my kitchen with bakeware from MORA, the well-known shop that specializes in pastry equipment and is a must for pastry chefs and bakers visiting Paris. So I asked one of the delightful white-smocked women there, who love to help me, where to go. (As with other shops in Paris, I've greased the wheels with *les brownies américains,* so when I walk in, they're sure to remember me. And, boy, do they ever.)

I was led out the door and pushed across the busy rue Etienne Marcel toward a weathered orange awning shading a couple of wood-framed windows packed with an incredible array of specialty foods, most of which I'd never seen before. I couldn't wait to go inside.

The name of the store, G. Detou, is a *jeu de mots,* a play on words. *G* in French is pronounced as "jay," so G. Detou when spoken becomes *J'ai de tout,* or "I have everything." And for a voracious baker like me, I'm happy to report that they live up to that promise. This tidy shop is my personal mecca, where I make weekly pilgrimages. The words in big block letters over the entrance, POUR PATISSERIE had the same impact on me as if they were rolling out the red carpet to welcome my arrival.

The shop sits near Les Halles, an area that writer Emile Zola famously characterized as *Le Ventre de Paris*—the belly of Paris. For nearly a thousand years, Les Halles was the the epicenter for anything edible in France. An impressive, soaring, glass and metal structure was built in the 1850s that dominated the neighborhood. Sadly, in 1971, the market was torn down and the wholesale businesses were exiled to Rungis, a modern, soulless structure near Orly airport. And what now sits in its place smack-dab in the center of the World's Most Beautiful City is the World's Ugliest Building, a glass and steel monstrosity filled with chain stores, fast-food outlets, pickpockets, and loitering teenagers.

A few cookware shops remaining in Les Halles retain the spirit of a bygone era. The ones that have managed to survive did so by conceding that a majority of their clientele are no longer professionals, who can easily order from supply houses, but out-of-town chefs and cooks. And, of course, *les touristes*. The most famous of these shops, and the most annoying, is E. Dehillerin, thanks to mentions from Julia Child, Martha Stewart, and Chuck Williams—whom the clerks are more than happy to quote when they see anyone vaguely American. It wasn't so long ago that if you wanted help, you'd have to pry the salesmen away from their rigorous duties, which involved leaning against the wall and enjoying a cigarette. Or sobering up.

Nowadays, I'm certain a commission system has been implemented, since even if I inadvertently brush my elbow against the handle of a spatula or saucepan, an ebullient salesman will race forward, pluck it off the shelf, wrap it up, then push me toward the eager cashier with a bill in hand—and they're happy to take most major credit cards. It can all happen in a matter of seconds, before I've even opened my mouth to murmer, *"Je regarde, s'il vous plaît"*—"I'm just looking."

If you're not paying attention, or are easily intimidated, you might not get off as easily as I do. Sure the stuff is great quality, and the prices (especially for copper pots) aren't bad. But I see people exiting, loaded down with shopping bags full of stuff they'll probably never use. More likely, it'll end up at their garage sale the following summer accompanied by a good story about the provenance of that kite-shaped (and -sized) copper turbot poacher, those pristine scalloped-shaped baking pans for madeleines, or the gleaming set of copper *cannelé* molds that they fantasized plucking little eggy cakes from, just like they saw Martha do on television.

Everything they have at G. Detou is stuff you really *will* use, since it's all edible, and their clerks are on the exact opposite end of the aggression scale. Many times I've seen either savvy locals stocking up or adventurous cooks checking out what's new that's worth trying.

One exception was the time a tour guide was bringing a group through. Eavesdropping, as usual, I felt sorry for her guests, because she didn't know anything about the wonderful items that are stacked on the shelves. So I spoke up, mentioning that the Valrhona Manjari chocolate she had described as "some kinda French chocolate" is actually unique, because it turns a lovely reddish brown when melted and has an unconventional, lush, raisin-like character that you don't taste in other chocolates. She stared at me and barked, "So what? Who cares?" and quickly herded her group away from the crazy man.

But I'm not the only one crazy enough to care about those kinds of details. Since buying the shop over a decade ago, cheery owner Jean-Claude Thomas has spent the following years revamping and constantly expanding what the store carries to reflect current gastronomic trends, as well as improving his selection of traditional French standbys.

And no one's happier than I am, since now I can easily find top-quality *couvertures* from almost every chocolate maker in France, facing off in the two opposing corners of the store. In one corner are three- to five-kilo professional-size boxes of *pistoles* and stacks of foil-wrapped *tablettes*. In the other are the bars from smaller French chocolate makers like Cluizel, Weiss, Valrhona, Bonnat, and Voisin. Monsieur Thomas told me that 25 to 30 percent of his customers are professionals, but the rest of his clientele is rather varied and there's no customer *typique*.

And he's right. The last time I was there, a frail little old lady with a cane came in, knew exactly what she wanted—three kilos of Cacao Barry white chocolate—and scurried out as quickly as she could. (Another cookbook author on a deadline?) Soon afterward a harried gent barged in, grabbed a stack of the three-kilo bars of dark chocolate, and loudly ordered a case of pistachio paste and a container of rose paste, all the while trading barbs with the salesman and carrying on a frenzied cell phone discussion while his car engine was humming impatiently just outside.

In another part of the store were two Japanese women, huddled together, oohing and aahing at everything with their hands covering their mouths. By the window, a man who was intently scrutinizing the shelf of teas almost *bousculé*'d me, so focused was he on finding the right one among all the elaborate Russian tins.

Aside from the chocolate shelves, which I always visit first, you'll find top-quality candied citrus peels (not the icky green kinds); hand-peeled fruits lolling around in jars of light syrup; artisanal horseradish (who knew there was such a thing?); tins of Breton-packed tuna studded with prunes, coconut, lime, and smoked peppers; true Dijon mustard and spicy mustard oil from Edmond Fallot; and a whole shelf of unpronounceable additives for molecular gastronomy, a movement that still mystifies me—didn't we just spend the past decade trying to get all that stuff taken *out* of our food?

Anyone in need of unsweetened cranberry juice will find it here, as well as electric-green Sicilian pistachios, Trablit coffee extract, lifetime-lasting bags of Venezuelan cocoa nibs (they're a deal, but find someone to split one with—unless you're planning to start your own chocolate factory), Worcestershire sauce (which my French friends find amusing, since neither of us can pronounce it), honest-to-goodness chocolate chips (which I almost cried upon finding), candied cumin seeds (you can keep those—I have a few bad dessert memories involving cumin), and everyone's favorite: cans of stuffed duck necks. And much to the delight of Americans, they have nonstick spray, albeit labeled "for professional use only," which made me realize why French home cooks have never heard of it: the professionals here are hogging it all for themselves. And yes, there are tubs of the elusive glucose.

When Monsieur Thomas took ownership of the shop, he started replacing the decades of dust on the shelves with French specialties like precious candied flowers from Toulouse and single-origin chocolates. He also kept track of cooking and baking trends by befriending Parisian chefs and began stocking unusual foodstuffs from other countries that the young renegades were looking for, including maple sugar and pecans, which have since become *très branchés* among the trendy *bobo* (bourgeois bohemian) crowd. And of course, are popular with certain Americans, too.

When I started shopping at G. Detou, the clerks eyed me with curiosity. I'd pop in, peruse the shelves, maybe ask a few questions about chocolate, pick out a box to buy, and split. After a while, I'd start weaving into my questions hints about what I did, which I'd season with technical questions, trying to show off a little, so they wouldn't just foist any old product on me. Most specialty stores in France will insist on selling you the better product if you show some inkling of interest or knowledge about it, because the clerks in these kinds of shops are professionals, not minimum-wage employees, and they make it their business to really know their stuff. I learned my lesson here when my Yankee thrift (a gift from my grandmother) once induced me to buy the inexpensive chocolate that's stored on the highest shelf possible, waving off their warning that it wasn't very good. And it wasn't. I suppose they stock it just to remain true to their mission to have everything, but paradoxically, keep it sufficiently out of reach to discourage customers from buying it.

It didn't take long for them to take a shine to me. Not only did I become a good customer, but I brought them brownies and copies of my books, and the French devour books like Americans wolf down brownies. In a nation of readers, writers are revered in France like pro football players are in America. And if you write about chocolate and ice cream, and make killer brownies, you're like the one who scored the winning field goal for the home team.

One day Monsieur Thomas lifted the rope tagged **RESERVE: *Accès limité au personnel,*** and we slipped underneath and headed to the backroom, where they keep their special ingredients hidden away for extra-discerning Parisian chefs and bakers. The wooden shelves were as neat as a pin and well organized, everything in easy reach. I made a mental note that when I got home I was going to completely reorganize my shelves of ingredients, too. (Which I haven't done yet but I swear I'm getting around to.)

We poked around and he showed me things like burlap bags of heavenly smelling roasted cocoa beans, which I like to nibble on just as is, carefully laid-out boxes of delicate candied violets, and a few others things he told me he'd prefer that I not talk about. We chef types are entitled to keep a few secrets to ourselves, *non*?

But what really thrilled me was when he asked me if I'd like to visit *la cave* downstairs, motioning to a staircase that led into dense darkness. It was somewhere he told me outsiders never get to see. Wanting to see it all, of course I said, "*Mais oui!*"

When we reached the bottom of a series of time-worn stone steps, he switched on a light and I gazed upward, reeling backward at the sight of magnificent stone arches and tunnel-like passageways leading off in various directions. "Wow!" was the first word out of my mouth and about all I could say for the next few minutes over and over again, like the village idiot. An idiot in awe. "Wow . . . wow . . . wow . . ."

As we walked around in near darkness, I was half expecting to trip over a few skeletons, like the ones resting in peace over in *les catacombes.* I ran my hands over the massive stonework, which he said were ancient fortification walls from when Paris was thirty feet or so lower than it is today. As with other ancient cities, buildings had simply been constructed one on top of the other over time, but who knew the little shop where I foraged around for chocolate, dried fruits, honey, and almonds sat atop such history?

Sadly, there wasn't much down there in terms of baking goods. Monsieur Thomas told me since it was so damp, he couldn't keep anything edible there. We walked around for a few minutes and I kept running my hands over the walls, which felt cool and damp, until I was satisfied that I'd really seen it all.

Now that I've seen everything they've got, from top to bottom, I can confirm that G. Detou certainly lives up to its name and has everything I could ever want. My fantasy is to move in permanently and spend the rest of eternity sampling French chocolate and candies there, until my time has come. If I did, I wonder what people would think a few hundred years from now, when they came across a skeleton in the basement clutching an empty burlap sack and a small plastic bucket of glucose. But should I get a proper burial down there, I suggest my tombstone read, "He Got Everything."

═══════════

MADELEINES AU CITRON

LEMON-GLAZED MADELEINES

MAKES 24 INDIVIDUAL CAKES

In spite of what Proust implied, I don't think the original little cakes had much of a hump, but merely a gentle curve. Somewhere along the line, a bit of baking powder was added, and *voilà*—a phenomenon was born. If you're one of those people who must have a large hump, note that I've included baking powder in my recipe. While purists may insist it isn't traditional, one could also make the argument that it's also not traditional for bakers to purchase eggs or buy flour—traditionally, people used to raise chickens and grow their own wheat. At some point, a lazy baker broke down and bought his eggs and flour from someone else, and ruined the entire system of traditional baking. Since it's already been ruined, you can comfortably add baking powder.

I bought my madeleine molds, the nonstick ones, at MORA. You still need to butter them, though, making sure you hit every little nook and crevice. I also found that it's best to place nonstick pans on an upper oven rack so both sides bake evenly, since their darker metal attracts heat to the bottom.

If you're one of those people who end up selling those pans at your next

garage sale, I invite you to enjoy your madeleines in Paris instead. The most perfect ones I've found are at Blé Sucré, an excellent little bakery overlooking a gorgeous square in the twelfth arrondissement. Fabrice Le Bourdat turns out the
loveliest, most delicious madeleines I've ever tasted, which prompted me to come
up with my own version. To ensure each little cake is just as moist as his, I swathe
each with a puckery lemon glaze.

For the madelaines

9 tablespoons (135 g) unsalted butter, melted and cooled to room
     temperature, plus additional melted butter for preparing the molds

3 large eggs, at room temperature

$2/3$ cup (130 g) granulated sugar

Rounded $1/8$ teaspoon salt

$1^{1}/4$ cups (175 g) flour

1 teaspoon baking powder (preferably aluminum-free)

Grated zest of 1 small lemon, preferably unsprayed

$3/4$ cup (105 g) powdered sugar

For the lemon glaze

1 tablespoon freshly squeezed lemon juice

2 tablespoons water

1. To make the madeleines, brush the indentations of a madeleine mold
with melted butter. Dust with flour, tap off any excess, and place in the
freezer.

2. In the bowl of a standing electric mixer, whip the eggs, granulated
sugar, and salt for 5 minutes, until frothy and thickened.

3. Spoon the flour and baking powder into a sifter or mesh strainer and
use a spatula to fold in the flour as you sift it over the batter. (Rest the bowl
on a damp towel to help steady it.)

4. Add the lemon zest to the cooled butter, then dribble the butter into the batter, a few spoonfuls at a time, while simultaneously folding to incorporate it. Fold just until all the butter is incorporated.

5. Cover the bowl and refrigerate for at least 1 hour. (Batter can be chilled for up to 12 hours.)

6. To bake the madeleines, preheat the oven to 425°F (210°C).

7. Using two teaspoons, plop an amount of batter in the center of each indentation that you think will expand to the top of the mold once the heat of the oven spreads it out. (You'll have to eyeball it, but it's not brain surgery, so don't worry if you're not exact.) Leave the dough in a mound; do not spread it.

8. Bake for 8 to 10 minutes or until the cakes feel springy and just set. While the cakes are baking, make a glaze in a small mixing bowl by stirring the powdered sugar, lemon juice, and 2 tablespoons water until smooth.

9. Remove the madeleines from the oven and tilt them out onto a cooling rack. The moment they're cool enough to handle, dip the cakes in the glaze, turning them over to make sure both sides are coated. Scrape off any excess with a dull knife. After dipping, set each one back on the rack, scalloped side up, letting the cakes cool until the glaze has firmed up.

STORAGE: Glazed madeleines are best left uncovered and are at their peak eaten the day they're made (which is not too difficult). They can be kept in an airtight container for up to three days after baking, if necessary. I don't recommend freezing them since the glaze will melt, but the unglazed cakes can be frozen in freezer bags for up to one month.

VARIATIONS: *For orange-glazed madeleines,* substitute orange zest for the lemon zest, and for the glaze, use 3 tablespoons freshly squeezed orange juice in place of the lemon juice and water.

For green tea madeleines, sift $2^{1}/2$ teaspoons of green tea powder (matcha) with the flour. Omit the lemon zest and add a few swipes of orange zest instead.

For chocolate chip madeleines, omit the lemon zest and stir 2 to 3 tablespoons cocoa nibs or chocolate minichips into the batter. Omit the glaze.

NOTE: If you have only one madeleine mold (you obviously didn't buy it at E. Dehillerin, where the guys would have talked you into buying two), bake one batch of cakes first. After you tip them out, wipe the mold well with a dishtowel, then rebutter. Freeze the mold for five minutes, then bake the remaining batter.

━━━━━━

GUIMAUVE CHOCOLAT COCO

CHOCOLATE-COCONUT MARSHMALLOWS

MAKES 36 MARSHMALLOWS

In France, you'll find marshmallows sold in long ropelike strands, not just in pastry shops, but in some pharmacies as well. The extract of the mallow plant is considered a remedy for respiratory disorders; the idea behind the long strands of marshmallows, or *guimauves*, is that the pharmacist will snip off a piece so you can "take your medicine." If this seems odd to you, think about those sweetened vitamins, candied cough syrups, and chocolate-flavored laxatives. For my money, I'll take marshmallows over any of them. (Although I do like that orange-flavored children's aspirin quite a bit.)

On the rue Rambuteau, a street that cuts through the Marais, is Pain de Sucre. It's not a drugstore, but arguably the best pastry shop in the quarter. In the window rest several glass apothecary jars filled with marshmallows of various flavors: angelica, olive oil, lemon verbena, chicory, rose, and saffron, all crafted by chef Didier Mathray. I haven't tried them all—yet. But my favorites, so far, are the pillowy-soft chocolate ones tossed in shredded coconut.

I'm not entirely convinced that marshmallows are the cure for what ails you. But I don't want to take any risks with my health, so I make sure they're part of my weekly regimen—just in case.

$1/3$ cup (80 ml) cold water, plus 6 tablespoons (95 ml) for the gelatin

2 envelopes (15 g) of gelatin

1 cup (200 g) sugar

$1/3$ cup (100 g) light corn syrup

3 large egg whites

Pinch of coarse salt

6 tablespoons (50 g) unsweetened Dutch-process cocoa powder,
     sifted if lumpy

1 cup (80 g) unsweetened grated coconut

$1/4$ teaspoon vanilla extract

1. Pour 6 tablespoons (95 ml) water in a small bowl and sprinkle the gelatin over the top.

2. In a small, heavy-duty saucepan fitted with a candy thermometer, combine the sugar, corn syrup, and 1/3 cup (80 ml) cold water and set over moderate heat.

3. While the syrup is cooking, put the egg whites in the bowl of a standing electric mixer with the whip attachment in place.

4. When the sugar syrup reaches about 225°F (108°C), begin whipping the whites slowly with the salt.

5. As the temperature of the syrup climbs, beat the whites on medium-high speed until they're fluffy and begin to hold their shape.

6. When the syrup reaches 250°F (122°C), remove from heat and scrape in the gelatin. Stir until it's completely dissolved, then whisk in the cocoa.

7. Increase the mixer speed to high and pour the syrup into the egg whites in a slow but steady stream. Avoid pouring the syrup on the whip or it will fling and cling to the sides rather than go into the meringue.

8. While the syrup is whipping, spread half of the coconut evenly over the bottom of an 8-inch (20-cm) square pan, leaving no bare spots.

9. Stop the mixer briefly and scrape down the sides and bottom of the bowl, then add the vanilla and continue to whip the marshmallow mixture until it's thickened and the side of the mixer bowl no longer feels warm. The mixture will still be a bit runny, like chocolate pudding, but will firm up as it sits.

10. Pour the mixture into the prepared pan and smooth the top as best you can. Sprinkle the remaining coconut over the top. Let cool at least 4 hours or overnight, uncovered.

11. To unmold, run a knife around the edge of the pan and turn the marshmallow square out onto a large cutting board or baking sheet. Use scissors or a pizza cutter to cut it into 36 squares. Toss the marshmallows with the excess coconut that fell off when you unmolded the large square, dredging the sides to coat them completely. Shake each marshmallow to remove excess coconut, then arrange on a serving plate.

STORAGE: The marshmallows can be stored in a container for up to five days at room temperature.

VARIATION: If you use a 9-inch (23-cm) square pan, increase the total amount of grated coconut to 1 1/2 cups (120g).

NOTE: Unsweetened coconut is available in natural foods stores. Sweetened coconut can be used, although the marshmallows will, of course, be sweeter. If you have only large-shred coconut, it's best to pulse it in a food processor or blender until the pieces are smaller.

LE BRONZAGE

I was minding my own business on a quiet, sunny morning, walking though the seventh arrondissement on the way to meet some friends for coffee and a croissant. Most of the neighborhood is relatively deserted, as the people who live there tend to reside in posh, expensive apartments and don't hang around on the sidewalks much. As usual, there was no one around, and although I find that neighborhood a little boring, I was enjoying the peace and quiet of being away from the hectic buzz of the Bastille.

As I approached a corner, my moment of bliss was broken when I heard a muffled thud. Then it was followed by another, then another. *Thump . . . thump . . . thump . . .* Soon the thuds were so close together they began to sound like a stampede. I could feel the sidewalk shaking so violently I became more than a little concerned about what was around the bend, which was for sure on a collision course with me.

As I rounded the corner, I saw what all the fuss was about. President Nicolas Sarkozy was heading right for me, followed by a trampling pack of photographers who completely encircled him, madly clicking away while he wore his customary glare as he barrelled through them. He had recently won the election, and the press was finding him and his personal life just as fascinating—even more so—than his political leanings.

Although Sarkozy was accused of a number of things, from being anti-Semitic and a racist, to having a violent temper and a penchant for serial monogamy, he had one addiction that no one seemed to want to talk about: tanning.

As I stood transfixed, just a couple of feet away from him, Monsieur Sarko's diminutive size didn't shock me. Nor did his famously fierce expression. It was the color of his skin, which was like none I'd ever seen before. His face had a glowing orange tint, the exact same shade as the flesh of a lush, ripe cantaloupe.

Flip through the television channels in France any evening of the week and you're bound to land on some round-table program where topics are discussed by notables in the news and entertainment industry. But there's no need to adjust the saturation mode on your *télécommande;* each guest seems to be brighter, and more tangerine-tinted, than the next. I don't know how those people can even speak without cracking through all that heavy-duty makeup they have caked on.

The French adore *le bronzage,* natural or not, and at the end of every summer during *la rentrée,* when millions of Parisians flood back home, the city comes alive in an artist's palette of cocoa-crisped cheeks and caramelized cleavages. And even though I've had interesting arguments with disbelieving Parisians who blow aside the notion that secondhand smoke is harmful, or that dragging a filthy rag from room to room is unhygienic, I'm proof that it's entirely possible to get secondhand damage from UV rays right here in Paris. My retinas are still singed from the day I came across my doctor's fifty-something receptionist sunbathing, bare-breasted, by the Seine one summer afternoon. God love her for being so brazen at her age, although the poor dear's dark skin made her look like a rolled-up chocolate crêpe. And the icing on that crêpe wasn't a mound of whipped cream, it's the fact that she works for a dermatologist. (I'll leave the cherries on top to your imagination.)

But there's no reason to limit melanoma, macular degeneration, skin cancer, and premature aging to summertime festivities. Since Paris is gray nearly 360 days of the year, there's no problem getting yourself *brûlé'd* at *l'espace bronzage*, the tanning salons that are a fixture as ubiquitous in the city as the *boulangeries.*

Actually, they outnumber them: a search though les Pages Jaunes (the Yellow Pages) lists 1,326 tanning salons, eclipsing the city's 921 bread bakeries. Apparently bread's not the only thing getting baked to a crisp here.

I've been seduced by lots of loaves in Paris, but I can't say the same about the tanning salons, which are manned by young people who are all several shades darker than the Africans up in the Goutte d'Or neighborhood. But there's something about going into a booth with a warning out front that says what you're about to do is likely to cause a fatal *maladie* that makes it less than appealing to me. The death penalty was abolished here in 1981, yet Paris is full of places where they're happy to grill you to an early death.

I stay out of the sun at all times, which makes me the whitest person in Paris—with the possible exception of the flour-covered young bakers working in the basement at Poilâne. Even more than my accent and pearly whites, my pallor pegs me as an *étranger américain.* But perhaps I'll outlive a few of the people around here who have been giving me a hard time over the years, like the women at the *préfecture* to whom I have to report annually for my visa renewal, or the particularly hostile saleswoman who presides over the chocolates at À la Petite Fabrique, where she refuses to sell me any of their chocolates, for some unfathomable reason. Outside of the window is about as close as I'm going to get to their chocolates until she's gone.

I've thought about sending her an airplane ticket to somewhere warm and sunny so she can roast herself to a crisp. Or maybe someday she'll find that working in a tanning salon is far more rewarding than safeguarding their chocolates from enthusiastic Americans.

Frankly, I don't care where she goes, as long as she goes somewhere else. I'm just terrified that I might run into her, and I can't think of anything more frightening than coming across her outside of the shop.

On second thought—yes, I can.

CREPES AU CHOCOLAT, DEUX FOIS

DOUBLE-CHOCOLATE CREPES

MAKES 16 CREPES

Crêpes are easy to make, and once you get the rhythm down, it's hard to stop. I always want to just keep going and going and going. The most important thing is not to be in too much of a hurry and to give them a good *bronzage* in the pan before flipping them over.

Once cooked, they can be stacked and filled with any filling you want, or simply eaten warm on their own. Crêpes are the quintessential French snack, and they're sold at stands all over Paris, often filled with a smear of Nutella (chocolate-hazelnut paste) or big chunks of melting chocolate. Either choice is good if you're one of those people like me who just can't get enough chocolate. (Which is true in my case, thanks to a certain nasty lady at my neighborhood chocolate shop.)

2 cups (500 ml) whole milk

3 tablespoons (25 g) unsweetened Dutch-process cocoa powder

3 tablespoons (45 g) unsalted butter, cut into small pieces,
  plus more for cooking the crêpes

3 tablespoons sugar

1/4 teaspoon coarse salt

4 large eggs, at room temperature

1 1/4 cups (175 g) flour

1 cup (160 g) chocolate chips or coarsely chopped bittersweet
  chocolate (or a jar of Nutella)

1. Heat the milk, cocoa, butter, sugar, and salt in a small saucepan until the butter is melted.

2. Put the eggs and flour in a blender and pour in the cocoa and milk mixture. Blend until smooth. Chill the batter for at least 1 hour.

3. To cook the crêpes, remove the batter from the refrigerator and let come to room temperature.

4. Heat a 10- to 12-inch (25- to 30-cm) nonstick skillet or crêpe pan over medium to high heat with a tiny bit of butter in it.

5. Once the pan is hot, wipe the butter around with a paper towel. Give the batter a good stir and pour in 1/4 cup (60 ml) of the batter. Quickly tilt the pan so the batter spreads and covers the bottom. Cook the crêpe for 45 seconds to 1 minute, until the edges are crispy, then slide a spatula under the bottom and flip it over. Sprinkle about a tablespoon of chocolate chips over the top or smear a tablespoon of Nutella over one quarter, and let cook for another minute.

6. Fold the crêpe into quarters (once in half, then in half again), enclosing the chocolate, and serve immediately.

STORAGE: These are best served hot off the griddle, like in Paris, and don't hold well, so they should be eaten right away. You can keep them warm on a baking sheet in a low oven as you cook them up, if necessary. The batter can be made in advance and refrigerated overnight.

====

PATE DE FOIE DE VOLAILLE AUX POMMES

CHICKEN AND APPLE SPREAD

MAKES 8 SERVINGS

The word *pâté* doesn't mean "terribly difficult, snooty French food." It can refer to any meat-rich spread, which is everyday fare in France and not meant to be reserved for special occasions. You can easily make and enjoy pâté no matter where you live, and this recipe takes less than a half an hour to put together, so there's no excuse not to give it a go. Especially true since I've replaced the slablike *baratte* of butter traditionally used in pâté with cooked apples, in case you're concerned about how you're going to look in, or out, of next summer's swimsuit.

3 tablespoons (45 g) butter salted or unsalted

1 medium tart apple, peeled, cored, and cut into $1/2$-inch (2-cm) dice

3 shallots or 1 small onion, peeled and finely minced

1 pound (450 g) chicken livers, cleaned of any veins or dark spots, rinsed,
      and blotted dry with a paper towel

Coarse salt and freshly ground black pepper

$1/4$ cup (60 ml) heavy cream

$1/4$ cup (60 ml) Calvados, Cognac, or Armagnac

Pinch of chile powder or ground nutmeg

A few drops of lemon juice or apple cider vinegar

Fleur de sel or flaky sea salt

1. In a large skillet, melt half the butter over medium heat. Add the apple and cook for about 6 minutes, stirring only once or twice, until the apples are browned and completely soft. Scrape the apples into a bowl.

2. Melt the rest of the butter in the same pan. Add the shallots and cook for a minute or two, stirring constantly, until soft.

3. Add the livers, season them with salt and pepper, and cook for about 3 minutes longer, until they're firm on the outside but still quite pink within.

4. Add the cream, then the liqueur, to the pan. (If you add the liqueur first, it can flame up.) Add the chile powder and continue to cook for about 3 minutes more, scraping the bottom of the pan to release any browned bits, until the pan liquids are slightly reduced. You'll know the livers are done when a test liver cut in half is just cooked through and the pan juices are the consistency of thin gravy.

5. Add the livers to the bowl of apples along with the liquid and all the appetizing brown bits left in the skillet. Let rest until no longer steaming hot.

6. Puree the livers, apples, and any juices in a food processor until completely smooth. Taste, adding more chile powder and salt if desired and lemon juice to taste. The pâté will seem runny at this point, but will firm up as it chills. Scrape the pâté into a decorative serving bowl, cover with plastic wrap, and chill for at least 4 hours or overnight.

SERVING: Bring the pâté to room temperature. Smear the pâté on little toasts, sprinkle with a tiny bit of *fleur de sel* or other delicate sea salt, and serve as an hors d'oeuvre. Ice-cold rosé makes the perfect accompaniment, especially in the summer.

STORAGE: Pâté will keep for three days, well wrapped, in the refrigerator. It can also be frozen for up to one month.

OF COURSE!

Finding anything in Paris can be a challenge, from the right printer cartridge (which is no longer being made, even though you just bought the printer two weeks ago) to a bath mat that doesn't set you back eighty-five euros. Everyone in Paris has pretty much figured it out: we all save ourselves a lot of trouble, and Métro tickets, and head straight to the Bazar de l'Hôtel de Ville, le BHV, the sprawling *grand magasin* that spreads its bulk over one enormous city block of the Marais.

You don't shop there because you're going to save any money—in fact, you're going to do just the opposite—but because you know that within one massive block-long building, you'll find whatever it is you're looking for. In America, I used to spend whatever time it took in pursuit of a bargain. But in Paris, bargains don't exist, so no one even bothers.

I am certain the BHV has scouts who look far and wide, combing the world, in search of the least-helpful people they can find. Then they bring them back to Paris and set them loose on the sales floor. But the surly sales-people aren't nearly as infuriating as the shoppers. If you think the *bousculeurs* on the streets are bad, they surely get their training wandering around the aisles of the BHV before the city of Paris releases them onto the streets. It's so bad in there the store had to erect prison-like steel rein-forcements at the base of each escalator to prevent people from cutting you off as you try to hop on the next escalator going down or up.

My mode of action when I'm ready to enter the BHV is to go on the offensive immediately. Which is pretty easy, since the second I take my initial deep breath and reach for the door handle, I can see everyone in-side redirecting themselves toward me and the door I'm going to open, ex-pecting me to move out of their way once I do. Except by now, I'm onto them and let go of the door at the last possible moment, quickly cutting away to another door, watching them panic and scurry around once their plans are thwarted.

Whatever cunning means I use to get inside, I enter with the assump-tion that no matter what it is I'm looking for, the BHV will have absolutely everything—except that one specific thing that I came to get.

Like the shoelace I broke and had to find a replacement for, one that was 110 cm long. There I stood in the shoe-accessories department in the basement, facing an entire wall devoted entirely to shoelaces. Really! You've never seen that many shoelaces in your life, and it's a sight to behold—leather or lanyard, woven or waxed, cotton or poly, round or flat, string or cloth; in white, brown, black, beige, tan, red, white, green, pur-ple, and blue. Not only do they have every color and style, they have every size that exists, from 60 cm to 120 cm and everything in between, all care-fully lined up on hooks pegged to the wall. Scanning the racks, I see 60 cm and 65 cm . . . and 70 cm . . . and 80 cm . . . yes, and 90 cm . . . and 100 cm . . . and 120 cm . . . all the way up to 150 cm. They have them all.

Except one.

Of course!

If every salesperson isn't busy avoiding customers or texting friends about what time he or she got home that morning, you might possibly be able to find someone to take an interest in you. And if you're really lucky, that person might even want to help you find what you're looking for.

"*Excusez-moi, monsieur, avez-vous des lacets de 110 centimeters, s'il vous plaît?*" I inquire, optimistically.

"*Oui, monsieur. Au 5ème étage,*" the salesclerk assures me.

Scratching my head at the logic, I ask why one pair of shoelaces would be up on the fifth floor when every other conceivable size and type and shape in the known universe is on the wall in front of us.

"It's because the hiking shoes are on the fifth floor."

Of course! How stupid of me! Even though my laces are for regular shoes, not hiking shoes, I find myself nodding in agreement. I can't explain it, but the logic around here is starting to make sense.

"*Mais oui, monsieur!*" he says, hoping he's done with me as he fumbles in his pocket for a cigarette and sidles toward the exit.

I used to fall for the oldest trick in the book they use in French department stores, which is sending someone to another floor for whatever they're looking for when it's actually just one aisle over. Now I've wised up: I don't budge unless I'm absolutely sure the item I want isn't just around the corner, where it often is.

The problem with the BHV is that you *have* to go there if you live in Paris. You have no other choice. Well, there is another choice. You can spend days and days searching through every obscure alley and passage to find that special shop that sells only laces for shoes with four eyelets, or the vacuum cleaner bag shop on the fringes of the faraway seventeenth arrondissement for those very special bags that only a French vacuum cleaner takes. But unless you have a couple of weeks to spare to search far and wide, you just suck it up and head toward the behemoth on the rue de Rivoli.

During the winter, if I have to go to the BHV, I wear as little as possible. It's worth freezing my backside off on the way over because I know that moments after I step inside, I'll soon be withering from the stifling heat and the lack of any sort of ventilation whatsoever. I've made the mistake of going in there bundled up against the cold outside—after a few minutes, I'm ready to keel over from heatstroke, and find myself staggering toward the nearest emergency exit in a sweaty stupor.

Come summertime, no matter how well prepared you are, whether dressed in wispy linen or a skimpy tank top, if you make it to the second floor without needing to call SOS Médecins, you're a hardier soul than I. They should just replace the bulbs with tanning lamps and Parisians could visit two of their most cherished institutions at the same time.

A trip to the BHV is always a test of not just my stamina, but the limits of my French vocabulary as well. If you want to see my favorite part of the BHV, you might be surprised to learn that it is not the well-stocked kitchenware department (where I once gave a cooking demo with cookie samples during the Saturday crush, and which ranks right up there with touching squid as one of the most terrifying experiences of my life). Instead, head straight down to the basement, where the hardware is. A mad jumble of hammers, windows, door jams, wine-making equipment, screws, power tools, lightbulbs, doorbells, heaters, insulating tape, locks, safes, flashlights, Beware of Dog (*Chien Méchant!*) signs, and lawn mowers.

It's not enough to prepare myself physically by dressing appropriately to go to the BHV; I need to prepare myself psychologically, too. It's barely controlled pandemonium. A friend went with her husband, who loved hardware stores and insisted on checking out the hardware department. As the president of a major American financial institution, he'd weathered some pretty stressful situations. Yet after three minutes in the madness, he had to find somewhere to sit and decompress: the floor of the New York Stock Exchange is simply no match for the basement at BHV.

Adding to the confusion for me is my lack of vocabulary for all the hardware. Anyone know what you call a "kickplate" in French? An *assiette à coup?* If I tell them I'm looking to "kick a plate," that's one time they'd be within their rights to send me upstairs to another department: housewares. What's window insulation tape called? I wasn't sure either, so I asked for "*Le chose comme le scotch à l'emballé les fenêtres pour l'hiver,*" otherwise known to me as "the stuff like masking tape for wrapping the windows for the winter." Or maybe they were wondering why I was asking for "the stuff like Scotch whisky to coat my windows for winter."

After a few years I got a bit tired of tripping over the loopy-length shoelaces that I settled for and I headed back to the BHV thinking that by now, they'd have the correct size. I pulled open the glass door, barging into Parisians as if they weren't even there. I've stopped apologizing when I run into people now and haven't had any repercussions. (Why should I? After all, who do they think I learned it from?) I headed for the grand staircase leading downstairs, peeling off articles of clothing as I started to feel the perspiration welling up on the surface of my skin. My fingers were poised on my cell phone, set to speed-dial SOS Médecins, as I strode past the smelly Chanel counter and the fancy eyewear boutique, dodging oncoming Parisians with the finesse of an Olympic slalom champ.

(Except a thought just occurs to me—I'm beginning to understand the relationship between *les bousculeurs* and those fancy eyeglass shops that are running rampant across the city. Parisians must have terrible eyesight from sitting in dark doctor's offices. They're not really rude at all—maybe they just can't see where they're going.)

As I sprinted toward the basement that day, I wondered if I might need glasses as well, because everything had changed. The place was clean and bright, and the sense of complete chaos was almost gone. There was actually some sense of organization. And on the wall—no, wait—over there. Could that really be a map of the aisles?

Breathing heavily from the excitement (or was it the oppressive heat?), I wandered around, amazed at the startling transformation. All the chainsaws and tree trimmers, so popular with city-dwelling Parisians, were lined up neatly against the wall. There were two fully stocked aisles of *joints d'isolation* (when you live in a drafty rooftop apartment, you learn the correct word for "insulating tape" pretty quickly). And I counted six shelves that held nothing but bells, from ones you'd hang around a cow's neck to the kind the town crier might ring to summon a town meeting. And to top it off, they were all on sale! A five-inch brass bell that I could use to call the gang to dinner was a mere €185, which I could now get for 20 percent off. I think I need to change my tune about there being no bargains in Paris.

Optimistically, I rounded the corner to the *cordonnerie:* the shoe repair department, which had been completely redone, too. I raced past the cobblers, tapping soles onto shoes with great concentration. There were dozens and dozens of insoles hanging from the wall, including those that promised to be *capteurs d'odeurs.* A good portion of display space was given over to all the various types of shoehorns (*chausse-pieds*), another obscure bit of vocabulary I learned during an earlier experience involving nylon hosiery and unintentional nudism.

But there still weren't any 110-centimeter shoelaces to be found. Because I didn't want my visit to be a total loss, I decided once and for all to find out the French name for kickplates for doors. It was driving me a little crazy and was something my French friends couldn't figure out when I asked them, even though I accompanied it with a demonstration on my door at home. But then again, it is pretty perplexing to be invited over to someone's apartment and to watch them repeatedly kick the bottom of their front door.

Next time my handyman comes, I'm going to ask him how to say it. He likes to come by my apartment, since it always means a scoop of homemade ice cream, a wedge of cake from a recipe I'm testing, or a handful of cookies in a little bag to take for his lunch break. Although lately, I've begun to suspect him of sabotaging my pipes, since a few days after he comes, another one suspiciously springs a leak, prompting yet *another* visit.

I'm not really worried about what he'll think of me, since we're on pretty good terms. And I don't mean hardware terms. After I find out that particular one, I'm going to forget about learning the rest of them for a while. I've got more important things to find around here—like shoelaces.

═══════════════════

SOCCA

CHICKPEA CREPES

MAKES 3 LARGE CREPES,
ABOUT 6 APPETIZER-SIZED SERVINGS

Many visitors come to Paris and ask me where they can find the best bouillabaisse or an authentic salade Niçoise, and they're surprised when I tell them they can't. Many regional specialties don't travel well out of their region, and because Parisians can't resist adapting other cuisines to their own tastes (which is why you'll disconcertingly find warm cheese served alongside *les sushis*), if you want to find an authentic version of a specialty, it's best to go to that particular region and taste it there.

Few Parisians would even know what *socca* is (which the Niçois should probably be thankful for), but on the Côte d'Azur, it's a very popular and well-known street food, cooked in huge rounds over a roaring fire. Once cooked, pieces are scraped off the griddle onto a napkin, sprinkled with flecks of coarse salt and freshly ground pepper, then handed over. After my first bite, I was hooked.

I played around with various techniques, trying to duplicate the same effect in my home oven. But it wasn't until Rosa Jackson, who teaches cooking in Nice, offered a few cooking tips, which included using the broiler, that I perfected *socca* in my Parisian kitchen. The best results were obtained using the well-seasoned 10-inch (23cm) cast-iron skillet that I lugged over from America, cooking one right after the other in the same pan. You can also use a similar-size nonstick cake pan, although you may need to add more oil between cooking each *socca*.

It's important to remember that this is street food, not something hanging in the Louvre. *Socca* isn't supposed to look precise or perfect: the more rustic, the better. But it does need to be served right from the oven. And just like in Nice, glasses of very cold rosé served over ice are an obligatory accompaniment.

1 cup (130 g) chickpea flour (see Note)

1 cup plus 2 tablespoons (280 ml) water

3/4 teaspoon coarse salt, plus more for serving

1/8 teaspoon ground cumin

2 1/2 (40 ml) tablespoons, olive oil, divided

freshly ground black pepper, for serving

1. Whisk together the chickpea flour, water, salt, cumin, and 1 tablespoon of the olive oil until smooth and lump-free. Let batter rest, covered, for at least 2 hours. (It can be refrigerated overnight, then brought to room temperature before cooking.)

2. To cook the *socca*, position the oven rack in the top third of the oven and turn on the broiler.

3. Pour the remaining olive oil into a cast iron skillet or nonstick cake pan, then place the pan in the oven to preheat.

4. Stir the batter, which should be runny (the consistency of buttermilk). If it's very thick and holds a shape, add a spoonful of water or two, to thin it out.

5. Once the oil is shimmering hot, ladle enough batter into the skillet or pan to cover the bottom, tilting the pan to distribute the batter.

6. Cook the *socca*, with the door ajar, 3 to 4 minutes, depending on the heat of your broiler, until the socca begins to brown and is blistered. Remove from the oven, slide onto a platter, and crumble with your hands into irregular pieces.

7. Sprinkle very generously with coarse salt and a few turns of pepper, and eat right away. Cook the remaining *socca* batter, in the hot pan, the same way.

STORAGE: *Socca* don't store well and they lose something when reheated. They really should be eaten right after they've been cooked.

NOTE: Chickpea flour can be found in stores that specialize in Indian or Asian foods. It's often labeled *besam* or *gram*. If using fine Italian chickpea flour, use only 1 cup (250 ml) water. Check Italian shops in your area for *farina di ceci* (or see Resources, page 271).

If you come to Paris and want to try authentic *socca*, visit the stand in the marché des Enfants Rouges, in the third arrondissement. The scruffy, but friendly, Alaen fries each *socca* to order, crumbles it into crispy shards, then hands it over with an avalanche of black pepper. (Tip: Unless you like a lot of salt, just tell him *"un petit peu"* when he reaches for the shaker.)

FINDING MY BALANCE IN A CHOCOLATE SHOP

On my first day manning the counter at one of Paris's finest chocolate shops, my very first customers were a less-than-elegant American couple. Forgive my cultural bias, but their nationality was easily discernible by his high-above-the-knee shorts, plastic flip-flops, and faded T-shirt, in marked contrast to everyone else in Paris—most people were bundled up in wool coats, scarves, and hats, it being mid-November. Dressed for a vacation at Orlando's Disney-World, he must have been freezing. It was obvious his wife wasn't faring well either, since her tight and dramatically low-cut stretchy shirt couldn't hide pointed evidence that she was feeling the chill of winter. Or was she just as excited as I to be around all those chocolates?

I greeted them in French. And to put them at ease, I followed up with a salutation in English right afterward.

"*Bonjour, monsieur dame.* Good morning."

"Uh . . . oh! . . . um . . . good morning," he replied, surprised, but obviously relieved.

"Oh . . . *hey* . . . you're an American, right? That's great. Uh . . . hey listen, buddy . . . can I ask you a question?"

"Sure," I said, assuming it would be a question about the exceptional chocolates spread out in front of him.

"Can I ask you how much you make working here? What's a guy like you get paid for working in a place like this?"

In one of my rare, speechless moments, I stammered—and told them that I was a *stagiaire,* working there as a volunteer to learn the *métier.*

Not embarrassed at all, nor content to leave it at that, he pointed with his chin toward the other salesperson who was working with me in the boutique.

"So, how much does *she* make then?"

Lifting my jaw back up into place, but barely able to muster a response, I said I didn't know. I explained that Corinne, who runs the shop, is the sister of the owner and chocolatier, and hoped this would put an end to his embarrassing line of questioning.

But after a bit more back-and-forthing, he still couldn't come to grips as to why I was working at Patrick Roger's chocolate shop, without pay.

His wife finally chimed in:

"So then . . . this Roger-guy must be your boyfriend or something, right?"

And people ask me why I moved to France.

After my experience working at the fish market, I realized that my forte was chocolate, and that I'm too old to learn new tricks and should stick with what I know best. So I went to work in the boutique of Patrick Roger, one of the best chocolate shops in Paris, which opens at the sensible hour of 10:30 a.m. and whose merchandise lacks beady eyes or tentacles.

It's difficult for Americans to grasp the French concept of a *stagiaire.* The idea of working for someone for free is shocking to us. When I tell aspiring chefs to volunteer in a restaurant kitchen to see if they like the work before plunking down the big bucks for culinary school, they look at me like I'm crazy. (One friend in Paris who's a fantastic cook asked for my advice about starting a catering company. When I suggested he hold on to his high-paying tech job and go work for a catering company on the weekends to see how he liked it, he was horrified: "No way! I don't want to work on weekends." He must have been planning on catering only the weddings that take place Monday through Thursday.)

In France, calling yourself a chef carries a lot of responsibility. It's not just someone who tosses a piece of fish on the grill, drizzles it with olive oil, and tops it with a sprig of thyme. That makes one a cook, not a chef. A chef is someone who has the responsibility for composing menus, managing food costs, overseeing a staff, and most important, has usually risen through the ranks the hard way. Many begin scrubbing pots and pans in the dishroom when they can barely reach the sink, and no job is too menial.

Although Monsieur Roger doesn't work in the shop (and no, we don't drink café au lait together either), the raffish-looking chocolatier commutes between his shop and workshop on his motorcycle. Despite his unshaven appearance, he holds the top culinary honor in France and can wear *le tricolore* on the collar of his chef's jacket signifying he's an MOF, Meilleur Ouvrier de France. That makes him part of the elite corps of chefs in France who are considered the very, very best at their craft. In order to obtain the privilege, one has to pass an extremely rigorous exam that includes creating intricate chocolate masterpieces, for which he's famous. His startling shop windows always feature an offbeat sculpture, like a garden of plants made of pure chocolate (including the soil) or a life-size replica of a man harvesting cacao. Corinne's out there several times a day, wiping nose prints off the front windows.

$\backsim$

I've become friends with many of the people who work in the chocolate boutiques in Paris because of the chocolate tours I've led. Hesitant about a newcomer in their midst, the people in the shops quickly took a shine to me and my guests, probably because I was sure to give each participant rules for how to behave, which included not wearing shorts and ragged T-shirts. (I never mentioned bras, but it never seemed to be an issue.) So when I asked her, Corinne let me come to work there as a *stagiaire*.

I had gone to chocolate school and worked in a chocolate shop before, but only spent time dipping and enrobing in the back kitchen. I thought it would be fun to dress up for a change, and find out what it was like in the front of the house. Waiting on customers requires a certain amount of patience and skill, quite evident if you've ever watched Parisian salesclerks filling boxes of chocolates ever-so-perfectly. Their ability to use delicate silver tongs to deftly tuck each chocolate-coated square, dome, and rectangle so they fit just-so into the box is really a marvel to watch. I wasn't sure I was up to snuff. I mean, in my own kitchen I drop things all the time (which, of course, I throw away afterwards) just using my hands. How was I going to handle those puny tongs?

The other concern I had was that I don't do "patience" very well. It's one of the skills I've not yet mastered, and I wasn't sure I had the restraint required to stand there silently while people pondered which two individual chocolates to buy. I'd scooped ice cream in my younger days and was always surprised how long it could take someone to decide on a flavor. Anyone who kept me waiting a particularly long time got a nice big scoop—that was hollow in the center.

Patience was a skill I admired, but only from afar. I had guests on my tours stand there, glassy-eyed, unable to make a decision, and I'd do my best to make it as easy as possible by offering my opinions and advice.

Still, there were plenty of unanswerable inquiries, ranging from "Do you think my father would like this?" to discourses like "Hmm. Well, I like almonds . . . and I like chocolate . . . but I don't like them together. I dunno, David . . . hazelnuts are okay. But I only like them with milk chocolate . . . they taste funny with dark chocolate. I do like almonds with milk chocolate, though . . . but only if there's almond paste in there somewhere . . . or liqueur. I don't like liqueur with hazelnuts . . . unless it's Cognac . . . though I don't like that with almonds. Rum is okay . . . at least I *think* it is. What do you think, David? I guess liqueur and walnuts are okay . . . if there's another nut mixed in. Can you ask them if they use light or dark rum, because I'm allergic to light rum, but not dark."

I like people. I really do. But I would just stand there, mouth slightly agape, hoping they'd answer their own questions, because I just couldn't. It drives waiters bonkers when customers ask them what they should order. How the heck do they know what we'd like to eat? Working in a shop all day was going to test my mettle.

The French usually know what they want and order it without second thoughts. More than once some harried Parisian would come rushing in and say, "I want twenty pieces. I don't care which ones; just fill a bag, *s'il vous plaît,*" before racing back out the door with our signature turquoise bag in hand.

Working in a shop and dealing with Parisian customers was also an unparalleled opportunity for me to finally nail down my comprehension of French numbers. For some peculiar reason the French don't have a specific word for seventy, eighty, or ninety. I've heard it's because some war was lost in a year ending with the number eighty, and the French were forbidden from uttering those numbers afterward; hence they came up with an alternative way of saying it—*quatre-vingts,* or four times twenty. (Which in turn elongates other numbers; ninety-eight becomes *quatre-vingt-dix-neuf,* or four times twenty plus ten plus eight.) Although I haven't found any evidence to support that theory, my war with French numbers was definitely real, and one I needed to conquer.

As luck would have it, France adopted the euro in 2002, conveniently around the same time I arrived, and there's still a bit of sentimental feeling about *le franc,* which seems to be missed by everyone around here but me. Many people still can't figure out prices in euros and some things they still have to convert to francs. Especially older folks, who, oddly, have less of a problem with a car that costs 163,989.63 francs than one that costs 25,000 euros. The big bonus for me is that all the numbers became much smaller, and simpler than they were before.

No matter how much easier the numbers are now, imagine people firing away at you, rat-a-tat-tat in French numbers, while you do all you can to avoid that *biche*-in-the-headlights look, mentally sorting out how many pieces of which chocolates they want while simultaneously sifting through your brain how you're going to say what they cost when you're done.

Fortunately the French are used to being obsequious to salespeople, so I learned to put on my Parisian face when I was asked a question. Hiding my confusion, I'd look them squarely in the eye, grimace, and look slightly taken aback, pause a moment, then imperiously ask, "*Comment?*" ("I beg your pardon?") so they'd have to ask again, buying me a little bit more time to think about it.

∾

Clerks in Parisian chocolate shops use dainty pairs of tongs to handle the wares. And since the *h* is silent in French, it's important not to confuse them with *les thongs*, which are flip-flops, or a thong, which is *le string.*

At Patrick Roger, of the forty or fifty chocolates that are handled with tongs (without the *h*), none is labeled. That would be too easy. Fortunately I'd memorized all of them from being a steady customer over the years, so I had a head start. I knew rum-raisin, which was a no-brainer, since it had a plump raisin poked into the top; *avoine* (oatmeal), which was also easy, since it had an oat on top; and sichuan pepper, whose tiny flurry of ground pepper in the corner was a giveaway. (I'm lying—those three were the only ones I had memorized. And since those were the only ones clearly "marked," one might accuse me of cheating as well.) Actually, I had no idea what any of the others were, and each had such subtle differences on the surface that I didn't see how it was possible to differentiate among them. Maybe it was time for me to start wearing glasses too?

Vanille had a few teensy dots in the corner, which differentiated it from *feuillantine* (crunchy nougat), which looked exactly the same, except for the microscopic markings that were so subtle, even Monsieur Braille would have had trouble reading them. *Citron vert* (lime) I kept confusing with *citronnelle* (lemongrass), since they both had some greenish powder on them. And I kept calling the chocolate square filled with chestnut paste *marron*, which confused the patrons until I was corrected by the other salespeople, since *marrons* are nonedible chestnuts and *châtaignes* are the edible ones. Yet I was the one who was truly confused since the shop also sold candied chestnuts, called *marrons glacés*.

When I mentioned that the chocolates weren't labeled, I wasn't being entirely truthful there, either: the boxes did have labels, but they weren't visible to the customers. Even if they were, I don't think it would have mattered, since their names weren't comprehensible to either of us. Using that special brand of French logic, instead of labeling the chocolates—say, "orange," "coffee," or "vanilla"—they used more helpful names like *harmonie, plénitude,* and *fascination.* Don't get me wrong, I'm all for *désir* and *amour.* But neither told me anything about the chocolates I was supposed to be selling. *Désir* was praline and *amour* was hazelnut, I later learned.

As I presided over the chocolates, squeezing my man-sized fingers through holes in the ladylike tongs, customers would scrutinize the offerings and invariably ask me to explain what all of the flavors were. Over and over again. Perhaps twenty or thirty times in one morning. Multiply that times forty or fifty chocolates and you'd think I'd have gotten them all under my belt pretty quickly.

I was also having trouble wrapping my mouth around some of the words, since my French accent is less than exemplary. *Amande* often comes

out of my mouth as *Allemand,* so people must have thought we were selling chocolates filled with ground-up Germans. After I learned that, I no
longer wondered why those chocolates weren't very popular.

Trying to describe the nuances between *orange* and *mandarine* is a challenge in any language. But to the subtle palates of the French, there's a
huge difference. "*Mais oui, Daveed!*" they all told me, emphatically.

The biggest stress for me wasn't the language or the descriptions. And
it wasn't learning the names of all the chocolates either. It was *la balance*—
the electronic scale.

It seemed simple enough: you put the chocolates on it, weigh them,
then press a button, and out comes a small receipt with the price. Simple,
no? *Non.* If there's a more complicated way to do something, the French
will find it.

When I'm finishing up with a customer, and I've packed the chocolates in a nice blue box, I place the chocolates on the scale. Then the real
fun begins: I need to find the right button out of the fifty-seven options to
press. So I've got these truffles to weigh and I have to dig deep in the re-
cesses of my shallow brain to remember what those little devils are called
("um . . . are they *mélodie? . . . katmandou?*"), then find the corresponding
button, hoping I guess right.

To complicate things even further, each button has two names on it:
tap once for the name on the top, tap twice for the name on the bottom.
But if you don't tap twice very quickly, it registers the top price. I'm sure
some people got some exceptional bargains when I was working, which
was likely balanced at the end of the day by other people who probably
paid more than they should have.

On the plus side, I did enjoy talking people into trying something new
and seeing the look of pure pleasure wash across their faces as they bit into
something divine, closed their eyes, then nodding in appreciation. I'm a big
fan of Patrick Roger's chocolates, which manage to combine unconventional, sometimes quirky, flavors with just enough subtlety to meld exquis-
itely on one's palate. When the thin *enrobage* of chocolate surrounding the

luscious filling melts away, your whole body just collapses with pleasure, and I loved watching our customers experience such bliss.

And they weren't the only ones enjoying them. I took the liberty of sampling as many of them as I could when I was alone in the boutique. More than once a customer walked in the door when I was midbite, and I'm sure they thought the big smile across my face was because I was so happy to see them. After jamming the other half of the chocolate in my cheek, saving it for later, I'd put on my best demeanor, grab the tongs, and mumble, *"Bonjour, monsieur dame."*

After all was said and done, though, I'm not sure I was meant to work in the front of a chocolate shop. For one thing, I'm really much more interested in the creative part of making chocolate, preferring to do the melting and mixing than all the memorizing and minding of customers. By the end of my *stage,* the *fascination* (honey) wore off, and I realized the *désir* (praline) to see life from the other side of the chocolate counter was a bit of a *fantasmagorie* (oatmeal ganache) for me.

Although I might be back at some point. If you're ever in a chocolate shop in Paris and you're being waited on by a fellow with a strong American accent, an odd bulge in one of his cheeks, struggling with the buttons on the *balance* and wrestling with the grip on a too-tight pair of tongs (the kind without the *h*), cut him a bit of slack. But for now, I'll stay on the other side of the counter, where the scales are decidedly tipped much more in my favor.

======

FINANCIERS AU CHOCOLAT

INDIVIDUAL CHOCOLATE ALMOND CAKES

MAKES 15 *FINANCIERS*

One story goes that *financiers* got their name because the tidy, dense little cakes are perfect for *les financiers*, the folks who work in the field of commerce and needed *un petit snack* that wouldn't mess up their fancy suits or dresses. Traditionally, *financiers* are baked in little rectangular molds to resemble bars of gold. But if you're like most people and don't have the molds, you can use mini-muffin tins or silicone molds for these moist little buttons of chocolate. If you want to increase the recipe and bake them in larger or rectangular molds, they're pretty adaptable. Simply fill your molds three-quarters full and bake them until they spring back lightly when pressed in the center.

6 tablespoons (90 g) unsalted butter, plus more for greasing the pan

1 cup (90 g) sliced almonds

3 tablespoons (25 g) unsweetened Dutch-process cocoa powder
(preferably Valrhona)

1 tablespoon (10 g) flour

1/8 teaspoon salt

3/4 cup (90 g) confectioners' sugar

1/3 cup egg whites, at room temperature

1/4 teaspoon almond extract

1. Preheat the oven to 425°F (220°C). Lightly butter mini-muffin tins or a silicone baking mold with 1-inch (3-cm) round indentations and place on a sturdy baking sheet.

2. Melt the butter in a small saucepan and set aside until room temperature.

3. In a food processor or blender, grind the almonds with the cocoa, flour, salt, and sugar. Transfer the mixture to a medium bowl.

4. Stir the egg whites and almond extract into the ground almond mixture, then gradually stir in the melted butter until smooth and fully incorporated.

5. Spoon the batter into the molds, filling them three-quarters full.

6. Bake for 10 to 15 minutes, until slightly puffed and springy to the touch. Remove from the oven and cool completely before removing from the molds.

STORAGE: Once cooled, *financiers* can be kept in an airtight container at room temperature for up to one week. The batter can also be made, then chilled, and baked up to five days later.

I SEE BREASTS

It's considered terribly rude in France to ask someone you meet what they do for a living. I didn't know that at first, and while at a party, I struck up a conversation with a man standing near me.

"So, what do you do?" I asked him.

"What do I *do*?" he cried. "You Americans! It's all about money! Why do you always ask what we do?" he huffed at me.

What I really wanted to say was, "You know, you're not very good-looking—actually, you're kind of unattractive—

and you're pretty rude, too. You should be glad someone's even talking to you."

But instead, I apologized and excused myself, because I didn't want to be rude twice.

If you tune in to quiz shows in France, you'll notice that the hosts would never be so impolite as to ask the contestants something so personal as their occupation. The questions are always about one's region; they might discuss an Auvergnat blue cheese or light *vin de Mâcon* specific to that area, a local dish like choucroute if they're from Alsace, or *confit de canard* if they're Gascon.

I've learned my lesson and now I wouldn't dream of asking people what they do for a living. When I led tours, and my guests were mostly Americans, I'm sure they said to each other afterward, "What a jerk! He never asked us what we do!" Little did they know how extremely polite I actually was.

We call questions like that "icebreakers." In France, the *brise-glace* is, "Where are you from?" Except I never know how to respond. I was born in Connecticut, went to school in New York, then lived in San Francisco for twenty years. So when someone asks, "Where are you from?"—I'm not quite sure what to say. And certainly being a pastry chef is more interesting to Parisians than the suburban town in New England where I grew up.

I usually assume they want to know my birthplace. But if I said, "Connecticut," they'd just look at me blankly, as it's a tough word to get your tongue around. Imagine if you asked a French person where they were from, and they told you they were from Ploudalmézeau, Xouaxange, or Quoeux.

∼

People ask me if I miss San Francisco, which is where I consider myself "from." I don't go back much, since I don't miss the twelve-hour flight.

But I do miss quite a bit about the city, and I love seeing my friends and doing things like having a burrito, enjoying a cup of good coffee at Peet's, sharing a plate of S'More cookies at Citizen Cake, or strolling through the Ferry Plaza Market, checking out all the plump peaches, the tangles of organic salad greens, freshly made tamales filled with butternut squash, and Rancho Gordo dried beans, which get valuable real estate in my suitcase for the return trip to Paris. Mexican food in the Mission is another draw, as well as the obligatory trips to Target and Trader Joe's.

Another thing I like to do is go to a yoga class when I'm back. Yoga is wildly popular in San Francisco and my instructors were exactly what you'd want in a yoga teacher: kind, caring, and always ready with a warm embrace. I'm not one to get all touchy-feely (I abstained from the group hugs), but one of the nice things about practicing yoga, aside from the physical benefits, is that it's calming, and going to a class fosters a sense of community.

A few months after I moved to Paris, because I wanted to keep up my practice, I started looking for a yoga studio. Scanning some of the newspapers, I saw that one place offered a complimentary class conducted in English on Thursdays, so I went to check it out. Midway through the class, the turban-topped teacher decided I was doing everything the wrong way and kept asking me over and over, "Where did you learn to do *that*?" And instead of speaking to me in a hushed tone, she broadcast her disapproval to the entire class. Maybe her turban was on too tight or something, but I think it would have been less rude had she simply asked, "What do you do?" instead.

Eventually I did find a school I liked where the teachers were good, although a wee bit short on compassion: in France no teachers tell you what a beautiful person you are, and no one gives you "permission" to go through any negativity or discover your inner tranquility.

Since I didn't find compassion in the doctor's office, I wasn't expecting to find it in a yoga class either. The upside was that I wasn't in any danger of being a part of a group hug. Yoga has been educational for me to practice, though, and I've learned all the obscure muscles, bones, and body parts in French, which surprises locals; they're shocked that I can toss out the word for the uppermost ridge of the shoulder blade, but curious that I can't figure out how much a box of chocolates costs.

The hardest part of practicing yoga in Paris isn't dealing with less-than-compassionate teachers. It's the changing room, which isn't much larger than a two-seater Smart car.

When we're all crammed in there, packed in elbow-to-whatever, it's difficult not to touch someone where they might not want to be touched or see things one might be unnerved to see bared in public. It's hard to act natural when you're carrying on a face-to-face conversation and Fabienne, Claudine, or Anaïs slips off her top with the same casualness that I pulled off my socks, leaving us both bare-chested. I'm not sure where the heck I'm supposed to look, and I feel hopelessly outnumbered.

When I explained this problem to my friend Gideon, he started pestering me to find out where I went to yoga. I'm not sure why, since there's no shortage of breasts around here. No matter where you are, you're never more than a few steps from a pair; they're on television selling deodorant, in bus-shelters, on the Métro, in store windows, and bursting forth from the covers of magazines at the newsstands.

⌒

When summer comes around and the temperature starts heating up, I can be sure even more skin will be on display. With the incendiary summer heat, the lack of air conditioning or even fans, and a refusal to open windows because people here are terrified of any fresh air that might come in, I see that most of my Parisian neighbors aren't fond of wearing much clothing at home. When the entire city of Paris is roasting away at debilitating August temperatures, *nudisme* becomes a necessity, rather than a cause for any lascivious thrills.

Luckily, *le voyeur* in the building directly opposite mine finally moved away. I'm hoping there are no shots of me walking around au naturel on the Internet. After getting tired of seeing him, shirtless, peering out from behind his curtains with a camera or binoculars at all hours, I finally took a flash picture of him at four a.m., brightly illuminating the entire city block between our buildings. Could it be that he was a government spy, scoping out the apartment below, and I blew his cover? Is that why he finally disappeared for good?

The last time I saw him, he was at the bakery downstairs. I have to admit I wasn't quite sure where to look, even though he was fully clothed. But then again, I'd seen all of him that I wanted to see before. And I'm happy to never have to see him again.

In spite of their supposed laissez-faire attitudes, San Franciscans are not quite the wild-and-crazy bunch you might think they are. Sure, people run marathons naked and the street fairs have public flogging booths, because there's an attitude of "Yes, I have the right to be nude." But overriding that attitude is another one that might be expressed as, "Yes, but I have the right *not* to see others nude."

I forgot about the uniquely San Francisco attitudes on a trip back when I went to a yoga class in the freewheeling Castro neighborhood. The Castro is a lively part of the city that once teeming with bars where all the confirmed bachelors in the city congregated. I remember a particularly raucous night when a group of drag queens became so entranced by my eyelashes that they threatened to kidnap me and give me a makeover in the hope I'd join their posse. It's a decision I sometimes regret I didn't take them up on and often wonder how much more glamorous my life would have been if I had.

On the way to my yoga studio, I saw that Lube 4 Less was still there, but it was now joined by a Sunglass Hut, Starbucks, Walgreens, and plenty of real estate offices. As I climbed the stairs to the yoga studio, I was passed by lithe women in unitards, clutching chai lattes and scrolling like mad on their BlackBerrys as they ran up the stairs.

I made my way to the communal changing area, a vast space far bigger than my entire apartment back in Paris. I tossed my mat against the wall, slipped off my trousers, and slid on a pair of blue gym shorts. It wasn't a big deal and took me perhaps all of three seconds. So I was surprised when a woman shrieked, "Ex-*cuuse* me!" from behind, breaking the moment of bliss I'd traveled halfway around the world to reexperience. "You know, there's a changing area behind that curtain!"

Gulp. I looked around, and yes, there was a curtained-off section in the corner. But heck, I had lived in this city for almost twenty years and seen far bolder displays of flesh on the streets, on streetcars, and at street fairs, than I'd shown in a momentary flash. And given all the toned, sculpted bodies around me, I doubted anyone was paying attention to the scrawny guy minding his own business. Heck, if anyone was, I would've been thrilled.

On my next visit back to the former let-it-all-hang-out capital of the world, I'll be more modest and will change only in curtained-off, specially designated areas, where it's okay to be nude, or partially nude. Like in the hosiery shops, at home, in Paris.

GATEAU BRETON AU SARRASIN ET FLEUR DE SEL

BRETON BUCKWHEAT CAKE WITH FLEUR DE SEL

MAKES 14 TO 16 SERVINGS

Brittany is famous not only for its salt, but also for its extra-rich golden butter, which they aren't shy about adding to cake and cookie batters, often in alarming quantities. Throughout the region, you'll find buttery local specialties in bakeries that are simple and need no adornment. I always find myself eating more than one would think prudent.

You'll find many versions of gâteau breton sold in the bakeries in villages throughout Brittany. I add buckwheat flour to mine, which Breton bakeries sell in kilo bags, since it's such an important ingredient in the local cuisine. The buckwheat makes for a slightly heavier gâteau, which is mitigated by its hearty goodness. If you wish, you can substitute one cup (140 g) of all-purpose flour for the buckwheat.

If you don't have *fleur de sel,* use a light-tasting sea salt, one that's not finely ground. In a pinch, kosher salt will work too.

For the cake

7/8 cup (140 g) buckwheat flour

1 cup (140 g) all-purpose flour

1/2 teaspoon plus 1/3 teaspoon fleur de sel

1/4 teaspoon ground cinnamon

1/2 pound (240 g) unsalted butter, at room temperature

1 cup (200 g) sugar

4 large egg yolks

1 large egg

3/4 teaspoon vanilla extract

2 tablespoons dark rum

For the glaze

1 large egg yolk

1 teaspoon milk

1. Butter a 10-inch (25-cm) tart pan with a removable bottom (or a 9-inch/23-cm springform cake pan). Preheat the oven to 350°F (180°C).

2. In a small bowl, whisk together the buckwheat and all-purpose flours with 1/2 teaspoon salt and the cinnamon.

3. In the bowl of a standing electric mixer or by hand, beat the butter until light and fluffy. Add the sugar and continue to beat until smooth.

4. In a separate bowl, beat the 4 egg yolks and whole egg with the vanilla and rum with a fork, then gradually dribble the egg mixture into the batter while beating. If using an electric mixer, beat on high speed so the batter gets really airy.

5. Mix in the dry ingredients just until incorporated. Scrape the batter into the prepared pan and smooth the top as flat as possible with an offset metal or plastic spatula.

6. Make a glaze by stirring the single yolk and milk together with a fork, then brush it generously all over the top. (You may not use it all, but use most of it.) Take a fork and rake it across the top in three parallel lines, evenly spaced; then repeat starting from a slightly different angle to make a criss-cross pattern.

7. Crumble the remaining 1/3 teaspoon salt over the gâteau with your fingers and bake for 45 minutes. Let cool completely before unmolding.

SERVING: I like a small wedge just by itself as a snack. You can also serve the cake with pears or apples poached in cider, or a compote of sautéed cherries.

STORAGE: Well wrapped in plastic, gâteau breton will keep for up to four days at room temperature. It can also be frozen, wrapped in plastic with a layer of foil around it, for up to two months.

ENFIN

The image people have of my life in Paris is that each fabulous day begins with a trip to the bakery for my morning croissant, which I eat while catching up with the current events by reading *Le Monde* at my corner café. (The beret is optional.) Then I spend the rest of my day discussing Sartre over in the Latin Quarter or strolling the halls of the Louvre with a sketchpad, ending with my sunset ascent of the Eiffel Tower before heading to one of the Michelin three-star restaurants for an extravagant dinner. Later, after toasting the day with glasses of Cognac in the lounge at the George V, I stroll along the Seine until

I'm finally home, when I tuck myself into bed to rest up for the next day.

One of my character flaws is that I'm not very nice in the morning, so as a courtesy to others, I refuse to leave my place until fortified with coffee and toast, which I eat while scrolling through the *New York Times* online and reading e-mail. And believe it or not, I've never been to the top of the Eiffel Tower. After the few hours I spent stuck in the claustrophobic elevator in my apartment building when the woman on the other end of the emergency phone told me to call back later—because everyone was at lunch—you can understand why I avoid elevators as much as possible around here.

As for starred restaurants, I can't justify a bowl of soup for a hundred bucks—unless a visitor is footing the bill. And you can imagine how many of my friends are going to visit me now, knowing how I feel about visitors.

One of the first words I learned in French class was *râleur,* which means "someone who complains." Maybe it's *la grisaille,* the dull, gray skies that hang over Paris, causing *la morosité ambiente,* the all-encompassing gloom that blankets the city at times. Complaining is such an important part of life here that my first French teacher felt it's a word we needed to learn right off the bat.

But living here, I now understand the pouting and the infamous French reluctance to change. From my daily baguette being baked just the way I like it, to the tomato vendor at my market who sings the James Bond theme song to me (even though I tell him that Mr. Bond is actually British), I like things to stay the same. And let's face it; most visitors come to Paris to bask in the glories of its past, not to marvel at the modern innovations of the present.

So it's annoying when you head to the market, clearing a path with your basket, and the tomato guy doesn't serenade you, and treats you just like any other customer. (And worse, you discover a couple of rotten tomatoes at the bottom of the bag.) Or worst of all, your corner bakery, where you go everyday, has changed bakers.

When I first moved into my apartment, the biggest plus—aside from sporting the world's most meticulous paint job—was the fantastic baguettes from the bakery just across the street. Each slender loaf was a dream, baked to a rough, crackly brown finish with little bits of flour clinging to the sharp ridges, which swooped down the loaf at curvy intervals. The counter clerk would rifle through the basket to make sure to pick out an especially good one for me, because she knew how much I appreciated it. Then she'd wrap a small square of paper around the center, give it a few sharp twists to seal the ends, and hand it over with a genuine, "*Merci, monsieur, et bonne journée!*"

The moment I grabbed my loaf, I could feel the heat radiating through my hand and could barely wait until I was outside before I tore off and devoured the prized crusty end, *le quignon.* By the time I reached the top floor of my building, I had polished off half the baguette, and there was a telltale trail of little flaky crumbs behind me to prove it.

One late summer morning, a few years later, the bakery reopened after *les vacances.* Excited they were finally back after their annual month-long holiday, I nearly burst through the door as soon as it swung open, but was startled to see a new woman behind the counter. After I ordered, she brusquely slammed on the counter a baguette she absentmindedly plucked from the basket, one that was remarkably smooth and pale, with nary a blemish. When I hefted it, I felt like I was lifting a sledgehammer. I didn't need to take a bite to know that something was wrong.

Outside, I ripped off the end and popped it in my mouth; the floury taste and gummy texture were a few steps in quality below what was on offer at my local Franprix.

✍

Despite my setbacks, I was proud I had survived *le bizutage,* the hazing one must endure when you move into a new neighborhood in Paris, spending a solid year befriending the local merchants so you get good service. Sometimes you're successful, like I was at my local *boulangerie;* other times, not so much, like the nasty lady at the chocolate shop a few blocks away, who I was never able to crack.

I knew I had made it here when the woman at the *charcuterie* finally responded to my friendly overtures and actually carried on a conversation with me, one that lasted for a couple of minutes, instead of her usual grunt in my direction. And our chat consisted of more than how many *saucisses* I wanted, and if I wanted regular wieners or the ones *aux herbes.*

That was after five years of visiting her *charcuterie* twice a week, which means I shopped there over five hundred times before I was met with something other than a disdainful grimace. No longer does she see how thick she can get away with cutting my four slices of *jambon de paysanne,* and sometimes she even lets me get away with giving her a €10 bill on my €8.50 purchase, without making me rifle through all my pockets for exact change. (The French like taking money, but they don't like giving it back.) Funny how one measures success around here—by no longer needing to have exact change, and by the thickness of ham.

Parisians have a reputation for being difficult, and sometimes kindness seems to be a priceless commodity, doled out parsimoniously to the lucky few. Yet I've managed to survive any wrath I've invoked with my special brand of American optimism (and brownies). I'm also grateful that I'm probably treated better than someone who moved to America would be, not speaking a word of the native language, trying to get by in a foreign land.

What helped was that I understood the food and tried my best to adapt to the culture, rather than trying to make the culture adapt to me. I arrived knowing a fair amount about the pastries, cheeses, chocolates, and breads, which impressed the French, and I also soaked up as much as I could. More important, though, I learned to take the time to get to know people, especially the vendors and merchants, who would patiently explain their wares to me. Plenty of people who move here arrive wide-eyed and excited, only to leave after a year because they miss their favorite brand of shampoo, or air conditioning, or customer service, or 110-cm shoelaces (which I finally found at Target, in Houston). I'll admit there are plenty of things that I miss, too, but I've also made new friends, had quite a few unusual experiences, and feel much more a part of the global community than I would had I stayed in the States.

Once I learned the rules and got past the inevitable emotional bumps and bruises that an outsider anywhere must endure, I became a regular fixture in my neighborhood: *l'Américain* and *chef pâtissier*. (I'm pretty certain the first distinction wouldn't have worked out quite so well if I hadn't had the benefit of the second.)

I do my best to act like a Parisian: I smile only when I actually have something to be happy about, and I cut in line whenever I can. I've stopped eating vegetables almost entirely, and wine is my sole source of hydration. I never yield to anyone else, physically or otherwise, and I've gotten so good at giving myself a shot that I'm beginning to think my mother was right—I should have been a doctor.

But I make sure to always stop for a handshake and a chat with the vendors at my market, who have become my friends—Jacques, who sells the best olives and tapenades from Provence, and José, at the Graineterie du Marché, whose bins are stocked with all sorts of lentils, grains, salts, *pruneaux d'Agen*, and *le popcorn*, which I think he carries just for me.

My Sunday mornings wouldn't be complete without picking up a *poulet crapaudine*, a spatchcocked salt-and-herb crusted chicken, roasted to a caramel-brown crisp by Catherine, the wacky chicken lady who loves to yelp over the other shoppers clustered around her fired-up rotisserie: "Daveed—howareyouIamfine!" in one nonstop greeting. And since the pork lady decided I'm okay, my life's become not just sweeter, but richer too. There are lots more *pâtés*, *boudins blancs*, and *saucisses aux herbes* in my life, plus an occasional *goûter* of *jambon de Bayonne* when she's feeling generous.

And, of course, there are the fish boys. Because of them, I now enjoy more fish than ever.

I've been fortunate enough to experience things that very few outsiders ever get to see in Paris: early mornings hefting slippery eels, overseeing chocolates at one of the finest boutiques in Paris, and an educational trip to harvest salt off the Atlantic coastline, which included a delicious detour (of which there are many in France) where I learned the secret of salted butter caramels from a native Breton chef.

I'll know for sure that I've made it here when I buy outfits specifically for taking out the garbage. And when it seems to make perfect sense to me that the switch that turns on the light inside the bathroom is located outside of it. When during the stifling heat of summer, I know enough to keep my windows firmly closed at all times, to avoid the possibility of coming into contact with any fresh air—which would make me very, very sick. And when the gap-toothed vendor at the marché d'Aligre stops feigning surprise when I point out that the bag of cherries on his scale (courtesy of his thumb) is off by more than just a few grams—a benefit of my pastry chef training.

I know I've finally arrived when my doctor no longer wonders why I've brought a flashlight to my appointment. When the change from my €1 purchase is 37 centimes, the cashier doesn't hand me back 37 individual centimes as punishment for not having the exact amount. And if someone says to me, "That new shirt looks terrible on you," I take it as a compliment—because in that special French way, they're actually doing me a favor.

On visits back to the States, I always anticipate the trip, thinking, "Ah, I can't wait to be around people who understand me." But that isn't always the case anymore, and nowadays I'm not quite sure where I fit in: here or there. And I'm okay with that.

Every day in Paris isn't always so sweet. Although I've tried my best to fit in, no matter where you plant yourself, there's certain to be ups and downs. I embarked on a new life in Paris without knowing what the future would hand me. Because of that, my life's turned into quite an adventure, and I often surprise myself when I find I'm easily mingling with the locals, taking on surly salesclerks, and best of all, wandering the streets in search of something delicious to eat.

It's the bakeries with their buttery croissants served oven-fresh each morning, the bountiful outdoor markets where I forage for my daily fare, the exquisite chocolate shops that still, after all these years, never stop astounding me every time I visit one, and, of course, the quirky people that really make Paris such a special place.

And I now can count myself as one of them.

———

BROWNIES A LA CONFITURE DE LAIT

DULCE DE LECHE BROWNIES

MAKES 12 SERVINGS

These opened a lot of doors for me in Paris. As soon as I started handing out these chocolaty squares with a swirl of *confiture de lait,* any problems I had seemed to vanish as quickly as the brownies.

I can't guarantee they'll do the same for you, but if you're coming to Paris, in addition to a guidebook, a sturdy (but chic) pair of walking shoes, and a good sense of humor, you could pack a few of these in your bag: they just might make things a little sweeter around here for you, too.

8 tablespoons (120 g) salted or unsalted butter, cut into pieces,
     plus more for greasing the pan
6 ounces (170 g) bittersweet or semisweet chocolate, finely chopped
1/4 cup (30 g) unsweetened Dutch-process cocoa powder
3 large eggs, at room temperature
1 cup (200 g) sugar
1 teaspoon vanilla extract
1 cup (140 g) flour
1 cup (100 g) toasted pecans or walnuts, coarsely chopped, optional
1 cup (250 ml) confiture de lait (see Note)

1. Preheat the oven to 350°F (180°C).

2. Generously grease an 8-inch (20-cm) square pan and line the bottom with a square of parchment or wax paper.

3. Melt the butter in a medium saucepan. Add the chocolate and stir constantly over very low heat until melted. Remove from heat and whisk in the cocoa powder until smooth.

4. Add the eggs one at a time, then stir in the sugar, vanilla, and flour. Mix in the nuts, if using.

5. Scrape half of the batter into the prepared pan. Drop one-third of the *confiture de lait* in prune-sized dollops, evenly spaced, over the brownie batter, then drag a knife through to swirl it slightly. Spread the remaining brownie batter over the top, then drop spoonfuls of the remaining *confiture de lait* over the batter. Use a knife to swirl the *confiture* ever so slightly. (If you overdo it, the whole thing will bake into a bubbly mess. Just drag a knife once or twice through the batter and leave it at that.)

6. Bake for 45 minutes, or until the center feels just slightly firm. Remove from the oven and cool completely. Cut the brownies and wrap individually, then distribute freely.

STORAGE: These brownies actually become better the second day, and will keep well for up to three days.

NOTE: *Confiture de lait* is also known as *dulce de leche* and *cajeta* (which is sometimes made with goat milk, which I like, but may not be to everyone's taste). Because it has become pretty popular over the last few years, you can generally find jars in well-stocked supermarkets and ethnic markets, especially those that specialize in Latin American products.

Resources

U.S. sources for French ingredients and other foodstuffs mentioned.

Amazon.com
www.amazon.com
Many fine food products and
cookware, available online. Search
under Gourmet Foods.

Artisan Sweets
www.artisansweets.com
925-932-8300
Prunes from Gascony, including
delectable *pruneaux fourrés
d'Agen*: prunes stuffed with prune
puree!

Bellwether Farms
www.bellwetherfarms.com
888-527-8606
Fromage blanc and crème fraîche,
made in the French style.

Bob's Red Mill
www.bobsredmill.com
800-349-2173
Chickpea flour, buckwheat, stone-
ground cornmeal, and other grains.

Chef Shop
www.chefshop.com
800-596-0885
French salt, chocolates, honey,
anchovies, Moroccan argan oil,
and Italian chickpea flour for
socca.

Chocosphere
www.chocosphere.com
877-992-4626
A well-chosen selection of fine
French chocolates, available in
tablets or in bulk.

Cowgirl Creamery
www.cowgirlcreamery.com
866-433-7834
American-made fromage blanc, crème fraîche, and Chèvre, as well as hand-crafted cheeses. The exclusive importer for Jean D'Alos cheeses from Bordeaux.

Gourmet Foodstore
www.gourmetfoodstore.com
877-591-8008
An impressive variety of French butters.

Kendall Farms
www.kendallfarmscremefraiche.com
805-466-7252
American-made crème fraîche.

King Arthur Flour
www.kingarthurflour.com
800-827-6836
Pearl sugar for *chouquettes* as well as flours, grains, and baking molds and equipment.

Made in France/Village Imports
www.levillage.com
888-873-7194
French fromage blanc, chocolate, and many condiments. San Francisco–area residents should inquire about open-warehouse sale days.

Rancho Gordo
www.ranchogordo.com
707-259-1935
Indigenous and heirloom varietals of dried beans.

Salt Traders
www.salttraders.com
800-641-SALT
Fleur de sel and other French salts.

Saltworks
www.saltworks.us
800-353-7258
Fleur de sel and other French salts.

St. George Spirits
www.stgeorgespirits.com
510-769-1601
American-made absinthe, eau-de-vie, and other spirits.

Vermont Butter and Cheese
www.butterandcheese.com
800-884-6287
French-style cultured butter, chèvre, and crème fraîche.

Zingerman's
www.zingermans.com
888-636-8162
Provençal olive oils, vinegars, anchovies, salts, and condiments.

Mes Bonnes Adresses

Here are some of my favorite addresses in Paris for chocolate and other edibles mentioned in the book. I've also included a few extras that I couldn't resist sharing.

Please note that shops in Paris have hours that vary or may be closed one or two days of the week. It's best to verify opening and closing times before venturing out.

If a shop has multiple addresses, a Web site may be given rather than all the addresses.

And last, a warning about French Web sites: If you're easily startled, you may want to switch off the speakers on your computer before visiting them. Some open with a fanfare of musical accompaniment. Consider yourself warned.

Angelina
226, rue de Rivoli
01 42 60 82 00
Rich, thick hot chocolate served in a classy pastry salon.

L'Atelier du Chocolat de Bayonne
www.atelierduchocolat.fr
89, rue de Rennes
01 53 63 15 23
Rustic chocolate from the Basque region and *piment d'Espelette* (smoked chile powder).

L'Atlas
12, boulevard Saint-Germain
01 44 07 23 66
Couscous and Moroccan cuisine served up in traditional surroundings.

Bazin
85 bis, rue de Charenton
01 43 07 75 21
Excellent bakery and pastry shop. Gorgeous exterior, which is perfectly matched by the lovely pastries and staff inside.

BHV
www.bhv.fr
14, rue du Temple
01 42 74 90 00
The Bazar de l'Hôtel de Ville is one of Paris's grandest department stores, where you can find (almost) whatever it is you're looking for. Great kitchen-ware and hardware departments.

biocoop
www.biocoop.fr
33, boulevard Voltaire
01 48 05 02 09
Well-stocked natural-foods store with several locations in Paris. I appreciate the American-style self-service bins.

Blé Sucré
7, rue Antoine Vollon
01 43 40 77 73
Lovely pastries, breads, and Paris's best lemon-glazed madeleines, tucked away in a charming square.

Boulangerie au 140
www.au140.com
140, rue de Belleville
01 46 36 92 47
Wood-fired breads and *viennoiserie*. Visit their pastry shop, Pâtisserie de l'Église, just around the corner on rue du Jourdain.

Brûlerie Jourdain
140, rue de Belleville
01 47 97 92 77
Coffee roasting done right on the premises.

Café de Flore
www.cafe-de-flore.com
172, boulevard Saint-Germain
01 45 48 55 26
The famous Left Bank café for the well-heeled, featuring thick hot choco-late. Great for people watching, but be prepared to pay for the privilege.

Café Le Moderne
10, rue Saint-Antoine
01 73 71 20 76
Simple café serving everyday fare, near the Bastille.

Cantada II
www.cantada.net
13, rue Moret
01 48 05 96 89
Sip absinthe among *les goths* of Paris. Black lipstick is *obligatoire*!

Aux Caves d'Aligre
3, Place d'Aligre
01 43 43 34 26
A favorite wine *cave*, in the marché d'Aligre. Helpful owner speaks excel-lent English.

Chez Omar
47, rue de Bretagne
01 42 72 36 26
Hip restaurant serving couscous, Moroccan cuisine, and *steak frites*. Always a scene, but no reservations, so you'll have to wait. (It's a good chance to practice your line-jumping skills.)

Da Rosa
www.restaurant-da-rosa.com
62, rue de Seine
01 45 21 41 30
Chocolate-covered spiced almonds, Christine Ferber jams, Rollinger caramels, Spanish hams, olive oils, and other specialties. Wonderful spot for a light lunch or dinner.

Debauve & Gallais
www.debauve-et-gallais.com
30, rue des Saints-Pères
01 45 48 54 67
One of Paris's oldest, most historic, and most expensive chocolate shops.

Le Dôme
108, boulevard du Montparnasse
01 43 35 34 82
This former literary hot spot is now an upscale restaurant specializing in seafood and oversized trays of *fruits de mer*, heaped with oysters and chilled shellfish. A Parisian classic.

E. Dehillerin
www.e-dehillerin.fr
18, rue Coquillière
01 42 36 53 13
Classic shop in Les Halles specializing in copper cookware and other items. Great cookware—but hang on to your credit card!

Eric Kayser Bakery
www.maison-kayser.com
8, rue Monge
01 44 07 01 42
Financiers, pastries, and exceptional bread. Reliably excellent. An ever-expanding list of locations across Paris ensures that you're never really far from good bread.

A l'Etoile d'Or
30, rue Fontaine
01 48 74 59 55
Paris's most unusual chocolate and candy shop. Find Le Roux salted butter caramels and Bernachon chocolate among Madame Acabo's treasure trove of sweets.

Fromagerie 31
64, rue de Seine
01 43 26 50 31
Compact and friendly cheese shop with a few tables for cheese tasting. Well located for visitors staying on the Left Bank. And they'll happily vacuum-seal your cheese to take home.

G. Detou
58, rue Tiquetonne
01 42 36 54 67
Chocolate, nuts, pearl sugar, and tons
of other products for professionals and
serious cooks, with a special emphasis
on baking ingredients.

Goumanyat
www.goumanyat.com
3, rue Charles-François Dupuis
01 44 78 96 74
Specialist in saffron as well as exotic
spices, nut oils, and culinary curiosi-
ties. Also sells ingredients for molecular gastronomes. Fine wines line the
walls of the *cave* downstairs.

Graineterie du Marché
8, place d'Aligre
01 43 43 22 64
A great place to stock up on grains, including *lentilles du Puy*, nut oils, and
old-fashioned French candies. A good
source for seeds and specialty foods,
with an empasis on organic.

Le Grand Colbert
www.legrandcolbert.fr
2-4, rue Vivienne
01 42 86 87 88
A Belle Époque traditional Parisian
bistro, which starred in the film *Something's Gotta Give.*

La Grande Epicerie
www.lagrandeepicerie.fr
38, rue de Sèvres
01 44 39 81 00
Paris's grand department store of
food, adjacent to the Bon Marché.
The chocolate aisle is a great place to
stock up on tablets from across
France.

Le Grand Véfour
www.grand-vefour.com
17, rue de Beaujolais
01 42 96 56 27
Elegant dining in one of Paris's most
historic and gorgeous dining rooms.
The fixed-price lunch, a relative bargain, is an affordable way to experience the *grand luxe* and cuisine of Guy
Martin.

Hôtel Royal Fromentin
www.hotelroyalfromentin.com
11, rue Fromentin
01 48 74 85 93
Sip absinthe in the same *quartier*
where artists imbibed before it was
banned. Now it's back!

Huilerie J. Leblanc
www.huile-leblanc.com
6, rue Jacob
01 46 34 61 55
Argan, hazelnut oil, and other fine nut
oils and mustards. Ask for a sniff of
each; the aromas will knock your
socks off.

Jean-Charles Rochoux
www.jcrochoux.fr
16, rue d'Assas
01 42 84 29 45
One of Paris's masters of chocolates,
well known for his dazzling sculptures.
Don't miss the tablets of chocolate
embedded with caramelized hazelnuts
and his *gianduja* (chocolate/hazelnut)
almonds.

Ladurée
www.laduree.fr
16, rue Royale
01 42 60 16 57
World-famous *macarons*, as well as exceptional morning pastries. The *kugelhopf* is my favorite of their breakfast
treats.

Laurent Dubois
47ter, boulevard Saint-German
01 43 54 50 93
Superb cheese merchant; knowledge-
able, well located, and will vacuum
seal for travel.

Au Levain du Marais
28, boulevard Beaumarchais
01 48 05 17 14
So-so baguettes, but fantastic croissants. Arrive early, while they're still
warm.

La Maison du Chocolat
www.lamaisonduchocolat.com
52, rue François 1er
01 47 23 38 25
The classic Parisian chocolates, available in several boutiques around Paris.
Each one is exquisite perfection.

A La Mère de Famille
www.lameredefamille.com
35, rue du Faubourg Montmartre
01 47 70 83 69
Confections, chocolates, and specialties from across France, including exceptional *pain d'épices* and a
surprisingly good *glace au chocolat*,
which rivals Berthillon.

Michel Chaudun
149, rue de l'Université
01 47 53 74 40
Extraordinary chocolates and sculptures from master chocolatier Michel
Chaudun. Be sure to try his *pavés*
(chocolate squares); each is a bite of
pure chocolate bliss.

Moisan: Le Pain au Naturel
www.moisan.fr
5, place d'Aligre
01 43 45 46 60
Hearth breads made with organic
flour and rustic, if underbaked, pastries. Multiple locations in Paris.

MORA

www.mora.fr
13, rue Montmartre
01 45 08 19 24
Madeleine molds and pastry supplies;
a destination for bakers from around
the world.

Pain de Sucre

14, rue Rambuteau
01 45 74 68 92
Homemade marshmallows galore,
plus gorgeous pastries and breads by
pastry chef Didier Mathray.

Au Pain Saint-Gilles

3 bis, rue Saint-Gilles
01 42 77 57 88
One of my daily breads, the seeded
baguette, is known as *la tradigraine*.

Paris Kléber Santé

www.parisklebersante.fr
21, boulevard Saint-Martin
01 42 72 72 11
The latest and greatest in orthopedic
hosiery.

Pascal Bellevaire

www.pascalbellevaire.com
77, rue Saint-Antoine
01 42 78 48 78
A well-chosen selection of cheeses,
but I come for the heavenly salted
butter.

Pâtisserie Viennoise

8, rue de l'Ecole de Médecine
01 43 26 60 48
My favorite hot chocolate in Paris,
which you can sip while eating classic
Viennese pastries and breads.

Patrick Roger

www.patrickroger.com
108, boulevard Saint-Germain
01 43 29 38 42
Contemporary chocolates featuring
traditional ganaches as well as modern
flavors.

Aux Péchés Normands

9, rue du Faubourg du Temple
01 42 08 47 73
Chocolate chip *chouquettes* and other
French bakery fare.

Ph. Langlet

Place d'Aligre
(Covered marché Beauvau)
01 43 45 35 09
Well-stocked *fromagerie*. The mountain cheeses are particularly excellent.

Au Pied de Cochon

www.pieddecochon.com
6, rue Coquillière
01 40 13 77 00
Well-preserved Les Halles restaurant,
still open 24/7. Famous for their
breaded pig's feet and French onion
soup.

Pierre Hermé
www.pierreherme.com
72, rue Bonaparte
01 43 54 47 77
Flavored *macarons* and other world-famous pastries in a jewel-box setting, with matching prices. His second location, on the rue Vaugirard, is much less hectic and more conducive to browsing.

Pierre Marcolini
www.pierremarcolini-na.com
89, rue de Seine
01 44 07 39 07
Fine Belgian chocolates and delectable chocolate-covered marshmallows.

Poilâne
www.poilane.fr
8, rue du Cherche-Midi
01 45 48 48 56
Home of perhaps the most famous bread in the world, *pain Poilâne*, as well as other outstanding breads. I'm partial to the rye with currants and the deceptively simple, but scrumptious, apple tartlets.

Sabah
140, rue du Faubourg Saint-Antoine and at the nearby marché d'Aligre
01 40 01 01 04
Spices, dried fruits and nuts, preserved lemons, olives, and many Arabic specialties.

Sadaharu Aoki
www.sadaharuaoki.fr
35, rue de Vaugirard
01 45 44 48 90
Exquisite Japanese-inspired French pastries and *macarons*. Some consider his the best puff pastry in Paris.

Sur les Quais
Place d'Aligre
(Covered Marché Beauvau)
01 43 43 21 90
Argan and olive oils, green olive tapenade, and very special foodstuffs from France, Spain, and Italy.

Vandermeersch
278, avenue Daumesnil
01 43 47 21 66
Delectable *kugelhopf* and other Alsatian-inspired pastries. Worth the trip, although the *kugelhopf* is available only on weekends.

I continually list favorite places in Paris on my Web site as I discover them. Follow along at www.davidlebovitz.com.

Index of Recipes